For

our very ~~good~~ neighbours
~~Kate~~ Kate & Gavin.

Gavin Stott

Summer 1991.

LORD ADVOCATE'S DIARY
1961-1966

LORD ADVOCATE'S DIARY

1961-1966

GORDON STOTT

ABERDEEN UNIVERSITY PRESS
Member of Maxwell Macmillan Pergamon Publishing Corporation

First published 1991
Aberdeen University Press
© Lord Stott 1991

British Library Cataloguing in Publication Data

Stott, Gordon
  Lord Advocate's diary, 1961-1966
  1. Scotland, Law
  I. Title
  344.11

ISBN 0 08 041399 4

Printed in Great Britain by
Antony Rowe Ltd, Chippenham, Wiltshire

Published in Great Britain
by Aberdeen University Press

CONTENTS

I HAVE ALTERED a few names in order to meet the requirements of the Rehabilitation of Offenders Act; and in the Introduction to each year (which was actually written at the end of the year) have changed the present tense into the past. Otherwise the extracts remain as written at the time.

1961

In 1961 I was appointed Sheriff of Roxburgh, Berwick and Selkirk: a recognition in very agreeable form of an ever-increasing practice. My diary was always well filled, with at least two proofs or jury trials down for each Tuesday and Thursday, and sometimes as many as four or five. The theory was that on a balance of probabilities all but one would be settled before the date of trial. Often they all settled, but something else turned up to take their place – debates and appeals had to be fitted in as best one could. I had a remarkably successful year, particularly before juries; but in the First Division I lost all my cases. The Border Sheriffdom suited me very well, since my four courts were readily accessible and it was a Sheriffdom which involved very little work. The world was peaceful, apart from continuing civil war in the Congo, and an extraordinary incident when the newly-elected American President, the white hope of world liberal opinion, decided in one of the sudden outbursts of idealistic mania apt to infect liberal politicians to support an invasion of Cuba in an attempt to overthrow the left-wing government. The invasion fizzled out, and the Americans were content to let their quarrel with President Castro remain dormant, while making it as unpleasant as possible for the Cubans by denying them food and fuel so far as in their power to do so.

JAN. 2. Airds Hotel, Port Appin. I retired to bed in a room looking out over the moonlit waters of Loch Linnhe to the island of Shuna and the snow-capped mountains of Morven.

JAN. 3. Everything quiet outside, but a persistent creaking of floorboards outside my door, where some collie dogs were sleeping. After breakfast we set off to walk round the route which is the subject of our right-of-way case: down the side of Loch Linnhe to Clash Thoule, the Eye of Appin, a natural crack in the cliff, of no particular beauty or interest so far as I could see. To Oban for the start of the case, in the Sheriff Court at 11. The defender has been laird of Airds since buying part of the estate in 1956 from Colonel Gordon Duff, and has become involved in controversy with the local inhabitants about the road round Clash Thoule. The villagers claim that it has always been a right of way, and the most popular walk in

2

the district. About 1958 Dundas started challenging children who were there with dogs, and Mrs Dundas challenged other children from the village who were bathing in Airds Bay. The hotel people took the matter up with the Scottish Rights of Way Society, whom I represent. The day was occupied by evidence from villagers that they had always walked along the route, and never thought they required permission.

JAN. 4. The case went well today. In the morning I got through no less than 15 witnesses, all telling the same story. Jauncey, who appeared for the pursuer, seemed to be despairing of shaking the evidence. Dundas was Jauncey's first witness. I not only got all the answers I wanted from him, but got him to the stage when he said he felt faint and had to go out and have some brandy — much to the delight of our party from Port Appin who thronged the public benches.

JAN. 5. Today I was confronted not only with two former lairds, who were fairly reasonable, but with two sisters of an earlier one — one a most obnoxious woman, who thought that the lower orders in Port Appin in the old days had far too good manners to use a road on the estate. The former laird told of an occasion when his father was asked if the main drive could be used as a short cut by people attending the parish church as well as the Free Church, and he had agreed, saying that so far as he was concerned the drive could be used by Hindus, Mahommedans and even Roman Catholics.

JAN. 6. A glorious morning for our last day in Oban: a full tide, the sun shining from a clear sky, and the snowy peaks of Mull glistening behind Kerrera. I had put in a lot of work on my speech, and I think it was pretty good. The Sheriff made no remark. When Jauncey was at a critical point in his argument, the Sheriff leaned forward, and we all perked up, wondering what was going to be said. But all the Sheriff did was to ask whether he would like a drink of water. Jauncey, who apparently had not thought he was suffering from hoarseness, seemed a little taken aback, but accepted the offer.

JAN. 7. I had been relieved on coming home last night to find there was no word of anything requiring my attention, but at Dundas Street there was an enormous pile of papers, with which I motored home. In the afternoon I had to go back, Norah having phoned to say that several more bundles had come in. Spent rather a frustrating day, never really settling down to work while at the same time feeling that I should not be doing anything else when so much work was hanging over my head.

JAN. 10. Elizabeth has got presents of two diaries, and finds it necessary to keep both, with slight variations between the two. "Daddy is at Oban". "Daddy is away, so saw Crackerjack".

3

JAN. 11. Douglas Johnston installed, with the judicial title of Lord Johnston. Margaret Kidd thought he would make a good judge, because he was so equable. She had never seen him excited or bad-tempered, even with the children — she knows him well, his wife being her sister.

JAN. 14. Finished reading *The Charm of Politics*, by R. H. S. Crossman. This collection of book reviews would dispel any theory that the author is haphazard and hasty in judgment. The essays, written at different times, show a consistency and maturity of thought which is distinctly impressive. Even when one disagrees with him, what he says is worth thinking about; if all our politicians showed his grasp of reality we should be a lot better off.

JAN. 15. Richard alarmed me by appearing on the roof, having climbed a ladder which the roof repairers had hung in a diagonally sloping position down the side of the house, ready to be re-erected when they come back tomorrow. From the top of this he had crossed part of the slated roof to the foot of another ladder leading up to the roof top. He seemed quite at home there.

JAN. 16. Parliament House: I got so absorbed in the draft of a case for the House of Lords that I failed to notice the passage of time, and suddenly realised it was 2.20 and I had an Appeals Committee at York Place at 2.15. Phoned Masson and told him I should be down in two minutes, and was almost as good as my word — Douglas James remarked that it had been 2½ minutes since I had phoned.

JAN. 17. Finished reading *The Day's End*, by Pamela Bright, vignettes of hospital life by a nursing sister, which make up a human, likeable book, rather out of the ordinary.

JAN. 18. The Church Deacons' Court, of which I have been appointed a member. A discussion of what was to be done about the pigeons which had been defacing the front steps of the church — a carpet laid down for a wedding last Saturday had been considerably damaged. It was felt that the pigeons should not come to any harm, but it would be a great convenience if they could be persuaded to move round to the back.

JAN. 19. A jury trial before Milligan: the pursuer a girl employed in Singers' sewing-machine factory. She went to the cloak room to get her coat, and slipped in a small pool of tea that had been spilled on the floor — injuring her leg. The whole case was over by lunch time; the jury returned a verdict for the pursuer, by 11 to 1, and awarded her £450. She was a nice little girl, and though the evidence was thin I had little doubt as the case came out that we should get a verdict. The defence was feeble — it was never even suggested that a pool of tea was perhaps not a very dangerous obstruction.

JAN. 20. Second Division judgment in Thomson v. Glasgow

Corporation. As I had feared, they refused the amendment and adhered to Wheatley's opinion. Thomson's judgment was entertaining in a cynical kind of way, likening judges to referees in a boxing match, with the contestants scoring points according to the rules. The idea with which judges sometimes deluded themselves that they were there to find out the truth was accurate, he said, only to a very limited extent. The powers of amendment were designed to get over technicalities, not to overcome difficulties caused by the ignorance or laziness of lawyers. Kissen thought this final remark was rude, and unlike Thomson — I daresay he had a bad conscience in giving what he must have known to be an unjust judgment. Strachan concurred, but said he did so with hesitation; whether that will prove good enough to get us Legal Aid to go to the Lords remains to be seen.

JAN. 21. Thomson's observations are reported in the *Scotsman* this morning under a heading across two columns, "Judge attacks ignorant, lazy lawyers". The names of solicitors and counsel concerned in the case are printed as usual at the foot of the report, and my junior and I found ourselves the targets for plenty of good-natured humour. This is all very well among those who know us, but the effect on those who do not may be more serious.

FEB. 9. Typing out a long argument to be submitted to my colleagues on the Committee as a note by counsel in an application for legal aid to take *Thomson v. Glasgow Corporation* to the Lords — encouraged by a letter McKechnie showed me from Normand, in which he agrees with McKechnie about the Lord Justice Clerk's remarks about the function of the court. "I was horrified by the report in the *Scotsman* and I can imagine certain members of the H.L. commenting severely". I used my Carlyle Society talk as an opportunity for getting in a shot myself, compiling a short press report in which I should be reported as saying that Carlyle would not have agreed with the Lord Justice Clerk's ideas. The *News* used the report.

FEB. 12. Greenbank Church: Rev. J. Michael Orr, minister of Jordanhill. He is an exceptionally eloquent young man, and preached as good a sermon as I have heard for many a long day.

FEB. 13. Elizabeth's diary for Feb. 12: "Went to different church, super minister".

FEB. 20. Glasgow Sheriff Court. Walked up to the station, where I spent most of the ten minutes until train time wrestling with an automatic machine from which I was trying to extract a bar of chocolate. It stuck when the drawer was half open, but a workman plied a corkscrew at one end of the chocolate while I worked with my pen knife at the other, and eventually we got it out, damaged but eatable.

FEB. 21. Glasgow. We finished in time to let me catch the 1 o'clock train home — having on this occasion failed to extract anything from the chocolate machine in return for my 3d.

FEB. 23. A jury trial before Strachan: Breigans v. Burgh of Alloa. The pursuer was shovelling material from round a manhole cover while another man, Bell, was dislodging the material with a pick. Somehow or other, he got struck on the top of the head with Bell's pick. He is a curious fellow with long black hair, who goes in for weight-lifting — he took a correspondence course with someone calling himself "Atlas". The pursuer's account of the accident was that he was bending down behind Bell, shovelling, when Bell swung the pick back over his shoulder and hit him on the head. This seemed an impossible story, and was contradicted by other witnesses, who said the pursuer was in front of Bell and got his head in the way as Bell was bringing the pick down. The Record had been kept vague on this matter — the case was based on the simple narrative that Bell had raised his pick and hit the pursuer on the head. The defenders' case is that Breigans, whom they describe as a "low worker", suddenly stepped in front of Bell when the pick was coming down; but this is not very credible either, since it is difficult to see how Bell got his pick high enough to hit Breigans on the down stroke. If both sides had not been agreed that Bell had indeed hit Breigans with the pick, it would be difficult to believe that the accident could have happened at all.

FEB. 24. The jury found for the pursuer by 8 to 4, and awarded him £500. I had been successful also in the Port Appin case, in which Kermack issued his judgment yesterday. On arrival home I learned that Bongo had been run over and killed: a quaint, likeable little dog with a personality of his own. He got on well with the cat, and it was a delight to see them playing together — running side by side down the pavement at night, or Bongo standing patiently while the cat laboriously washed his coat, first on one side and then on the other.

FEB. 25. Nancy phoned to ask me to go and see a black mongrel puppy in the Fleshmarket Close. I found two black puppies in a cage in the shop, one woolly and one smooth-haired. In the afternoon Nancy and Elizabeth went to town to buy the smooth-haired puppy. Richard had not noticed Bongo's absence, and was much surprised when the puppy arrived; its arrival seemed to put Bongo pretty well out of mind.

FEB. 28. A jury trial before Migdale. The pursuer, a deckhand on the *Caledonia*, had to take an anchor light down an accommodation ladder. His foot slipped and he fell 10 feet to the foot of the ladder. He says the accident happened because the steps of the ladder were worn and greasy. The case had never been properly precognosced, and it turned out that our only supporting witness was almost totally blind, and had seen the ladder only once, six months after the accident. But we were assisted by a helpful policeman who was led for the defenders and said the steps were worn, and the jury found unanimously for the pursuer.

MAR. 2. A debate before Carmont, sitting in the Outer House: Hill v. Stewart. Dick appeared for the defender, to argue that the case be sent for proof instead of jury trial. He went at once to the Record, which told of a cart horse of the same name as himself which was standing below a hay loft while the pursuer was on top of the cart helping another man to hand up bales of hay to the farmer in the loft. The horse moved forward, and the pursuer lost his balance and fell to the ground. The defender says Dick was a " one-man " animal whose master was the pursuer, and was a quiet animal. This is admitted, under explanation that a horse is liable to move forward irrespective of its disposition. The pursuer says the defenders should have had a man to hold the horse's head, or should have had brakes on the cart, or should have used an elevator. Carmont seemed to keep quite well awake, and took a lively interest in the case, saying that he was of an age to remember about horses. He took the case to avizandum.

MAR. 3. A debate before Clyde. The pursuer was hit by a stone which fell from the roof of a mineral working where he was employed. His case is founded on a breach of the Mines and Quarries Act. The defenders say the accident was caused by the pursuer's failure to examine his working place and secure any loose part: a duty imposed on him by the Miscellaneous Mines Regulations. C. H. Johnston opened the case for the defenders, obviously confident that he would have no difficulty in persuading Clyde that such a case was unsuitable for jury trial. However, he is even less *persona grata* than I in that quarter — Clyde hardly gave him a civil hearing. My junior, Sutherland, made a tactful reply, exactly what was required, and I was not called on; Clyde gave judgment forthwith, allowing a jury trial.

MAR. 4. An interesting half-hour on television: the Winston Churchill film — this week, the fall of France. The children stayed up to watch it, and obviously found it very interesting. It is a pity that they must put up with so much rubbish in their normal viewing hours.

MAR. 5. We have had to move the cat's bed up on to the top of the refrigerator, where the puppy cannot reach it, so as to let the cat have some peace. The puppy never leaves it alone, and though it is still only about half the cat's size flings itself on the cat with such force that it knocks it over, and then proceeds to stand on it. The cat seems happy on top of the refrigerator.

MAR. 7. Elizabeth came home with a poem she had written, on "Love":

"It is immortal.
He is your pull, for ever.
The heather, of your arms. Ashes for his.
In a prison, you from, her
Your thoughts with him.
No thought of sin. You are together.
A few words on a flyleaf, of a book
Makes your belief (in a shady nook).
More real, more gaily, in a sense
That pain can't cure.
so leaning forward tease,
Your reply, unshy, unguarded, yet I love you".

Finished reading *The Cunning of the Dove*, by Alfred Duggan, a novel based on the life of Edward the Confessor which not only rings true but is attractive and interesting, with many delightful touches.

MAR. 9. Working on a question about the validity of a restriction imposed as a real burden in a conveyance of property. I felt sure it was invalid, but extensive research among authorities yesterday failed to bring anything to light that would support this view. Just before going to bed, however, I found a case which said just what I wanted, and satisfied me that my impression had been correct after all.

MAR. 10. Judgment in *Hill v. Stewart*, disallowing a jury trial on the ground that the case raised problems of law rather than questions of fact: a fantastic decision.

From Mr J. O. M. Hunter:

42, India Street, Edinburgh, 3.   11th March 1961.
Dear Gordon
It may interest you and give you pleasure to know that, in the course of the hearing of the appeal in *Warden v. Warden* last week in the Lords, Viscount Simonds who was presiding referred to you as "a Counsel whose abilities are well-known to their Lordships". Unsolicited testimonials are hard to come by in our profession — & from such a source they are, in my humble estimation, worth a great deal.
Yours ever

MAR. 18. We all motored to Cramond, taking Nicholas. We had intended crossing the ferry, but a very high tide, with north wind blowing into the river mouth, had brought the water over the landing stage on the Dalmeny side and made the crossing impossible. We had a pleasant walk up the river to the dell — Nicholas delighted with the place, which oddly enough he had never been to before and thought was the next best place he had been after England. We motored home, and passed a house with one of the ornamental lamps outside which marks the home of an Edinburgh bailie; Elizabeth remarked that that was where one of those beagles lived.

MAR. 20. Glasgow Sheriff Court. A restaurant recently opened close to the court was quite elegant, and we had an 8/6 three-course lunch which was satisfactory, plentiful and speedily served.

From Mr William Muir:

H.M. Prison, Edinburgh 20.3.61
Dear Gordon Stott Sir. it is with deep regret I send you this address now why I am here I cannot remember I have tried to dive deep into the Dark Regions of my mind but I fail. Now Sir. the position is this I must be ill. Now I have had a Dr mental Dr to see me from where or who sent him I do not know. He is aquinted with Dr Boyd a fine old Gentleman who once examined me in Inverness Prison I feel now it is from the results of the Beatings & Bashings about I got while I was serving that last sentence It is very cruel to throw an old man who has given evidence in a High Court to the wolves as you no once a man has helped the Police he is a marked man & subject to much abuse and assaults I got plenty of it Bashed behind the ears & Head all because I helped the Police
Now I am going to ask you will you be good enough to bring this matter before the Court I want to go into a Home for old people on any conditions the Court may impose on me . . . their are in Prison a certain class of men who delight in making life miserable for one who has squeeled as they call it you are my only hope . . . I am very deaf now & subject to Black outs I hope your Dear little ones has completely recovered from the Flu as far as I can remember here is one of the charges A small hold was advertised for sale I went look it I called at Rathlaw House to make enquiries the Lady invited me in for a cup of coffee She was a gracious Kindly Soul. She further wanted me to have Breakfast I stayed about 4 hours with her in her Bedroom I want to say right here she was a honest good women only wanted to be kind I told her I must be going as I had to get some money for the week end She offered me a Blank Cheque from her Cheque Book & loaned me £8 I signed my name at the bottom of the Cheque.
she filled it in I dont no what became of the Cheque. Their are other similar cases all gave me a Blank Cheque from their Book I am satisfied that the cause of my breakdown is from the threats & Bashings I received in Prison I feel it is only fair that this matter should be brought before the Court and I plead to you to help me.
Yours sincerely
W. Muir.

9

I will not let the Court down if the impose on me certain conditions & gave me a chance to go into a Home. I see the question of my age has interested some people Well tho it is impossible to say what I am but I must be in the region of 75 or 76 I enlisted in the HLI at Hamilton for the Boer War I was in the 1914 war got badly wounded I do no when a person becomes 3 score & 10 he is a child again some people possess all their faculties much older but not after the Bashing about I have received & illness Your sincerely

MAR. 21. William Muir is back in Saughton as an untried prisoner. It is not clear from his letter what he is there for, but it seems to be something to do with a forged cheque.

MAR. 23. My colleagues on the House of Lords Legal Aid Committee have been considering my application in *Thomson v. Glasgow Corporation*; and Courtney phoned to say that our application had been granted. I have every hope that the Lords will see that Mrs Thomson gets justice. It is ironical that the only two House of Lords applications granted so far were both submitted by the chairman of the Committee.

MAR. 28. Glasgow Sheriff Court. As I was leaving court, I encountered two girls, with high heels and very much painted and powdered, who asked if I could direct them to the Salvation Army Hostel — which fortunately I was able to do, though a little surprised by their request.

MAR, 30. Glasgow. Wilson's charge was very prejudicial, and the jury found the accused guilty of reset. Haberstich, my client, seemed a nice little man, and got an undeservedly heavy sentence for a crime in which I thought he was very mildly involved. The trouble was that throughout the case I was completely outgunned and out-manoeuvred by the Depute-Fiscal, Smith. The evidence against Haberstich was the flimsiest possible, and it was bad luck that he came up against a Sheriff who has a reputation for taking the Crown side and a Fiscal who on this occasion at any rate was much too good for defence counsel.

From Mr William Muir:

H.M. Prison, Edinburgh. 3rd April 1961.
Dear Sir: I humbly appeal to you to help me to be given my last chance. I am going to plead guilty. I am really not guilty I have plead guilty before when I was not guilty. What is the use of me trying to prove my innocents. When I stood in the dock 1949 I was not guilty fear made me plead guilty I was glad to get away from Barlinnie where I was threatened with my throat cut if I gave evidence against Dickson & Duffy . . . that is twice I plead guilty because of fear and the last two times I defended my self another foolish act if I had a had

10

proper Counsel I would never a had the record I have. . .
I am writing a book it will be a true story off my travels & interesting
People I have met in America Canada Mexico & South America. it
will be sold at 48/6 What a story I can tell I have travelled much seen
a lot of life the Title will be The Fox versus the wolf.

AP. 5. With Nancy and Richard to the Dominion cinema: "The
Man in the White Suit", a cruel picture, and all too true: a scientist
who discovers a new fabric which never wears out, and whose
discovery is sabotaged by a combination of millowners and workers
who see their livelihood threatened. The material proves unstable,
and the inventor's suit is torn off him by the mob, leaving him
standing in his shirt-tails in the street. It says much for the audience
that few of them laughed at this denouement, but I am not at all sure
that the makers of the film did not mean them to laugh. That is the
film's weakness; but it is effective and exciting, and brilliantly
played by Alec Guinness. We arrived in time to see the later part of
the main picture, "Doctor at Large", which I found surprisingly
likeable and entertaining.

AP. 6. In Dundas Street, when I was turning the car to go up the
hill, the lining of my raincoat caught in the indicator lever and the
coat wrapped itself round the steering wheel, so that I could not get
the wheel turned. I had to stop dead in the middle of the street,
holding up the traffic for quite a while until after a struggle I
managed to get myself free.

AP. 6. Potato Disciplinary Committee: mostly producers
charged with having knowingly or recklessly understated their
potato acreage, on which a levy is payable to the Board at £11 per
acre. In most cases, the producer had written in explaining that a
field was difficult to measure, by reason of patches of weed, or a pit
ventilation shaft, or something of the sort. But my farming
colleagues were not disposed to accept excuses of that kind; if the
producer had understated his acreage, that was good enough for
them. We found all the contraventions proved, and fined the
offenders sums ranging from £10 to £20. The offender was liable
also to make good the loss sustained by the Board through not having
collected the proper levy. Finally we had a producer from Nairn who
had sold potatoes that were too small — a very small-scale producer.
We fined him £5 on an assurance that he had provided himself with
the proper size of riddle and would not do it again.

From Mr William Muir:

H.M. Prison, Edinburgh   6.4.1961
Dear Gordon Stott Sir. Thank you a million for your kind litter it is

very thoughtful of you to help me out of my difficult position Yes if the Crown Office gets the facts I am sure they will not be hard on me. as you know Barlinnie & Peterhead have some vicious men, will stop at nothing when you have helped the police you are doomed as far as the underworld is concerned The majority of the Officers are very efficient and would not allow any man to be Bashed about They cannot always be watching & ready to pounce on the aggresor some men in Prison will do anything for a $\frac{1}{2}$ oz of tobacco yes cut your throat Saughton is quite a safe Prison for any thing like that to happen. I served a 4 year sentence here and was out all the time I never contacted the Prisoners their was no question of security I was trusted and I never let any Official down — it is places Barlinnie & Peterhead it was unfortunately not expected to be assaulted in Inverness Gordon is a fanatac

I dont no what the court is going to do I would like to be given one last chance I am not a bad man. I have been foolish & easy for some people I could not face the wolves again it is a horrible thought now about my book I will dedicate it to Gordon Stott it certainly will be worth reading Conin Doyle well not have a look in poor man he done so much for a ungrateful man — Oscar. Slater. I have met some men in the Prison service that have been helpful & sympithic

However if the Crown Agent takes a interest as you say he will I may get another chance I am certain you will do what you can for me old age is a killer it just seems like yesterday since I was a boy when I used to walk out through Blackhall to Crammond Kirk Oh if I could only go back to those happy days to see some of the faces I knew then . . . Please Sir help me if it is only to be given a chance I cannot afford to engage D McKay at a £150 I believe Mr Veitch at Linlithgow can help me he has represented me the last two times at the Court I remain Sir

AP. 7. With Nancy and the children to the Empire: "Tokyo 1961", a Japanese musical, lavishly staged and dressed, with an enormous chorus of gaily-dressed girls, all wasted on what was just a colossal bore. Whoever devised it had no imagination, and microphones turned all the singing into a monotonous mechanical shout from a square box at the side.

AP. 8. Motored with the children to Crichton. Stephen Barr was halted by gorse bushes, and after encouraging him as best I could to push past them I carried on while Stephen howled dismally for five minutes. He then pushed his way through a gap in the bushes, and came cheerfully after me, announcing that he had got through by himself. The others had meantime reached the castle, and came back excitedly with the news that it was open and it was only 3d to get in. With some misgivings, remembering the worn stone stairs and the precipitous unfenced drop from the top of the walls, I let them go in,

12

and followed the party up the steep ladder to the top. Stephen fortunately was content to stay below, and on the whole everyone behaved sensibly. But I was glad to get them all safely away, after the castle had been thoroughly explored.

AP. 9. We all motored to church. Mr Reid preached on Job, 42, 1-2. I fell asleep in the course of this sermon, which lasted for half an hour. A television documentary on Britain just made by the Columbia Broadcasting Company of America for its own audiences: a curious hotchpotch. Topics discussed and people interviewed seemed to have been selected in a very arbitrary manner, but in its crazy, muddled way it presented an interesting picture of this country, one that I daresay was not far off the mark.

AP. 10. Finished reading Beatrice Webb's Diaries, 1924-1932, an interesting account of contemporary events and personalities seen through the eyes of an exceptionally clear-sighted writer who views them dispassionately, without the slightest emotional overlay. She is never offended by what is said to her or about her, but simply considers the extent to which the remark may be true. It is the same with her estimates of other people. Her judgment is usually justified by events, but occasionally I felt there was a certain lack of human sympathy. She is a likeable person — good at seeing her own limitations just as much as others'.

AP. 13. Finished reading *Lloyd George*, by Earl Lloyd George. The author is mainly concerned with his father's liaisons with various women: a novel aspect of Lloyd George's life, and not a very interesting one. On the political side, this is a naive production. It comes to life briefly, in one chapter, with the indignation of a serving soldier at Haig's policy of mass murder on the western front.

AP. 14. The children have a society called S.A.C.S., which appears to stand for "Society for Annoying Colin Smith" — a small Academy boy who lives at the foot of the street. They were castigating Stephen Barr this morning for telling Betse the Society's secrets, to which he replied that he had not told Betse. "I was talking to myself, and Betse was there". Television relay from Moscow of the reception given to Major Gagarin, the first man to be launched into outer space. It was notable for masses of flowers with which everyone was loaded, including Mr Kruschev, who took the first opportunity to hand his over to Major Gagarin. He at once passed them on to a lady — who may have been Mrs Kruschev.

AP. 16. Letter to William Muir. I was able to inform him that he was not to be put before the High Court, but simply Sheriff and Jury. I got Mr Gordon to speak to the Prison Commissioners about Willy's desire to serve his sentence in Saughton and not be exposed to his enemies in Barlinnie or Peterhead.

AP. 17. We all motored to the Dominion cimena to see the Tony Hancock film, "The Rebel" — funny in parts and, though it has its dull moments, amusingly worked out. On television tonight we had Selwyn Lloyd on his Budget. He made a better show as Chancellor than he ever did as Foreign Secretary, though his defence of his financial proposals was not particularly convincing. Raising the exemption limit for surtax from £2000 to £4000 is commended on the ridiculous view that this lightening of the burden on the rich is going to provide some incentive to industrial effort, though at the same time the Chancellor has introduced what he regards as a counterbalance in the form of increased profits tax on companies. The only people that can profit will be higher-paid professional people, and financiers; but in the *Tonight* programme earlier in the evening we had an extraordinary example of the ability of the British to delude themselves when random interviews with members of the public in the street, people obviously nowhere near the surtax level, showed that this was regarded as an excellent proposal, put forward in the best interests of the nation as a whole.

AP. 18. Switched on the television to see the three candidates in the Paisley bye-election. The first impression of the Labour candidate was far from favourable: an AEU official, a mere party hack. I was not greatly impressed either at the first sight of J. M. Bannerman, the Liberal. The Conservative seemed easily the best, unattractive in appearance, but quiet and sensible enough when he came to speak.

From Mr William Muir:

H.M. Prison, Edinburgh   19.4.61
Dear Gordon Stott Sir I am very grateful to you for your kindness in taking a interest on my behalf and also the Crown Agent I will never be able to repay you in this world only I predict you will someday b e a judge I may never see it I can assure you it will happen. I have had a vision of the future state I had passed on from this Earth. This sojourn on Earth is a Probation Period We pass on from life to Death Our Bodies are buried in mother Earth Our Spirit travels immediately it leaves the body to another Body in another Planet that is the test God puts us to. We live our future life there We are tempted to Sin and if we Sin we perish our Soul is cast to damnation. destroyed for ever I was in a beautiful Garden (not the Garden of Eden) you arrived I knew you and identified you as Gordon Stott. I was made a God . . . I was the big shot up there I met many people I had known on Earth I met many lawyers. Lord Milligan came along many judges Lord Milligan's record on Earth was bad. He was a Tory. . . He became a Christian up yonder & lived for ever but many perished. . .

MAY 2. William Muir appeared in court today: a sentence of 9 months, a lenient sentence in view of his record.

MAY 3. Bowen, speaking of William Muir, told me of one of his latest escapades, typical of the elaborate way in which he sets about defrauding of even small amounts. A small farm in West Lothian was advertised for sale, at the price of £6000. Willy went to see it. His father, he said, had just died at the age of 103, and left him £20,000, and he would like to put in an offer for the farm if it was suitable. He was conducted all round, and said he liked it, so much so that he was prepared to write them out a cheque for, say, £300, as earnest of his intention to put in an offer. But feeling in his pocket he found he had lost his wallet with a cheque book in it. He was sure that it must have been lost while they were going round the farm, so an elaborate search was made, without result. Willy concluded that the pigs must have eaten the wallet, and that made it awkward for him, because it left him without any ready money. Perhaps the farmer could lend him £10? So the farmer handed over £10, and Willy went off; and nothing more was heard of him or his offer.

MAY 10. Church Deacon's meeting. I made my maiden speech, Mr Reid having invited me to express an opinion on where the title deeds of the manse and the beadle's house should be kept — a subject upon which I did not hold any strong opinion.

MAY 11. Ewan Stewart told me that Milligan had a jury trial in which there was a very long-winded pursuer, incapable of answering a question without a lengthy exordium or explanation. He complained of suffering from breathlessness, which might come on at any moment — at which Milligan asked: "Is there any hope of it coming on just now?"

MAY 16. A divorce proof before Walker, Taylor v. Taylor. The pursuer is an electrical engineer whose wife left him in December 1959. According to him, she neglected the household from the start. She would not get up in the morning, and he had to make breakfast and get the two children off to school. Something was always wrong; no butter, or the sugar was finished, or no food at all in the refrigerator. The wife seems to have been neurotic and unbalanced, but it is all vague and general, and I doubt whether it will be sufficient to establish a case of cruelty.

MAY 17. The defender went into the witness box. She was obviously peculiar, with a macabre fascination about her which made the situation easy to understand.

MAY 18. Mrs Taylor did not turn up. Shortly before 12 word came that the defender had arrived; she explained to Walker that she had slept in. In her evidence yesterday, when asked about her alleged neglect of her home and family, she had said it was impossible for her to get up in the morning, and today's incident seemed to establish her credibility on that point. She was a frank witness, explaining her emotions and difficulties at length, and accepting most of what I put to her. I felt a real sympathy with her, and we got on well together — I enjoyed cross-examining her, and I think she enjoyed telling me all about it. She told us about a sensation she had had of snakes in her arms, which made it impossible for her to remain in the Crichton Royal hospital. When I came to address Walker on the evidence I found him unexpectedly difficult. Perhaps like me he had felt attracted to the defender and wanted to let her have her way.

MAY 25. A jury trial before Migdale. The defenders had averments based on hospital records, to the effect that the pursuer's incapacity had been due to deep-seated emotional and mental disturbances, and chronic alcoholism. A psychiatrist in a letter to another doctor said his main complaint was that he had a certain Sister C. on his mind. "Rather belligerently he wanted me to tell him why she was still on his mind. It was ever since she gave him an injection . . . I think there is a good deal of aggression and although I seldom get frightened this was one patient I did not care to be alone with for too long". In 1960 he was admitted to hospital as a day patient, but kept going out for drink at lunch time and "returning to play cards with alcoholic patients". The pursuer turned out to be rather delightful: frank, spontaneous, good humoured, answering all Kissen's questions with complete candour and in a racy, friendly manner. He was quite unselfconscious, moving about in the witness box with constant gestures, and sitting down or standing up as he felt inclined. He candidly admitted that he went drinking every Friday when he got his pay, and often found himself miles from where he started. He would be in Glasgow, and wake up to find himself in Largs or Saltcoats. When asked about playing cards with alcoholic patients, he had no recollection of it, saying in surprise, "I was the alcoholic patient". After the accident he was supposed to have gone on working; but the foreman, he said, had told him to sit down against a bulkhead and he sat there doing nothing for the rest of the shift. When Kissen asked why he had not gone home, he replied, "To tell the truth, I was getting double pay — it was a Sunday shift". There was a very amusing interlude while in answer to a question from Kissen about a period when he worked as a tictac man he gave us an illustration of how tictac men operate, to show it was a skilled job, one that he was not really qualified for. The pursuer's account of the accident was supposed to be corroborated by a workmate, but when adduced as a witness he maintained stoutly that he had never seen the accident, and there was no answer to Kissen's motion that the case should be withdrawn. The only hope lay in the fact that Migdale was the judge, but even he had no hesitation in acceding to the motion.

JUN. 1. London — Stanhope Court Hotel: the clientele much the same — last night I heard a man refer to "that infernal nigger Nkrumah", and two separate people this morning were objecting because their eggs had been hard on successive mornings. The food is actually very good; and I told the head waiter that I did not know anything about boiled eggs, but he could tell the chef with my compliments that he was one of the few people in London who knew how to make porridge. He said the chef would be very pleased to get that message, particularly coming from me. The dermatitis case, *Gardiner*, did not take long. A short reply left me with 20 minutes to catch the 4 o'clock train. O'Brien got me a taxi, and I had an enterprising driver who did his best. His efforts were foiled by a cleansing lorry which proceeded to back into a pend in a narrow street south of Russell Square, manoeuvring back and forward three or four times. It was exactly 4 when we reached Kings Cross. I grabbed a porter and ran, but the train had gone. Finding the call boxes all occupied, I crossed the street to a box on the pavement, but found I had no pennies. Efforts to get some in a ladies' dress shop opposite were unavailing, and having tried the local newspaper seller — he had just started and had no pennies — I went down to the Underground and bought a newspaper. This gave me two pennies, and I got two more by taking a 10d ticket at the booking-office. Thus equipped, I dialled the BEA number and asked for "Reservations Edinburgh", but forgot to press Button A, so that my request would not be heard at the receiving end. Not realising this, I stood patiently holding the phone to my ear for 10 minutes, thinking that Reservations were slow in answering. At last I realised what was wrong, and pressed Button A, but by then I was too late. I should of course have pressed Button B, and started again, for I had now left myself again without any pennies. It occurred to me to buy a packet of cigarettes — of which I use quite a lot at consultations — and this gave me 4d change. This time I got through to Reservations at once, but was told that bookings for tonight had reached the stage of being dealt with at West London Airport, to which the girl offered to put me through. The line was occupied, and she suggested she should give me the number and I could ring the Airport on an outside line. This offer I had to decline for lack of any more pennies, and she agreed to keep trying to put me through — which after another 10 minutes she was able to do. But there were no seats available on any Edinburgh plane tonight. I returned with my bags to the main-line station and enquired about sleepers; all sleepers, I was told, were booked. The Tyne-Tees Pullman was standing at the platform, and it occurred to me that I might join it and get as far as Newcastle, where I might spend the night in the Station Hotel and go on by the early train tomorrow. This, it seemed, might be preferable to sitting up all night in the Edinburgh train. But the Pullman too turned out to be fully booked. So I thought I should go to the Reeds' and phone John Taylor as a last resort. Found Ann entertaining about 20 women, some Old Girls club. The party seemed to have just finished tea, with quantities of cake and other foodstuffs on the table, from which I was invited to help myself. Phoned Portland House, and was relieved to find Taylor there. He said he would phone me back in 15 minutes, and did so with the welcome news that there was a sleeper for me on the 11.35.

JUN. 2. Woke between 3 and 4, and finished reading *Jampot Smith*, by Jeremy Brooks. It is about teenagers at school at Llandudno during the war, and is rather a lovely book, written with sympathy and affection by an author who knows his young people through and through, and brings them delightfully to life.

> "Love has a baffling logic of its own. One falls in love with a person about whom one knows nothing, and only then, after the first impulse has been obeyed, does one start slowly to discover those qualities which, in later years, seem to be the essence of one's love. Thus with Kathy I came first to realise how little I knew of her, and then to uncover the treasures which in retrospect I would have said made me love her. Yet I loved her first".

In Parliament House at lunch time, after I had remarked on the fact that the Lords had not known the meaning of "stoor" when I read it out in the evidence in the dermatitis case, Shewan told a story about Dr Tennant of Clydebank. The morning after the blitz, when a large part of the town was destroyed and many inhabitants killed, he was going along the street and stopped as was his custom to exchange a word with an old resident. "A terrible night", he said. "Aye", said the old man, "it was awfu' stoory".

JUN. 4. We all motored to Mayfield North church, a handsome church with a good organ and choir, and a big congregation. Rev. W. J. G. McDonald, the minister, preached a fine sermon: thoughtful and to the point, with up-to-the-minute illustrations.

JUN. 7. Finished reading *The Life of John Middleton Murry*, by F. A. Lea. Murry was a queer fish, but this interesting biography succeeds in bringing out the fundamental integrity underlying his soul-searching tergiversations.

JUN. 9. Finished reading *Wake Up Stupid*, by Mark Harris, a novel about an unusual professor in a university in California, written entirely in letters. I much enjoyed its witty characterisation and rabelaisian humour. The letters bring vividly to life the

18

professor's correspondents, ranging from a bishop to the manager of a prize-fighter of whom the professor owns a share. The book is sprinkled with amusing Johnsoniana, the professor being a student and admirer of Dr Johnson.

JUN. 10. We were wakened about 6.30 by Nicholas shouting and whistling for Richard outside the window. I got up and ordered him to clear out. He had laid out a lot of things on trays under the hedge, for Richard to look at, and sadly gathered them up, exactly like a man who comes to the door selling things when one tells him one does not want anything today.

JUN. 12. Glasgow: a fatal accident inquiry arising out of a fire on a German ship *Peyannel*. Fire had broken out in the hold while the ship was in the North Sea. The master ordered the hatches to be battened down, and continued through the Pentland Firth and round to Glasgow. On her arrival in the Clyde the firemaster decided to have the hatches opened. The officer in charge, McIntyre, dropped down with Station Officer Mearns on to the top of the cargo, both wearing breathing apparatus. It was presumed correctly that after two days of burning the hold would contain a dangerous concentration of carbon monoxide, and in some mysterious way both men were overcome. Other firemen and officers dropped down to assist them, and were themselves overcome by gas so as to require to be pulled out. When Sub-Officer Kelly came aboard, he found a chaotic situation, with men being pulled out unconscious from the hold and laid on the deck as their rescuers in turn collapsed and had to be hauled out. Kelly at once got hold of three sets of breathing apparatus, and he and the two other men got down into the hold. Some difficulty had been occasioned in getting a rope round Mearns, but this was eventually done and both officers got out. By this time however Mearns was dead. A jury of 7 had been impanelled when one of them got up and announced that he was a docker who had been working on the *Peyannel* on the day of the fire. This seemed an extraordinary coincidence; but Smith, who as Depute-Fiscal was in charge of the proceedings, did not think it afforded any reason for not having the man on the jury, and as I agreed with him the man was allowed to remain. In my cross-examination of McIntyre, he insisted that I was treating him as if he were on trial, and appealed to the presiding sheriff, A. D. Gibb, formerly Professor of Law in Glasgow University. He dealt with the situation calmly and competently, soothing the outraged officer while permitting the cross-examination to proceed. I thought Gibb's conduct of the inquiry was excellent throughout: impartial, reasonable and fair.

JUN. 15. Finished reading *Laughter in the Dark*, by Vladimir Nabakov. Despite a kind of compulsive force which one sometimes

19

feels in it, and one horrifyingly effective passage when a man who has been blinded wonders why nothing happens when he switches on the light, this is an unpleasant story which never rings true.

JUN. 16. High Court: *Haberstich*. Guthrie was in our favour, and I hoped he might be able to persuade the others; but after the three judges came together to make their decision it was obvious that Clyde was saying the evidence was sufficient. Guthrie shook his head, and without any discussion whatsoever Clyde proceeded to give judgment refusing the appeal — a shocking judgment, which did not deal with any of the points raised. Carmont of course merely said " I agree ". Guthrie then delivered an excellent dissenting judgment, covering all the points succinctly and effectively, and concluding that in his considered opinion there was no evidence whatever that Haberstich knew the goods were stolen. I regarded this as something of a moral victory, though it did no good to my unfortunate client, who will have to go off to serve his 18-month sentence. The time taken with criminal appeals meant the Court had not yet started its roll of Stated Cases, of which I had the last. As this was a very short case, it was agreed to take it right away. The appellant had been charged with assaulting his landlord by punching him on the face. A Glasgow police judge had found him guilty, and fined him £5. Attempts had been made by the solicitors to persuade the appellant that the appeal was hopeless, but he insisted on going on with it. His real grievance was that he had been kept for some days in prison before being bailed out, with the result that he had been unable to attend a compulsory paratroopers' training session, thereby losing an efficiency bounty. This of course was irrelevant, but I told the Court all about it, and they listened in a friendly way before refusing the appeal — no doubt about the justice of this decision.

JUN. 27. Judgment in *Taylor v. Taylor*: for the defender, on the view that any of her activities that had affected the pursuer's health had been the result of her mental illness and could not be regarded as cruelty. I daresay this is right.

JUN. 29. The Lord Advocate called me out into the hall and asked if I should like to be Sheriff of Roxburgh.

JUN. 30. Coming on the Lord Advocate in the lobby, I told him I should like to be Sheriff of Roxburgh.

JUL. 6. News reached Parliament House that the House of Lords had decided *Gardiner*'s case in my favour, unanimously reversing the First Division and restoring Kilbrandon's award.

JUL. 11. A. E. Pickard, aged 87, spent the whole day in the witness box in Wheatley's court, giving evidence in his case against my clients: *Pickard v. Pickard*. He was unexpectedly reasonable, only occasionally making an irrelevant remark. Ian Macdonald told me that while answering one question he took a half-crown out of his pocket and passed it to the shorthand writer. I certainly saw him offer her a box of matches — which Wheatley told him to put back into his pocket.

Jul. 12. Pickard startled everybody by his reply to a question by Ian Robertson about what his intentions were as regards the future of all these properties. "I'll give them all to you", he said.

Jul. 13. *Breen v. Breen*: the Second Division judgment. We had won this one, Cameron's judgment refusing decree being sustained on the ground that insanity is a defence to an action of divorce for cruelty. I think this is probably wrong.

Jul. 15. Elizabeth produced a notebook in which she had written an account of what happened to her yesterday at Blackford Hill on her way back from the school playing field. Nancy said she had seen Elizabeth writing it, sitting on the wall at the foot of the street before she got home.

> "When walking through the park I stopped at an ice cream van, and purchased an ice-cream. Just after I had bought it a crowd of small boys, one armed with a stone asked me ' for a sook hen '. I refused and walked on, one boy took my purse (very clever), without my knowing, the other boys shouted out 'He's got your purse hen'. The boy then gave me it back. When I had turned the corner I looked to see what he had taken. I had about 6d in my purse and a key, only the key was left. I then walked home".

The other item in the book is short:

> "When waiting at the bus-stop, I saw three ambulances pass in 5 mins. No one was in the front except the two ambulance men. Footnote: The bus stop is near Parker's store".

Jul. 18. Evidence in the first Pickard case ended, and old Pickard went into the box for the second time, to give evidence about the properties involved in his case against his daughter Dorothy. He insisted on telling us the origin of the name of one of the properties, Formakin: "for makin' money", he said.

Jul. 20. Addressing Wheatley on the evidence in the Pickard cases. He was against me all the time, evidently determined to find for old Pickard if he can; but my clients were not at all disconcerted. They are a nice family, and have throughout shown a remarkable absence of illwill against their father, for whom they all have great veneration.

Jul. 28. Finished reading *The Road to Harpers Ferry*, by J. C. Furnes. I learned for the first time who John Brown was, and how his soul comes to be marching on after his capture of Harpers Ferry.

AUG. 1. Finished reading *The Manchurian Candidate*, by Richard Condon, an immensely powerful story brilliantly told, which holds one's interest from the start and goes on inexorably to its climax. It includes a wealth of satirical observation, but there is more to it than that: a magical, almost religious awe that reminded me strongly of Charles Williams' books, however different their subject matter and however greatly this author's view of life differs from his. Selsey: our house, Bushy Ruff, at the very end of the road, right above the shore.

AUG. 4. Portsmouth. We went to see the *Victory*. I was surprised at the size of the ship, which I had imagined as quite small. Actually, as we were informed by the guide, it carried 800 men at Trafalgar. We crossed in a little steam ferryboat to Gosport. Here we lunched in a low-class cafe, which served some very good food. Richard's 4/6 lunch was mostly wasted, as there was nothing he wanted to eat, but the lunch I ate myself would have cost a lot more than 4/6 in most places.

AUG. 5. To the local cinema, the Pavilion: "Tom Thumb" — terrible. The fairy story had been turned into an American musical too puerile for adults and too slow for children.

AUG. 6. Motored with the children to the parish church, where the Rector of Selsey, Rev. Prebendary G. Handisyde, preached to a smallish congregation: a simple sermon, nothing much in it, but sensible, dignified and quite interesting. Richard did not think much of the Church of England service, and I rather agreed with him. After lunch we all set off for a motor-cycle scramble at Butser Hill. The course went down a steep descent into a hollow called Grandfathers Bottom, and up again by a long, steep, dusty climb. There was a radar station at the top, and spectators were asked to keep their cars as much away from it as possible, as they were causing interference and affecting the control of aircraft coming in to London Airport. Elizabeth has been keeping up her diary: "I asked dad what we did Friday morning, he said we'd gone to Pourtsmouth — I'd forgotten . . . It is a very busy place with an enormous lot of sailors. We went round Victory with very amusing guide. He told us all about capstans, pikes, where Nelson fell, etc."

AUG. 7. Alton Show. Near Petersfield the heath had a cricket ground tucked away in the middle of it, and then a golf course. Though it looked an attractive course, golf did not seem to be taken very seriously: people were picnicing and sleeping in the middle of the fairways, and children playing in the bushes, the golfers having to steer their way round these obstructions. At Selsey, Broncho Bill's Circus has just set up its tent: a circus that has been criticised in the

World's Fair as advertising turns which never appeared. Selsey has been liberally plastered with similar advertisements, and I was interested to find on a small slate in front of the tent a message to the effect that some of the leading turns might not appear today, having been held up by road trouble after appearance at a big gala at Swansea. The whole circus equipment visible here seemed to be four small waggons, two old horses, a mule and a monkey. I went also to look for the golf course, which typically of Selsey is hidden away, with no advertisement whatever, at the end of a stony little lane — nothing on the clubhouse or elsewhere to inform visitors about admission or charges. The weather continued fine — just the kind of day to bring out Bank Holiday crowds, so that it was all the more surprising to find the roads I travelled along almost as deserted as on any ordinary day: some traffic to get past from time to time, but nothing to support the view that motoring at holiday time in the south of England has become impossible.

AUG. 8. Finished reading *Trumpets from the Steep*, by Diana Cooper, the final volume of her reminiscences. I read a scathing review of this book not long ago; and certainly it is odd to read of her having a premonition of danger to her husband when he was flying back from France during the war, and ringing up "Clemmie" Churchill so that she could ask her husband to send up a squadron of Spitfires to protect him. But what the reviewer failed to realise was that it was the author's own candour that revealed the more foolish and weaker aspects of her character, she knowing well how weak and foolish they are. Like its predecessors, this is a completely honest book, and gives a genuine picture of its author's personality. It is worth remembering too that in spite of all her fears and forebodings she is always ready to tackle the task that comes to hand and carry it through to completion — keeping and milking a cow, or running an embassy, or loving two men at the same time. Through it all runs her devotion to the egregious, sentimental, matter-of-fact Duff her husband. I like her when she says "Before we married I used to ask him if he felt equal to the heavy task of keeping me happy. He never doubted it for a moment". I like too her delightful vignettes of Churchill himself — for instance, on a picnic in North Africa when he is hauled up a steep mountain track by means of a tablecloth knotted round his back and under his arms. "He had no thought of being ridiculous (one of his qualities)". Her judgments of people are shrewd: she does not go far wrong. I found her rather lovable, and I am sorry that there are no more books for her to write. We all motored to Bognor: a surprisingly tawdry, trippery place, with practically no shops of any quality. Back to Selsey. The top of the circus tent had blown down in the gale, and all today's performances were off; so Broncho Bill here met with an appropriate penalty.

AUG. 9. Bognor: a fete in the hospital grounds. I paid 6d to get in, but won 1/- flicking pennies. There was "dancing" in a cleared space in the grass, where 20 or 30 teenage girls were rocking and rolling — one of each couple jigging up and down in one place, while the other spun round first one way and then the other, all with completely vacant expressions. It looked crazy.

AUG. 12. A petrol station on the Arundel-Chichester road with a machine labelled "Fresh Farm Eggs". For a half-crown put in a slot, one got half a dozen eggs and 3d change.

AUG. 14. Finished reading *Emergency Exit*, by Sylvia Foot. Lady Foot's husband was Governor of Cyprus during the troubles which preceded the final settlement, and she has written a remarkable little book about her experiences. She has a very human and obviously delightful personality, with malice towards none — a writer of great sensibility. Her moods range from the humour of a Cypriot workman who, like all others working at Government House, has a soldier allotted to him to see that he keeps out of mischief and is found searching wildly around, complaining that he has lost his soldier — to her mental response to some high-up military person whom she has approached with an enquiry on behalf of a Cypriot wanting her husband's release, and who has advised her to "save her sympathy" for the widows of soldiers and civilians who have been murdered. How, she asks herself, is it possible to save one's sympathy? Surely there is enough to go round. The author herself has understanding and sympathy for all, and although very sensible of the tragedy and horror never loses her belief in the joy of living. I liked this book very much; it has magnanimity and courage and loving kindness. West Wittering: the church an old building with a simple but attractive interior, set in a pleasantly unkempt church-yard full of old gravestones and surrounded by trees. We got back to the Selsey road by lanes winding through flat country and threatening constantly to land us back at the place we had started from.

AUG. 15. We took day tickets to London, and the 9.56 train. To Ede & Ravenscroft's, where I was measured for a new wig; they told me blandly it would be ready in 5 or 6 months. Then to Tower Wharf, where we embarked on a cruise to Greenwich. Elizabeth was unwilling to go, on the ground that it would be rough. We assured her that it was perfectly smooth, but it turned out to be very rough indeed. The boat was small, crammed with passengers, including some who could not find a seat, so that it was low in the water, with waves breaking over the bow. Every time a boat passed, our helmsman shut off the engine and turned the boat head on into the wash, and there was a great heave and splash — quite alarming. So, although it was interesting to see all the wharves and ships, it was a relief to reach Greenwich in safety. I remarked to Elizabeth that she had been right about its being rough, to which she replied, "It wasn't rough at all".

AUG. 16. With Richard to the golf club, where we paid 5/- and 2/6 respectively and had 9 holes of golf. It is a 9-hole course, and we could have gone round twice for the same money. A pleasant enough course, flat but not uninteresting. At two holes I lost my ball, in one of numerous wide, reedy ditches in which it is utterly impossible to find a ball. Chichester Granada: "One Hundred and One Dalmatians" — the animation brilliant, and some of the animal characters very funny, but Disney's humans are always tiresome, and for all its cleverness I did not find the film particularly interesting. The children enjoyed it immensely, as they do most films. Everybody goes to bed early in these parts, and we had a speedy, unobstructed journey back to Selsey.

AUG. 20. We went to see the polo at Cowdray Park. By a misunderstanding, we went into the members' enclosure, and got a good seat on the grass in front of the members' cars: everything very peaceful and elegant.

AUG. 21. Chichester cathedral: the organ playing, the organist a young man who played on steadily, apparently for his own amusement. An excellent recital, marred by the noise of babies which were being carried through the cathedral in considerable numbers. One which emitted a loud yelp at regular intervals seemed to be making a complete tour of the building.

AUG. 23. Elizabeth has completed her diary for Sunday: "We went to see a Polo match. It was great. There are two goals, the men ride on horses and try to hit the ball into their own goal with things like fly-swatters. Jimmy Edwards was playing".

AUG. 30. Home. The holiday quite a success — Selsey does not make the best of itself, but it avoids all the abuses, even the most trivial: ice-cream stalls, for instance, or bathing boxes. So the beach is delightfully quiet. The house very charming; and delightful to get straight from it to the sea. I lost a pound in weight, due no doubt to the sea bathing.

SEPT. 18. St Boswells: a meeting of the Probation Committee. Lady Elliot presided — masterful, full of her subject, and despite her courtesy to other members obviously quite unable to understand how anyone could hold a point of view other than her own. I thought she was very much on the mark.

SEPT. 20. Parliament House: 4 consultations. In the course of one of them I had to order out the wife of my client, who kept interrupting me when I was advising her husband. I had had to put up with this woman on a previous occasion, and had made up my mind not to put up with her again.

OCT. 2. STV had a programme on "You and the Law", for which they claimed to have had the cooperation of the Faculty of Advocates. But after a few minutes of drivel — little sketches played in a manner that would have disgraced any Women's Institute dramatic society — I was glad to go off and feed the cat.

OCT. 4. As Sheriff of a seaboard county, I am *ex officio* a Commissioner of Northern Lights, and had a Board meeting to attend in their offices in George Street at 4.

OCT. 5. Parliament House. In talk about the Irish labourers who come over from County Donegal and become involved in actions of damages in the Scottish courts, A. A. Bell remarked that the office of the local solicitor was known as the Grotto, because the clients who came away from it with their awards of damages always left their crutches behind.

OCT. 6. Finished reading *Flight into London*, by David Storey, a love story told by a Yorkshire miner's daughter who goes off to London with a married man: a simple, unpretentious story, none the worse of recognising that besides its idyllic moments love has its periods of doubts and despondency. The drab anti-climax of the ending may be right too.

OCT. 8. The Wolf Cub packs in the district were all attending morning service in Morningside parish church. Mr Wood preached on II Kings 13,16. He never seemed to me to get to the root of the matter, and indeed it might be a most misleading sermon to preach to boys. Finished reading *Lifeboat Number Seven*, by Lieut-Commander Frank West — one of about 80 men who packed into a small lifeboat when their ship was sunk by a raider in the South Atlantic. Most were Indians who were more of a liability than an asset, but there were also three young officers whose navigational skill brought the lifeboat to the coat of Brazil in a 39-days voyage — within a day in time, and a few hundred miles in reckoning, of what they had calculated at the start. More than half of those in the boat died en route. Written in a straightforward, matter-of-fact way, it is an enthralling story: remarkable evidence of what men can go through and still survive.

OCT. 9. Yesterday's *Observer* prints some letters written by Rose Macaulay to an Anglican priest in Boston, Massachusetts, including one about her late uncle.

"He had been an agnostic (very noble in character) from his undergraduate days on; but when he was dying he said to his sister, who had mentioned God and a future life: 'Well, there's nothing so rum it might not be true', which pleased my aunt very much".

On getting into the car to go down to the library, I found the cat sleeping on the shelf behind the back seat. I did not trouble to move it, but it woke up on the way down and made such a noise that I had to bring it home. Finished reading *Storyboard*, by John Bowen. I was misled by the title, and the design on the jacket, into thinking that this was intended to be a funny book, but though it has amusing passages it is really rather grim — the build-up of suspense effectively done. The book is about an advertising agency, but though it throws an interesting light on that industry it is more concerned with the agency as people than as an abstraction: an absorbing novel.

OCT. 10. To the National Library to borrow two books for the children on Duffes' list, both books I had enjoyed as a boy: *The Rival Submarines*, by Percy F. Westerman, and *The Adventures of Lieutenant Lawless RN*, by R. Bennett.

OCT. 11. A debate before Jack Hunter, who was installed on Friday as a judge of the Court of Session, on the phoney view that an additional judge is required to cope with pressure of work. His first extempore judgment was very competent, as one would expect from Hunter.

OCT. 12. A jury trial before Migdale: Lamb v. British Transport Commission. The pursuer, a blacksmith's striker employed by the defenders in their smithy at St Rollox, was helping to turn a 10-foot connecting rod. His foot caught on the base of an anvil standing in the centre of the floor, and he fell and hit his head on a table. The case is based on the unpromising ground that the defenders should not have had the floor obstructed by an anvil, and I was not hopeful of being able to persuade a jury that it was negligent to have an anvil at a blacksmith's fire. Emslie got the pursuer to admit that it was the natural place for the anvil to be.

OCT. 13. Before the trial resumed, I did some work on the speech I had prepared before it began, and had quite a nice speech to make to the jury — anticipating an attempt by Emslie to laugh the case out of court. Migdale was an excellent judge for this kind of case, giving us a charge which was perfectly fair and indeed rather favoured the pursuer. The jury found for the pursuer by 11 to 1, awarding him £750.

OCT. 15. We all motored to church, where Rev. John Birkbeck, of John Knox Church, Aberdeen, preached on Galatians 6,17. He never got his points or his illustrations quite right, but he had a good point and good illustrations, and what he said was worth saying.

OCT. 18. When Nancy went out with the dog at night she found a hedgehog on the pavement. I went up and brought it home; put it in the back garden, but when I went out with bread and milk it had disappeared.

OCT. 23. Had to go to the Central Hall to preside over a meeting called to support a project for a national theatre to Edinburgh: Sinclair Shaw's present craze. He had roped me in for it, though privately I regarded it as a fantastic notion, considering that Edinburgh is completely unable to support the three theatres it has. I opened the meeting by saying that if it were thought that a national theatre was desirable Edinburgh by reason of its setting and traditions would seem to be the appropriate site. In the past few years, unfortunately, we in Edinburgh had been too busy putting up lamp posts and raising the level of pavements to give much thought to theatres; and when one reflected that in the week following the Festival not one of Edinburgh's three commercial theatres found it possible to remain open it did not look as if Edinburgh deserved any theatre at all, much less a national one. That however was a counsel of despair which was not shared by those who had organised the meeting. Shaw was interesting though not particularly convincing; he was more concerned with detail of where the theatre should be than any purpose it might serve. Professor Butt, of the chair of English Literature, was more convincing, with references to the National Gallery and the National Library as analogies.

OCT. 25. Appeal: Stanley v. Baxters Bus Services. Sheriff-Substitute Young found there was negligence on both sides, and having assessed total damages at £3250 awarded the pursuer £1625. Both parties appealed to Calver, who held that there was no fault on Stanley's part and awarded £3250. The defenders have now appealed to the Court of Session. The case raises an interesting medical question. At the time of the accident the pursuer's injuries seemed trivial. Four weeks later he was found to be suffering from angina pectoris, and the medical witnesses for the pursuer have concluded rather halfheartedly that there was a causal connection. Young concluded that the angina, on a balance of probabilities, had resulted from the accident. Calver agreed, remarking that he had read the medical evidence many times but without any confidence of his understanding it. The evidence is lengthy, and the solicitors conducting the case pursued the matter with great diligence down every conceivable byway. They took from each of the doctors what was his opinion of the qualifications of the other medical witnesses, and questioned them at length about unimportant symptoms about which there had not been any factual evidence:

"If a person like Stanley had a habit in the course of his work of placing both his hands on his chest and leaning backwards and breathing in as though gaining relief from something, would that small mannerism in your opinion be related to any kind of heart trouble? A. — I do not think that we in the hospital or in a doctor's

28

surgery would relate that without further evidence. Q. — But I am asking you this question apart from whether there is other evidence or not? A. — Then I would say no. Q. — Assume that there is no other evidence and you don't know about the other entries; this is just one symptom? A. — I do not think that such symptoms are frequently related to any condition of the heart. Q. — What would make a man do that then? A. — I would say in the first instance one would be much more likely to think it was just a simple habit, that he was just in the habit of doing this, possibly through general tiredness and fatigue, but it would not give us a clue as to which particular systems in his body were diseased or, indeed, if any system in his body was affected. Q. — If you have a man who is in fact suffering from some condition of the heart over a period would it be a natural thing from him if he feels pain or tightness, which I understand are the normal symptoms, to put his hand or hands on his breast and breathe? A. — Usually the left hand over the left side of the chest, but if I understood or observed Mr Hamilton correctly I think he put both hands. Q. — Is it a natural thing for a man to place both hands over his nipples and seek to breathe deeply and at the same time lean back? A. — I think it is possible, but in my experience it is not the usual way. Q. — Supposing a man is suffering from a heart condition which causes him chest pain or discomfort, what does he do naturally? A. — I think we must distinguish between the very acute pain which may strike a man in dire agony, in which case he might well do that, but in that case he is usually lying and not moving himself about. Then there is the other occasion when a man is afflicted from time to time with discomfort in his chest, and as a rule they adopt an almost Napoleonic attitude whereby they put their hand in here. I have in fact seen woollen vests with a hole rubbed in them which is a result of this habit or method of response to the pain and discomfort that they feel ".

The defenders had put in a tender of £1625 at the same time as they lodged the appeal. The pursuer had turned this down, but knowing the First Division I had arranged for him to come through this morning to see me. But though he listened to the argument for sometime, and it must have been obvious to him what was likely to happen, he would not consider accepting the tender. In the afternoon he got fed up with it and went off home, leaving his case to go on to what I am afraid is almost certain disaster.

OCT. 26. The *Stanley* case: Mitchell still speaking. Just before the Court adjourned for lunch he referred to a passage in the evidence dealing with the famous Dr Hunter who had angina for 20 years and had remarked that he was always at the mercy of any fool that made him lose his temper. "It's a good thing he wasn't a judge", said Clyde, "or he wouldn't have survived long". "Or counsel", I remarked in an audible aside, which without thinking Mitchell proceeded to repeat to the Court. Clyde laughed, but Sorn looked a little taken aback; and Mitchell, realising that what he had said might be taken personally — as I had intended it — hastily remarked, "I think I had better pass on from the medical evidence as quickly as possible". But when the Court resumed after lunch I thought it right to get up myself and express my apologies for having by an "injudicious aside" led my learned friend into making an observation that might be construed as discourteous to some senator of the College of Justice. My learned friend, I added, was the most courteous of pleaders, and it was entirely my fault that he had been led into saying something that might be thought discourteous.

OCT. 27. I duly addressed the Court in *Stanley v. Baxters Bus Services*; although I had not much hope of any success, it seemed worth while to present as good an argument as possible. They gave me a fair hearing, and when they came together at the end for the pretence of a discussion Carmont unexpectedly took it upon himself to stand up for the pursuer, apparently saying to the others that it would be unjust to exonerate from all blame a bus driver who reversed blindly into collision with a pedestrian. But Guthrie was not sitting, and Clyde and Sorn had their opinions written last night, so that modification was impossible; and after a few minutes' argument they overbore Carmont and in the end he simply said "I agree". Clyde and Sorn read out their "extempore" opinions word for word, without even a passing reference to the argument presented this morning. The Court reversed both Sheriffs on the ground that no negligence had been proved against the bus driver.

NOV. 2. A divorce proof before Wheatley: the pursuer seeking to divorce his wife for desertion. He came in one day and found her smoking a clay pipe, and there were quarrels about this.

NOV. 4. Four consultations. One client, brought from Glasgow to discuss, with senior counsel, junior counsel, and solicitors, whether to accept an offer, replied to me when we were all assembled and I asked him what he thought about accepting it, "I'll need to see my lawyer about that".

NOV. 16. Wheatley had been delivering himself of his 100-page judgment in the *Pickard* case. He found against Angus and Dorothy all along the line, but had been unable to avoid assoilzieing the other three. Angus did not seem at all downhearted, and said that a sale of some of the others' properties would provide plenty of funds for taking his and Dorothy's case further.

DEC. 1. McShane v. McShane. I appeared for the wife, now Mrs Rockingham, who had brought a divorce action in 1955 against McShane on the ground of cruelty. McShane belonged to the so-called Scottish Republican Army, and was at one time tried on a charge of setting fire to the Ministry of Labour office in Glasgow. They are both Catholics, and in the course of the divorce proceedings McShane bombarded his wife's solicitor with scurrilous letters, advising him to read Cardinal Spellman's recent speeches on excommunication. Before the date of the proof he had returned to sea in the course of his occupation as a wireless operator, and was prevented from getting to Scotland by a hurricane. The proof was postponed, but he still did not turn up, and the divorce went through undefended. Nothing was heard of him until last month, when he appeared at the wife's house at 10 pm, demanding to see the child. He claims to be an American citizen, and had spent the intervening years in America, where he remarried. The wife refused to let him see the child, and he arrived at her school next day and had to be locked in a room by the headmaster until the police arrived and persuaded him to go. He then lodged a Minute for access, but as he had paid nothing towards the aliment of the child a motion was enrolled to ordain him to find caution, and Douglas Johnston ordered him to find £50. He has marked a reclaiming motion, and the motion today was to ordain him to find caution before proceeding. When Layden mentioned the case to me yesterday, it seemed to me rather fantastic that anyone should be asked to find caution before being allowed to argue whether he had to find caution or not. But I was persuaded that in the peculiar circumstances of the case there was something to be said for the motion, particularly before the First Division; and in fact I had no difficulty. They showed no sympathy towards Mr McShane, who appeared on his own behalf and made a number of wild allegations against his wife. He was ordained to find caution of £50 before proceeding with his appeal, and Sorn pointed out to him that it would be much better to find the caution that the Lord Ordinary had ordered him to find, and so get on with the merits of his claim to see his child — which he had come 7000 miles from California to do. To the New Club, where the Lighthouse Commissioners were giving a dinner to Wakelin, their retiring secretary. Albert Russell proposed Wakelin's health. Wakelin himself was quite good, and took the opportunity of having a dig at his old enemy Jack Hunter, saying that among many members of the Bar who had been Commissioners he had had a father and son: the father a gentleman, and the son a gentleman's son. Gilchrist insisted on speaking, and was followed by Lillie as senior commissioner. It occurred to me while they were speaking that I should have done it better, but none the less it was something of a surprise for me to be called on to speak, as the junior commissioner present. Everyone had referred to Wakelin as "Glen", his name being Glencorse Wakelin, and I remarked that the only Glens I had known had been dogs, but perhaps a collie was not an inappropriate symbol for one who had to round up a motley flock of Sheriffs, as well as bring home many wanderers all round the Scottish coasts from Muckle Flugga to the Mull of Galloway. By no means a polished speech, but I thought it was probably not bad for one who had never known Wakelin at all and was speaking entirely extempore.

DEC. 2. Five consultations, including two arising out of the same accident. I interviewed one of the clients and was halfway through a consultation with the second when it turned out that the solicitors had got them mixed up and I had advised the first man on the footing that he was the second. As they were a couple of good-for-nothing layabouts from Glasgow docks, it did not make a great deal of difference.

DEC. 4. Richard, Nicholas and Gordon went off to Blackford Hill to sledge. They returned with Richard's sledge broken, and Nicholas incapacitated by a cut on the eye; Mr Heggie was on his way home to take him to the Children's Hospital. So on my way back from town I bought a new sledge for Richard at the price of £3.

DEC. 7. A jury trial before Migdale.

DEC. 8. Alex Thomson, with his usual candour, had told me that his remaining witness would be Stabler. As I find Stabler the most difficult of the engineering experts, I spent a useful half-hour this morning preparing a cross-examination. As Alex in his speech committed some curious indiscretions, and Migdale when he came to charge the jury was as indecisive and off the point as usual, I had some hope that this unpromising case might come off. So it did; the jury by a majority of 11 to 1 awarded the pursuer £2,800. It was lucky for him that Kissen, who was to have taken the case for the defenders, was occupied elsewhere — Kissen would have torn the case to pieces.

DEC. 10. Television in the evening: an interesting film of the new Hiroshima which has arisen on the site of the ruins, the acme apparently of Americo-Japanese vulgarity, but with death always hanging over it in the form of delayed-action symptoms of radiation sickness.

DEC. 12. A jury trial before Douglas Johnston — watched by a party of schoolgirls from Stobswell School, Dundee, to whom I gave a little lecture during the lunch interval, on procedure and what the case was about.

DEC. 13. Finished reading *Russians as People*, by Wright Miller. It is concerned less with personalities than with general principles, and is uninterestingly written, but it gives an instructive picture of present-day Russia. It suggests that standards of values there are at least as high as in the competitive societies of Britain or America.

DEC. 14. A jury trial before Kilbrandon. He gave a delightful charge which gave no indication of his own views but explained to the jury what they had to decide, in easy, non-technical language, with complete lucidity and in the fewest possible words, without any any of the usual legal jargon about "onus of proof" or "balance of probabilities".

DEC. 15. With Nancy to the Lyceum: "The Big Killing". This thriller was excellent — witty, ingenious, full of character — and every part was played to perfection, Naunton Wayne particularly effective. We enjoyed every minute of it.

DEC. 16. To National Library to get two books for the children on Watt's list — including "Timothy in Bushland", which came back to my mind the other day as a book I had always enjoyed as a boy.

DEC. 17. The cat was out all night, and when we got up was perched on the very top of the lilac tree at the gate. It looked very odd, sitting on a bare twig.

DEC. 20. *McShane v. McShane*: a motion by the husband that he be allowed interim access was refused, much to the indignation of McShane and his American wife, who spoke to me afterwards more in sorrow than in anger about the number of lies I had had to tell. I rather liked the American wife, but McShane is pretty objectionable. Presided over a meeting of the Advocates Clerks Committee, to consider a request for an increase in writing fee from 2/- to 3/- per sheet.

DEC. 22. The start of the vacation, marked by the pile of papers that always seems to arrive when the Court rises.

DEC. 25. To Leith Street in quest of milk. We found a milk-vending machine outside a cafe and got 4 half-pints — the first two for 6d, presumably because the last user had failed to press the button to get his carton.

From Mr Alex M. Young:

110 Brora St. Glasgow, E3   Dec. 29. '61
Dear Gordon Stott,
Please accept this diary which might come in handy for Parliament Sq. or Dundas St. . .
Alexis is now 6 years old — and bright in singing — but not so "hot" at counting and reading; I'm tired of her singing about our little Lord Jesus — altho' I say nothing. Me being an Atheist. She is also quite good at dancing tho' not an expert.
Was at an anti-polaris demonstration — but couldn't help feeling that things were not the same — Pat Arrowsmith was in gaol at the time. Young people coming to me asking me to join the movement and selling me "Peace News" etc. I don't mind. *But* I thought they should have been down at Greenock Prison tearing it down brick by brick. . .

1962

1962 was another uneventful year – if a year in which the world probably came as near to complete destruction as it has ever been can properly be described as uneventful. The Cuban crisis, which blew up seemingly out of nothing and threatened for a week to engulf civilisation, subsided as suddenly as it had arisen; and in retrospect gave some ground for optimism as indicating how close our rulers could come to destroying us without actually taking the last fatal step. In the courts I was kept fully occupied, and should not have been surprised to find that my practice was the largest at the Scottish Bar – there was no means of telling. The novel feature of the summer was a week's cruise on the Pharos as a Commissioner of Northern Lights, with a Sunday in Barra and a sail up the coast of the Long Island to Stornoway.

JAN. 12. The McShane case came up in the First Division, on a motion for the wife to ordain McShane to find caution before proceeding with a reclaiming motion he had enrolled against Johnston's refusal of interim access. He appeared on his own behalf, and was a good deal less effective than on his previous appearance, harking back to injustices that had been done in the divorce action seven years ago. His American wife, sitting behind him, tried to get him on to the right lines, but he did not stay there long. Clyde harried him unmercifully, and eventually browbeat him into withdrawing his reclaiming motion, on the view that he ought to go back to the Outer House and get an early decision on the merits of the case. I think Clyde misled him in this: the first thing that will have to be done in the Outer House is to decide whether the Court has jurisdiction, and there will be a lot of legal argument before the merits can be reached.

JAN. 22. London: *Thomson v. Glasgow Corporation.* At first it looked as if we were not going to get very far — Simonds obviously took the view that amendment was a matter for the discretion of the Court of Session and that there was no ground for interfering. But in the afternoon they began to get interested and, I thought, to see that there was no reality in the suggestion of injustice to the defenders.

JAN. 23. It appeared that feeling had hardened overnight. Even Denning, who had seemed in my favour, was obviously swithering, and another half-hour was sufficient to bring the proceedings to a close: Kissen was told that they did not require to hear him. I was disappointed in the result: it appeared to me that the equities were overwhelmingly in the pursuer's favour, and there was no substance in the excuses that were given for failing to give her justice. To Portland House to call on John Taylor. Miss Flynn positively beamed on me, and said she thought a visit from me would be just the very thing; in his present frame of mind she believed it might do him a lot of good. This may have been so, though all I did was to sit in an armchair for half an hour drinking a glass of milk while he talked at me. He came out to the lift when I left, and stood talking for another five minutes, he on the landing and I in the lift, while the liftman waited patiently for him to stop. On the way down the liftman remarked to me that he had to be on duty by 8 o'clock, " but quite often 'e's there before me ".

From Biddy Derham-Reid:

9, Kenilworth Road, Lytham St. Annes, Lancashire   Jan. 31st 1962.
Dear Gordon/
Thank you very much for your letter . . . I'm sorry I failed to sign the voting paper — and my signature is *so* expansive — I always write the lot — Eulalie D. Derham-Reid — I thought, when I got my first cheque book — that that was the correct procedure — and though I have since suggested to the Bank — that I drop half of it — & omit writing Eulalie in full — " they " implored me not to — " Oh Miss DR — you are our only Eulalie — & we do like it when your cheque comes through. . ."

FEB. 1. A jury trial before Wheatley. With some hesitation, Wheatley was persuaded not to accept a motion by Kissen to withdraw the case. This point came up in the afternoon, when the evidence for the pursuer finished, and Scotland was standing by with a case for me for tomorrow in the event of this one's coming to an untimely end. He went off to find someone else to take tomorrow's case, and we were then mainly concerned with preventing what has happened in Wheatley's court two or three times lately: evidence finishing about 3.45, and his deciding to sit late and finish the case. Kissen and I agreed that we should play out time on the evidence, and I cross-examined a surveyor at length on a plan he had prepared — though nothing really arose on it.

FEB. 2. I made a good speech, and Kissen, I thought, erred as he often does on the side of over-violence. Wheatley gave a longwinded but perfectly fair charge, though it was obvious that he would have found for the defenders. The jury thought otherwise, and found unanimously for the pursuer, assessing damages at £6,000 — too good an award to stand without an appeal. My first victory this term.

FEB. 4. On television tonight Roy Thomson, the newspaper owner, was needled by John Freeman, and encountered Freeman's questions with imperturbable good humour and frankness. Freeman did not seem to understand the great merit of a newspaper proprietor who left his editors to follow out their own policy, good or bad: an attitude which has had excellent results so far as the *Scotsman* is concerned, the editorial policy of which has become much more liberal, unpartisan and courageous since Thomson became proprietor. Despite the lateness of the hour, I was kept riveted to the screen by the following programme: Jacqueline du Pre playing the cello with grim, unsmiling devotion, tossing her hair back from her forehead with the vigour of her playing — an almost mesmeric attraction about her.

FEB. 5. Pike in Scotland for a couple of days. He told me that when London traffic was paralysed last Monday by a one-day strike on the Underground he cycled to work from Ealing, 12 miles each way, across London. Cycling was a much faster mode of travel than by car, car traffic being pretty well brought to a stop by traffic jams.

FEB. 6. A proof before Walker. The pursuer had been working in the hold of SS *Venetia* at Princess Dock, loading cartons of milk. They were slung on board by a Clyde Navigation Trust crane. The crane suddenly swung the hook across the hatch, and the hook hit the pursuer on the face. Unfortunately the pursuer is a complete humbug. The blow he received seems to have been trivial, but he was off work for a long time, complaining of headaches, dizziness, and defects of hearing and eyesight. He has equipped himself with a hearing aid and spectacles, though all the doctors agree that he can hear and see equally well without them. But though he was strongly cross-examined on credibility, and our medical witness could find little to say in his support, his supporting witnesses on the facts were good, and when I put the hatchmouthman into the box he gave the show away, insisting that what had happened was pure accident, through his thinking that the hook would pass safely between the pursuer and another man. It was obvious that the accident could have been avoided very easily by ordering the crane to lift the hook a little before swinging it; and I do not see how even James Walker can fail to find for the pursuer, though he may make only a nominal award of damages.

FEB. 7. Judgment assoilzieing both defenders — apparently on the view that all the evidence was wrong, and the accident had happened because the hook had swung after one of the pursuer's mates let it go. There was no evidence to this effect, but as Walker has gone on to say that if he had been in the pursuer's favour he would have awarded only nominal damages there is probably no point in attempting to take the matter further. Letter from National Commercial Bank: I have been corresponding with them about payment of school fees, which by a Merchant Company ruling have to be paid to the bank, and an instruction has been issued that an additional sum of 6d must be paid with each fee to cover the bank charge, and a stamped envelope sent for return of the attendance slip bearing a receipt. Since the parent is given no alternative to paying through the bank, I queried whether this charge should not be met by the Merchant Company, and on the last two occasions sent only the bare amount of the fees. The bank in a long reply explained that the arrangement has been made for general convenience, but give no justification for the instruction that the parents should pay the charge. They have accepted my payment, and sent back the attendance slips duly stamped.

FEB. 8. Finished reading *No Signposts in the Sun*, by V. Sackville-West, a neat, rather moving vignette of a man who is told by his doctor that he is soon going to die, and who in fact does, just after he has realised, too late, that the woman he has come to love reciprocates his affection. With the children to the Dominion at 5 to see " Seven Brides for Seven Brothers ". We had asked Nicholas, but Mrs Heggie thought it unsuitable for children : a strange view, when the Heggies allow Nicholas to spend hours watching American television rubbish in which the " characters " spend their time shooting at one another and a blow is the answer to every problem. " Seven Brides for Seven Brothers " seemed if anything better on a second visit. We all enjoyed it thoroughly.

FEB. 13. A jury trial before Migdale. The pursuer, an apprentice dresser in the defender's foundry, was working on a circular casting. The wedges worked loose, and the casting fell over, injuring the pursuer's wrist. His ground of action was that the defenders failed to provide a vice to hold the casting secure. In addition to the pursuer and his father, I put in three fellow-workmen as witnesses, and Dr Muir ; and the odd thing was that each of them had a different description of how he wedged that type of casting. Dr Muir and the pursuer's father were the only two who agreed, and their description of how it should be done was quite different from the pursuer's. But they all agreed that the job could not be done properly with the casting lying on its side, as the defenders suggested. They put in their works manager to support this, but he did not know much about it, and fortunately agreed with me that if the casting had to be set on edge wedges were a very insecure way of holding it. The jury found unanimously for the pursuer.

FEB. 14. Second Division : a motion for a new trial following a jury verdict in favour of the pursuer. The pursuer, a cranedriver, went with his crane to work in the premises of British Oxygen Company. A man named Mitchell went with him, to walk along the street in front of the crane and keep the way clear. The pursuer asked the

British Oxygen people for a slinger. They had nobody, and he had to make do with Mitchell, who had never done any slinging before. The crame overbalanced and fell, with the result that the pursuer was seriously injured. The case was based on Mitchell's negligence in overloading the crane and slinging the load badly. Nobody said the load was badly slung, and both Mitchell and the lorry driver said the slinging was all right. The pursuer insisted it must have been badly slung, and rejected all suggestions that there was overloading. He was responsible, he said, for seing that his crane was not overloaded, and if anybody had come and told him he was overloading his crane he would have told him where he got off. Lord Kilbrandon had been asked to withdraw the case from the jury; Alex Thomson for the defenders today said that Kilbrandon had gone so far with him, telling the jury that there was no evidence of faulty slinging but he would leave the case of overloading to them. This seemed to me to be right, for although the pursuer had insisted that the crane was not overloaded he seemed to be under the impression that there were only 12 tubes in the heave, the same number approximately as had been in the others, while Mitchell and the lorry driver said clearly that there were 16. Taken along with the fact that the crane had overbalanced, I thought the evidence might be just enough, before the Second Division; and so it turned out. When my turn came, I contented myself with a very short summing-up of the evidence, to the effect that this was a bigger load than usual and Mitchell had been responsible for slinging it. "Put like that", said my junior to me, "it all seems very logical and simple". The pursuer was highly delighted, rushing round shaking hands with everyone, including Douglas Fairbairn, who had nothing to do with the case but happened to be standing near. He was lucky, for if there was anything at all in what the pursuer had said in evidence the accident had happened mostly through his own pigheadedness.

FEB. 16. A debate on the McShane case, about jurisdiction — McShane appearing on his own behalf. He abused his former wife and former solicitors, and lawyers in general, with an occasional mild rebuke from the judge. I think most judges would have had McShane downstairs in the cells long before he finished his diatribe, but Johnston contented himself with remarking from time to time that he was doing his case no good. McShane during my reply came across and leaned over my shoulder while I was citing authorities, to study the passages I was quoting. He put me right about some averment in our Answers, remarking that he did not know how some of the boys on the other side had ever got their practising tickets.

FEB. 22. Johnston in the McShane case dismissed the Minute on the ground that he had no jurisdiction.

FEB. 24. Took an opportunity to approach young Clyde about a matter which had been troubling Duffes and to a less extent myself: a conversation Duffes and I had been having earlier in the week at the fireside in Parliament House about the shortcomings of the First Division and its President — how much the courts had deteriorated since Cooper's death, and how Lord Clyde was the worst judge that one could imagine. This is a normal topic of conversation round the fire in Parliament Hall, but we had failed to notice that young Clyde was standing a little bit along. As we both have a great respect and liking for young Clyde, we felt sorry about this. But today Clyde assured me that he had not overheard this conversation, and in any event felt we should have full liberty to criticise judges, including the Lord President, to our hearts' content. Actually, apart from my dislike of the Lord President's conduct of the court, I am on fairly friendly terms with him just now — he signed a chit for me the other day to get two books for the children from the National Library.

MAR. 2. Special Constables' dinner at Dryburgh Abbey Hotel. Ex-Provost Landles of Hawick told me about a man who had come before Sheriff Macleod on a charge of poaching, having been found with a ferret standing beside him. He maintained that the ferret was not his, and had appeared by chance when the police arrived on the scene. After quite a long trial, Macleod found him guilty, whereupon he asked for the return of his ferret. "Well", said Macleod, "that's not a very good thing when we've spent a whole day here by your insisting that the ferret wasn't yours". "I have", said the man, "but what your Lordship said convinced me that it must have been mine".

MAR. 3. An interdict case: Donaghy v. National Union of Scottish Mineworkers. Scottish miners have been up in arms against a decision of the Coal Board to close several Scottish collieries, and suggested to the National Union of Mineworkers, of which the Scottish union is a section, that there should be a mass lobby of MPs at Westminster. The National Union rejected this, and advised the Scottish union to proceed with consultation at area level. The Scottish union decided to go on with its own scheme; and the pursuer for whom I was appearing, a Kilsyth miner, has raised an action to prohibit the Scottish Union's trustees from paying out any of the Union funds for the purpose of this trip. Ian Fraser, who appeared for the respondents, was persuaded to give an undertaking that the trustees would not pay out any of the funds standing in their name. The action, though in the name of an individual Scottish miner, has the secret backing of the Union's national officials in London, who have inspired the action with a view to curbing activities which the Scottish union under its Communist leader Alex

Moffat has been carrying on in opposition to the Union's official policy.

MAR. 13. A proof before Milligan — the case based on failure to provide a safety bar across a doorway into a hatch. There is a sharp conflict of evidence as to whether a bar was there. The pursuer and his mates were all quite clear that there was none, but one of the unfortunate things about having a case tried before a judge is that he is liable to prefer the evidence of some officer or other "responsible person", and I think that may well happen here.

MAR. 14. It was obvious that Milligan was going to accept the "responsible" witnesses and disbelieve the pursuer and his mates — though I felt no doubt myself that the pursuer was completely honest. This case looks like being a classic example of the injustice which results from having a jury case tried by a judge.

MAR. 22. Bradley v. Cruickshank: an appeal by a bookmaker who was convicted at Ayr Sheriff Court on a charge of failing without reasonable cause to produce his bookmaker's permit for examination when required to do so by a policeman. The appellant had been operating at Bogside races under the name of John Classic when two policemen came up and asked if he had a permit. He said he did not have it with him, explaining that he had changed his suit and forgot to change the permit from one suit to the other. Sheriff Frame held that this was not reasonable cause for failing to produce the permit, and fined him £5. I argued that there could be no more reasonable cause for failing to produce a permit than the fact that the bookmaker did not have it with him. Where the Sheriff had gone wrong was in considering whether it was reasonable for the appellant not to have had his permit with him, when there was nothing in the Act to say that a bookmaker had to have his permit with him when operating at a race course. The Court were left in a quandary. They obviously did not want to quash the conviction, but on the other hand could see no answer to my argument that if a bookmaker did not have a permit with him he plainly had reasonable cause for not producing it to a policeman. In the end, after a long discussion among themselves, they took it to avizandum. I daresay they will find some way of allowing the conviction, but I at least got farther than I had had any expectation of doing, and I certainly enjoyed the argument — as, I think, did my listeners, if I could judge by sounds of mirth coming from the benches behind.

MAR. 27. The Second Division's decision in *Bradley v. Cruickshank*: they upheld the conviction, holding that it was for the Sheriff to decide what was reasonable cause.

AP. 1. Completely hoaxed by an *Observer* "Profile" of Sir Timothy Cargill, distinguished physicist and administrator who though seldom mentioned in the newspapers had held positions of effective political power. I read without a qualm that he was "still remembered in College as the last scholar to score a goal in the Wall Game", and how at King's he had set up a new record in the quarter mile and rowed in the defeated Cambridge crew of 1923 — "itself a distinction in these years of monotonous Cambridge victories". His influence with Macmillan I readily accepted, as also his Lithuanian wife and his entertaining in his Somerset home, where he was a renowned connoisseur of burgundy. It seemed odd that he was "prouder that his daughter, Mairi, is art editor of a monthly review, PROG, than that his son, Hugo, was recently appointed Assistant Keeper of the Queen's Statistics at Windsor Castle"; but it was not until I read of his circle of acquaintances — "which includes Ian Mikardo, Charles Clore, Arthur Schlesinger, Tony Snowden, Huckleberry Hound and John Osborne" — that I began to wonder what I was reading. Even then I merely thought it was oddly expressed, and only when I turned the page found that it was all a hoax, and the distinguished portrait at the head of the article had been Peter Sellers with a stiff collar.

AP. 3. Nancy stayed in bed with a bad cough. As it was raining hard, I motored Elizabeth to the bus, then came home for breakfast. Surprising how much time housework occupies: the routine jobs of breakfast, washing up, fires and shopping took me most of the forenoon.

AP. 4. Had things better organised today, and had breakfast all finished in time to take the dog round and get off to town soon after 9. Tonight's television included an interesting half-hour about W. R. Hearst and his white-elephant castellated mansion in California — which seemed to me distinctly attractive.

AP. 5. Norah phoned to say I had better come in, as there was a big pile of papers; on arrival at Dundas Street I found ten different sets of papers awaiting my attention.

AP. 6. Walked down with the dog to Morningside to buy a postal order for Elizabeth's foreign stamps — she gets a monthly sample book from Bridgnorth Stamp Co. When I got to the post office I found a notice on the door, "Dogs Not Admitted"; as two ladies were having a lengthy chat on the pavement outside, I asked one of them to hold the dog for me. *Tonight* on television included Gerald Gardiner attacking the regulations which require dogs and cats to be imprisoned in quarantine for 6 months on coming into this country. I was impressed by him: courteous, unperturbed, knowledgeable, convincing.

AP. 7. A slight contretemps this morning owing to Richard setting fire to the curtain in his bedroom. It appears that he lit a

43

firework with the intention of throwing it out of the window. By the time he reported to Nancy, he had put the fire out, but quite a bit of curtain had been consumed. It was a wonder that he did not have the whole house alight.

AP. 8. St Annes: Hotel Glendower — the hotel practically empty.

AP. 9. We had been puzzled by information that Biddy had given us that the hotel was expecting a visit from Lady Mason this week but afterwards would be free to attend to us. It turned out that what she had been told about was a visit of lady Masons. The ladies began to arrive by ones and twos immediately after lunch, all in their sixties, all wearing long evening dresses — mostly black — almost all with motheaten fur coats on top of the dresses, and all with frizzed-up hair of varying degrees of blondness. We were much entertained by this spectacle; Nancy suggested I should phone Biddy and tell her to come round and see the sight. Biddy as easy and vivacious as ever, prepared to talk happily away at any length even if it means telling us the same thing twice over as she often does. Television news: a report of Selwyn Lloyd's budget, a stupid, pointless affair putting up purchase tax on some things and reducing it on others.

AP. 10. We motored to Fairhaven boating lake, a big expanse of water thoughtfully provided by the municipality to take the place of the sea, which is miles out for most of the day. The children were keen to go back to the Blackpool "amusements", and we motored there after lunch. I went into Woolworths, the most enormous glittering, glamorous Woolworths I have ever been in, where I was served with a glass of milk by a brilliant blonde with pencilled eyebrows. In the hotel everything had returned to normal after the invasion of the women.

AP. 11. Blackpool: the Tower menagerie. The big carnivores, to my surprise, all looked extraordinarily healthy, well groomed and clean, and gave every appearance of contentment, particularly one lioness lying on her back with her paws in the air. Biddy came for dinner, and a succession of card games. I motored Biddy home. When we arrived in Kenilworth Road, an old lady was walking along the pavement and opening the door of a taxi standing at the kerb, in order to peer into it. "That's Miss Marshall", said Biddy. "I must try to get her to go home. She has delusions". She certainly had — the particular delusion being that two girls were hiding in a small cherry tree opposite Biddy's gate and came into Miss Marshall's house through a crack in the floorboards. She had been to the police, she said, and they explained to her that the crack was too narrow for girls to get through. They said she was seeing things that were not there, but she had seen them. She had not been well, and had been going to a psychiatrist — it was these girls who upset everything in the house. They were going into the drawers, and sitting on one of the seats which was not doing it any good. She told us all this in a matter-of-fact way. I tried to explain to her that the girls might have nowhere else to go, and might not intend any harm. They might be quite friendly; but Miss Marshall agreed with Biddy that they were not at all friendly. By slow degrees, with a great deal of discussion, we got her back to her gate and persuaded her to go inside. She was good humoured about it. laughingly rebuking Biddy as a "naughty girl" when she suggested that some of her complaints must be an exaggeration. Back to the hotel, to be received somewhat coldly by Nancy, who not unnaturally wondered why I had taken half an hour to take Biddy home.

AP. 12. Home today. Richard bought a plastic rugby ball which he saw in a toyshop window. He had 12/8 left, and was delighted to find that the ball was 11/6. The girl went downstairs to fetch one; and better things still were in store for him, for when she came up it was to say that they had none left exactly like the one in the window but while he could have that one if he liked she had brought up another very much the same which cost only 7/6. Out hotel bill came to £27.10.6, which we thought very reasonable — no extras, not even the numerous glasses of milk that Elizabeth ordered, or the Daily Express which we got every morning.

AP. 16. George Thomson's death reported in this morning's paper; he had gone to Spain with Gracie for a holiday, and taken a coronary thrombosis. There was an element of good fortune in his getting to the position of Lord Justice-Clerk, but he was well fitted for the job. His offhand manner was misleading, concealing as it did not only brilliant intellectual qualities but a degree of determination and drive. He was not interested in publicity, and since he did not care whether he got the credit for reforms he was able as Lord Advocate to do far more than others who liked to beat the big drum. Any sort of opposition would put him off, but his own views were remarkably sound and progressive, and provided he could achieve his aim without arousing antagonism he was prepared to go to quite a bit of trouble. He had the reputation of being lazy — and he was, in the sense that he did not trouble to pursue a point if it was not generally acceptable; he liked things to go along on an even tenor, without fuss or argument. Within these limits, he was always helpful and friendly, with an essential kindliness which pervaded his judicial work as it did the rest of his activities. His early death is another misfortune for the Court of Session, which could so much more readily have spared some of its other judges. *Panorama* included an interview with Prince Rainier of Monaco about his troubles with the French government. He seemed eminently reasonable: a wholly benevolent dictator if he is a dictator at all, and much more sensible than most present-day parliamentarians.

AP. 17. Finished reading *The Franco-Prussian War*, by Michael Howard. From this detailed, fairminded study it was possible to observe the utter triviality of the grounds upon which the people of the two countries enthusiastically committed themselves to war: the point at issue had actually been settled before the war began. As usual, after peace was made, everything at once settled down in a manner completely contrary to the gloomy forecasts of disaster by those who had been urging the continuance of the war.

AP. 18. Motored to Hawick to take the Vacation Court. The zip fastening on my trousers broke, so that I had to obtain two safety pins from the police inspector.

AP. 20. Sinclair Shaw to tea: amusing about Harald Leslie, saying he could put up with a sham Viking and even a sham Highlandman, but the combination of sham Viking and sham Highlandman was too much

AP. 21. Longniddry beach: we found a curious green creature, about a foot long, lying in wet sand, something between a snake and a lizard. It was alive, and wriggled when we prodded it.

AP. 30. Probation Committee: Lady Elliot in devastating form. A question arose about the conduct of some lady Adoption Officer, who it was suspected was a representative of an Episcopal adoption society. Lady Elliot at once got on to Hon. Mrs Scott, a frail-looking, dresden-china old lady who regularly attends the meetings. "You should do something about it", she said. "You're a pillar of the Episcopal church". "I have done something about it", said Mrs Scott quietly but confidently. "I prayed, and my prayer was answered. We have a new secretary now". "Well, you'll have to pray a bit more", said Lady Elliot, pointing out that this was a question about an adoption officer.

MAY 1. Three cases in Procedure Roll, before different judges. I succeeded in speaking in each of them, but was feeling quite tired after all this, and annoyed at having to walk up and down the hall for twenty minutes with Lillie, while he explained why we must resist a proposal by the Sheriffs-Substitute that they should be known as "Sheriffs". His main reason for opposing this seemed to be that it had been opposed before, and this involved going through the whole history of the matter over the past 30 years.

MAY 2. Procedure Roll before Hunter — Ewen Stewart with me for the defenders. Hunter delivered an excellent judgment allowing a jury trial. Not often that one comes out of court after complete defeat with the feeling that justice has been done, but the way Hunter put it left one in no doubt that he was right. His long record of acting for defenders does not seem to have affected his judgment in any degree.

MAY 9. Proof: Wright v. British Transport Commission. Wheatley seemed in my favour when I addressed him, and I purposely put some of the propositions a little bit wrong so that he would be able to correct them and tell me what my case really was. He always likes to be able to do that. Deacons Court — rather a waste of time: a lot of trivial points such as whether the notice of services should read "Sunday" or "Sabbath".

MAY 11. Valuation Appeal Court. The case concerned two cupola furnaces in an iron foundry which projected above the roof with spark arresters on top like a metal helmet. "Rather like a hat", Sorn remarked, to which Jauncey, appearing for the Assessor, at once replied, "Yes, a lum hat". Two questions arose: whether the furnaces could be said to be in a building when they projected beyond the roof, and whether disturbance of the sand floor when the furnaces were removed should be regarded as removal of part of the building.

MAY 15. First Division: a motion for a new trial. The accident was only spoken to by the pursuer and one other witness, and Kissen now argued that the two accounts being materially different could not corroborate one another. This was the kind of point that appeals to the First Division, and I had not much hope of holding the verdict. But Clyde while Kissen was speaking was unusually silent. Sorn was engaged in his usual ploy of seeming to be impartial while preparing to come round and go with the tide when the time was ripe. Today he left it rather late; and when he began to show signs that he was ready to turn he did not get the customary encouragement from Clyde, while Guthrie had already taken a definite line in support of the verdict. So, much to everyone's surprise, when Kissen sat down they held a short confabulation and gave judgment for the pursuer without calling on me. Carmont alone seemed anxious to hold out for the defenders, but as usual was suppressed and merely said "I agree". So one never knows what will happen, even in the First Division.

MAY 16. The rhubarb and custard which Nancy served tonight had a peculiar taste; this was explained when it turned out that she had put salt into the custard in mistake for sugar.

MAY 21. East Kilbride: a gymkhana at Lymekilns — the field a morass of mud. In the prevailing conditions, it seemed pointless to pay for admission, and I climbed in over the fence. Got home before 6, and opened a tin of sardines for my supper. Went out of the kitchen to wash my hands, and when I got back found the dog had been up at the table and only 1½ sardines were left.

JUN. 1. A meeting of Sheriffs, to whom Lillie expounded the history of the controversy with the Sheriffs-Substitute. When Lillie had gone on for half an hour, Ross McLean — who was sitting beside him and so in a position to make him hear — told him of this fact, and added that it had been very boring. A vote resulted in 4 for No Change, 3 in favour of granting the Sheriff-Substitutes' request, and T. P. McDonald declining to vote.

JUN. 3. Craiglockhart Church: a small barn-like structure, seats in the gallery not much more than a set of forms erected on a steep little flight of steps. Rev. Thomas Balfour, the parish minister, preached on Matthew 28, 18-20: an interesting sermon. He wrestled painstakingly and often adequately with problems of baptism, with little regard for the capacity of his listeners to understand what he was talking about — though occasionally he let out some homely and often violent truth about their shortcomings.

JUN. 4. To Players to enquire about a Ford convertible: none now being made, an open car not being an economic proposition in this country.

JUN. 6. Miss Kidd dragged me off to a meeting of a small committee of Sheriffs to deal with amendment of the law regarding registration of births, marriages and deaths. As none of us knew anything about it, the meeting did not last long.

JUN. 9. Finished reading *Fights Guns and Debates*, by Anatole Rapaport. The author is professor of mathematical biology in the University of Michigan, and most of his book is an attempt to reduce conflicts to mathematical formulae. In the final part he forgets about his mathematics, and making what he calls an " assumption of generality " puts forward the ingenious idea that to get some sense into international discussion the best thing is for each side to state the other side's case in the best possible way

JUN. 14. A jury trial before Migdale: an odd reference in the medical records to an occasion when the pursuer had volunteered the information that whenever he took a deep breath he felt a burning pain in his thumb. At lunch R. J. Wallace, who has recently retired from being Sheriff-Substitute at Lerwick, recalled the first visit paid to Lerwick by T. B. Simpson after his appointment as Sheriff Principal. It was at a time when tuberculosis was rife in the islands, and Simpson on opening the local paper found a big heading " T.B. the scourge of Shetland ". " Well ", he said, " they haven't taken long to cotton on to me ".

JUN. 15. With Nancy to the Regal: " A Kind of Loving ", a picture of working-class life in an industrial north-country town, with a young couple starting off together in the home of the wife's mother and not unnaturally coming to grief: not much of a story, but carefully observed and set forth with sympathy and not without humour. All very understandable, and the human problem, which must be a very common one, presented fairly and truly. The weakness of the picture is that it is all so true to life that it fails to make any particular impact.

JUN. 17. Finished reading *First Hand Report*, by Sherman Adams, Eisenhower's right-hand man during his election campaign and most of his presidency. He is an Eisenhower admirer, and makes out a good case for his chief. Considering the difficulties he had from Congress, his policy and views seem to have been more reasonable and farsighted than I appreciated. His attitude towards McCarthy is typical: "I will not get into the gutter with that guy".

JUN. 18. Called at the Lighthouse office to see Robertson about the inspection voyage on the *Pharos* at the end of July. Places are allotted to Commissioners on a reckoning of the number of meetings they had attended, and I wanted to know whether my attendances had been enough to qualify.

JUN. 20. The annual abstract of the Advocates Widows Fund: an entry under the head "Contributors who have changed their Names", narrating that "Charles Campbell Ross, Younger of that Ilk" was now "Charles Campbell Ross, of that Ilk, Younger".

JUN. 24. Blackbarony for tea: the usual attractive, plentiful repast at a total charge of 16/6 for the five of us — which seemed very reasonable.

JUN. 28. Finished reading *Ten Rillington Place*, by Ludovic Kennedy: not a very good book — a lot of repetition, and written from a frankly partisan angle, on the assumption, of course now amply justified, that it was Christie and not Evans who murdered Mrs Evans and the baby. But the story is so extraordinary and its implications so horrifying that it holds one's attention throughout. It is not only that a man was hanged for the murder of his wife and baby when he had nothing to do with it, but it is apparent that police, being certain that they had the right man, concocted a confession for him and then suppressed any evidence which turned up and did not fit in with the confession they had devised. The defence, which happened to be true, being so fantastic that no one could ever have accepted it, the rest followed as a matter of course. One can hardly blame those engaged in the Evans trial for failing to consider the possibility of such an extraordinary character as Christie; but the author is clearly right in his condemnation of Mr Scott Henderson's whitewashing report — a shocking demonstration of what a second-rate legal mind can concoct in defence of the establishment.

JUN. 30. Galashiels: a luncheon to the Braw Lad and Lass in the Douglas Hotel. Provost Kemp, somewhat to my dismay, asked me if I would say a few words. By good luck I had happened to notice the Burgh crest on my invitation card, 2 faces looking up at a tree, with the odd motto, "Soor plooms" — apparently a reference to some incident concerning an invasion by the English in 1337. So I was able to comment on the Gathering as a link between traditions of the past and prospects of the future, and say it would not do to concentrate too much on the good old days. The only person who knew about the good old days was Adam, and we had no record of what he thought, except that I had it on good authority that when he had to surrender the apple after one bite his only comment was in two words, "Soor plooms". Having made my joke, and my mind being otherwise blank, I brought my remarks to an immediate close. My speech had the merit of brevity, and no one else offered to say anything. The party broke up with everyone shaking hands, wishing me goodbye and thanking me for coming. As I had undertaken to attend the sports in the afternoon, this too was a surprise; but I felt it would be out of place after it for me to go to the sports, so I made my way to the car and motored home.

JUL. 1. With Nancy to Greenbank church. The children preferred Mr Reid, and went off by themselves to South Morningside. At Greenbank a young minister, Rev. E. P. Lindsay Thomson, preached on I Peter 1, 8-9. He seems to be a local boy in the course of making good, but though well intentioned his sermon was more notable for clerical jargon than for any significant thought. Finished reading *Candles in the Sun*, by Lady Emily Lutyens. She writes disarmingly and in spite of her weird ideas and neglect of her husband and family one can see what a nice person she must be. But this account of her lengthy connection with Mrs Besant and the Theosophical Society is all too remote from reality to sustain any profound degree of interest. The "Masters" who dwell mainly on an astral plane but incidentally on a physical plane, two in Tibet and one in a mysterious castle in Hungary which no one has ever seen, the expedition which sets off hopefully for Hungary to see him and for some unexplained reason never gets there, the squabbles about whether the Society's bishops are speaking with a Master's voice — it is all so crazy that even Lady Lutyens' sympathetic, matter-of-fact narrative can hardly bring it to life.

JUL. 2. To Leith with the object of buying some oilskins for the inspection voyage. Finding myself at the dock gates, I decided to go in and have a look round: a small American warship being towed in through a lock gate with tugs ahead and astern. A man standing by me remarked that every time a Yank came into Edinburgh Dock he must go bump up against the side of the dry dock; but so far as I could see this one did not go bump against anything. In evening with Nancy to Duns for the dinner to the Reiver and his Lass. Major Askew, the county convener, proposed the Burgh of Duns: a resumé of the industrial situation in Berwickshire. Though not altogether appropriate to the occasion, it was admirably succinct and interesting — a big improvement on the string of "funny" stories which is the usual feature of such occasions. But the hit of the evening was the Mayor of Berwick, Councillor McKay. I sat between the mayoress and the wife of the Provost of Lauder, a buxom lady who quickly disposed of everything set before her — relieved, as she said to me, to find it was a real hot dinner, not just a cold supper which would have been a repetition of the meal she and her husband had had before they left home. Things slowed down when the local schoolmaster was on his feet. "You can tell a schoolmaster a mile off", the lady from Lauder remarked, when he was well launched into his anecdotes.

JUL. 3. The royal garden party at Holyrood. Cameron's court had risen early so that he could change into an Archer's uniform; and a story was circulating in Parliament House about a previous occasion when he was similarly dressed and had almost fallen when trying to get on a bus while it was in motion. "Now, Robin Hood", said the conductor, "you should remember to get on at the proper stop next time". The Queen looked pleasant in a yellow coat, and beamed cheerfully on her guests.

JUL. 5. Turned on the wireless shortly before 6.55 to hear the weather forecast, and was fortunate enough to hear a talk in the *Lift Up Your Hearts* series by Rev. Werner Pelz. There was a fatal fascination about his voice and manner, so that one felt one must accept everything he said; and what he said was remarkable — even his casual asides such as "Jesus of course had no interest in mere morality". He was speaking about the hope that can transform the whole of life, so that happiness and everything else cease to matter. "Shall we ever attain to such a hope?" he asked; and answered that at any rate we can hope that we shall. Motored with Nancy to Melrose to meet the Queen. At the station we found the Duke of Buccleuch, who is Lord Lieutenant of the county, with the Duchess, Lord Stratheden & Campbell, and his daughter Myra. We lined up on a red carpet laid on the platform and down a steep flight of steps. The Duke went down the steps to the bottom and up again, to try them out. The Duchess seemed mainly concerned to let the press know that she had arranged for hounds to be out at St Boswells so that the royal party could see them in passing. At 11 precisely the royal train rolled in, drawn by two engines. The Queen stepped out, and each of us moved forward to be presented. Nancy and I were not concerned with the Melrose ceremony at the Greenyards, and were missing out St Boswells, rejoining the royal party at Hawick; so we strolled back to the car and motored up the Dingleton road, stopping beside the reservoir at the top for a sandwich. The official party must however have gone much faster than we had expected, for when we got down to Bowden Toll we were halted by a policeman who said the outriders had already passed and we could not get through. After some discussion, he agreed to let us proceed, provided we went quickly. We accordingly drove on along the royal route as fast as we could go, by undulating, winding country roads to Hawick. All the way along we passed groups of spectators, some of whom waved to us, and at every crossing we had to encounter policemen — some of whom stopped us and on being told I was the Sheriff waved us on, with an injunction to "step on it", while others simply gazed at us in surprise. Before lunch there was an exhibition of knitwear, modelled by local girls who all did their part very well. Drinks were served in a small ante-room. "We've got rid of all the knitwear people, have we?" said the Duke of Edinburgh in a loud voice. Fortunately we had. We were hurried along to the dining-room, where I was between the Countess of Leicester and Myra Campbell. The Countess was pleasant and friendly, and Myra equally so. She lives and works in France, but had travelled quite a bit, and expressed great admiration for Australia — somewhat to the surprise of the Countess, who had heard it was difficult to get any help in the house there. Lunch started off with cold salmon, a big helping, very good. Then, when we were expecting a sweet, an enormous plateful of cold roast beef was set before us, again with a pile of salad. This was good too, but far more than anyone wanted. Finally there was a big dish of fruit salad. The Duke of Edinburgh remarked that it had been a very nice lunch, but rather too long. Nancy and I this time were content to tail on at the back of the traffic following the royal party. We got ahead of the Queen by cutting out Jedburgh, and at the village of Heiton turned down to Heiton Mill, Ronald McLarty's little farm on the river. He showed us round his house and garden; but knowing the speed at which the Queen travelled we could not stay long. At Coldstream we found Major Askew walking about in an agitated way near the hotel door. Inside we could see Provost Linklater in his robes of office, getting instructions from the Earl of Haddington, the Lord Lieutenant of Berwickshire. Like the Duke of Buccleuch, he was in uniform, but unlike him the Earl is a small man, and he was hampered by an enormous sword trailing on the ground at his side. When the royal party arrived, we all walked along the street and by a nice walk with a grassy slope down to the river. There was barely room for two to walk abreast, and we strolled round in an informal way, the Queen and the Provost leading. A gap in the wall led up a steep flight of steps to a small grass park where a marquee had been erected — a marvellous affair of billowing coloured fabrics, like what one imagines would have been Saladin's tent at the time of the Crusades, brightly furnished inside with chintz-covered chairs and one or two little tables with tea things set out on them. The Queen was set down at one of the tables with the Provost's wife and the local minister, Mrs Linklater pouring out tea for her while someone else did the same for the Duke of Edinburgh. After tea Linklater presented a bottle of whiskey to the Duke in a wooden casket, the key of which he professed to have lost and was searching round for on the grass — though he found it easily enough when he wanted. " We don't need a key for this", said the Duke, " we need a corkscrew". The Queen and the Duke were paying a private visit to Lord Home at the Hirsel, so we did not wait to see her out of the Sheriffdom. A very entertaining day: a remarkable absence of formality or constraint. I met McCallum in the tent, and congratulated him on the police arrangements; he agreed that everything had gone well, remarking that so far as he had heard only one car had got on to the royal route.

JUL. 6. Motored to Duns, where I had an appeal, and as I had arranged with C. de B. Murray took the routine court work — mostly motoring cases. A lady had collided with another car coming in the opposite direction. According to the letter she had sent, addressed to the " Prosecutor Physical ", she had been driving with a lot of children and having had her attention distracted by one of them looked up to find herself running into the other car. I fined her £6, and imposed a similar penalty on a young tractor driver who had come round a corner on a country road, riding a motor cycle, and collided with a cyclist. He appeared for himself and said he had had to come out to the wrong side to be sure he was clear of anyone walking on the road side round the corner. " But what would happen if something was coming the other way ?" I asked, to which he replied " I don't know ". The appeal was in an action of separation by a young wife, based on two assaults just before the wife left her husband. Sheriff Murray, in granting the decree, did not seem to regard either assault as important, but founded on the history of the marriage which showed, he said, that the husband had never shown any affection for his wife. The question in the case was obviously whether this constituted cruelty so as to entitle the wife to live apart from the husband at his expense for the rest of their lives; but neither of the two solicitors who addressed me even remotely approached the point at issue. They contented themselves with comments on odd bits of evidence, of no importance, and niggling criticisms of discrepancies between evidence and pleadings. It did not seem to have occurred to either of them that their task was to persuade me that Murray had been right or wrong in his finding of cruelty. So I shall just have to apply my own judgment to the evidence. My inclination is to reverse the Sheriff-Substitute's decision, on the view that the whole affair was trivial and there is really no reason why these two young people and their baby should not come together again.

JUL. 7. Arranging with Layden that he would get someone else to take two cases I had for him next Thursday, when I shall be otherwise engaged. He asked me to say nothing about this meanwhile, as there was still a possibility of negotiation and he did not want the other side to know I was no longer employed. "Without wanting to be fulsome", he said, "I can say that you're generally regarded as the best counsel available, and it's an advantage to be able to say that you're to be in the case".

JUL. 9. St Boswells: a Probation Committee meeting. Lady Elliot conducted the proceedings with her usual enthusiasm, and informed me afterwards that she had been on a tractor most of the morning.

JUL. 23. To Gourock to start our voyage of inspection of lighthouses — Ailsa Craig our first port of call, then Loch Ryan. Shearer, who served in Malta throughout the siege, from 1940 to 1943, gave us his impressions of the generals he encountered: Lord Gort, who had been brought there to tighten things up after the loss of precious cargoes through the Maltese refusing to unload ships on a fast day, but who Shearer thought had a pretty antiquated outlook so far as generalship was concerned. He had a great admiration for Alexander and Scobie. He told us about being trained by an officer of the Hussars, who informed his men that the cry for attack was "Hurrah", not "Hooray".

JUL. 24. Alastair Robertson told us that at the beginning of the war there was an idea among high-ups in the Navy that aeroplanes could not attack at night, with the result that officers found themselves manning anti-aircraft guns on board wearing a dinner jacket and steel helmet. He and Ross McLean were swapping reminiscences, McLean recalling that he had been one of the last to get out of Singapore. He did it under sail, coming to Sumatra in a tompan. Much earlier in the war he had brought out his wife and family to Singapore, thinking they would be safer there than at home in the bombing. They got away a week or two before he did, and after his own escape he met up with them by chance in Colombo, and they all came home together. From Stranraer we set off for Ireland, and as we came to anchor in Bangor Bay saw the three lighthouse vessels we had come to meet: the Trinity House *Patricia* and two Irish ships. A cocktail party on board the principal Irish ship. The Trinity House men came aboard all togged up in uniforms with ribbons and blue cloaks. An English business man who was on the *Patricia* as a guest had apparently been very successful, and had a house with a private beach at Angmering-on-Sea, but he became maudlin at the thought that he had never been able to learn to play golf. This he found most humiliating. The wind had got up during the party, and I congratulated Lillie on the agility with which he got off the boat on to the ladder. He took this, like everything else, as a matter of course, merely remarking that one of the officers had once told him he was the most sure-footed of all the Commissioners.

JUL. 25. A meeting on board *Patricia* in the forenoon, to be followed by a sherry party. I cut that out, and went off on my own. Train to Belfast — which seemed a humdrum place — and bus to Donaghadee. Lunched in a cafe where the food was good but service poor. Three who came to my table had a long wait for their main course, the waitress remarking when she at last served them that she would take their order for a sweet " when they're in the mood there for giving things out ". Dinner at the Royal Ulster Yacht Club. The Trinity House people had decided it was too stormy for coming on board at night from Bangor, and we were to go to Belfast and lie alongside the quay. This had been decided without any consultation with us — the other boats had just upped anchor and sailed, leaving *Pharos* alone in the bay. Our people poohpoohed the idea that there would be any difficulty at night, but we were left no choice but to follow. The sail up Belfast Lough in bright evening sunshine was delightful.

To Elizabeth Stott (Picture postcard):

M. V. Pharos   26/7/62
The Isle of Man is a nice place, but unfortunately it is an island and quite a long way from anywhere — and I can assure you that the sea today was very different from how it looks in the picture. Better fly there, I think, if you want to enjoy the I.O.M. Meanwhile give my love to Nancy.
PS: A *glorious* day at Islay!

JUL. 28. Dhubheartach, an isolated rock in the Atlantic southwest of Mull: the lighthouse a forbidding sight, a dun grey tower, with red in the central portion, standing on its rock with the top of a reef just visible in the form of two low rocks to the west of the lighthouse rock — not visible except at low tide. We anchored some way off, and a boat put out, dropping a big red buoy with a long rope attached, which was led out as the boat proceeded until an anchor was thrown overboard. The boat could now come in close to the rock, and we were slung ashore on a derrick. Each in turn grasped a rope and put it through between our legs where there was a toggle on it, about 8 inches in diameter, forming a kind of seat, and sitting upright on this was hauled ashore. Lillie had asked me if I had a good head for heights, remarking that when Watt had been going up the similar light at Skerryvore he had stuck halfway, feeling unable to go farther. I could not understand how anyone could stop halfway, but when I got on to the rock I realised what he meant: the door of the lighthouse was still a long way overhead, reached from the rock by a series of metal rungs on the vertical lighthouse wall. I learned later that there were 32. Ross McLean was already shinning up, and there seemed nothing to do but to follow. It was only when I got in at the door that the lighthouse keeper remarked that a safety belt is provided for climbers, with a rope attached; not knowing of its existence I had not of course waited for it. At Barra we anchored in the bay, opposite the village — the Catholic church in a commanding position in the centre. We went off in a boat to the pier. Ross McLean engaged in conversation with the priest, Father John McCormick. I suggested we might go in and see the church, and when we did so we found what McLean described as "the starboard side" full of kneeling people of all ages, from children to grannies. In answer to my enquiry, Father McCormick explained that they usually came along on Saturday nights to prepare for Sunday. They were all on the one side so as to be ready to go in one by one to the confessional room at the end of the passage. McCormick invited us in to the Presbytery next door, and putting his hand in behind some books produced a bottle of whisky, 32 over proof. "If your sermons are as powerful as your whisky", said Ross, "they must do a power of good". "Ah", said McCormick sadly, "perhaps they don't go down so well". Ross invited him to come aboard with us at 6.45. Meanwhile I climbed a little way up the hill to the rocks above. A cow was grazing there, and while I was coming down a woman emerged from one of the houses with a pail, walked along the hillside to the cow, and having hobbled it sat down on the grass and proceeded to milk the cow where she stood. At 6.45 Father McCormick came off with us in the boat. He is an Islander, from South Uist, with real Highland charm and humour, and a soft voice to match the grace of his manner. The conversation turned to the subject of his near namesake, the singer, and McCormick recalled that when he had been stationed a long time on one of the other islands, I think it was Eriskay, he had a visit from Bishop Grant, and sang him the song about the old house. And there and then, sitting with us in the after saloon, he launched into the last verse of the song, singing in a delightful melodious voice: "Gone are the children" and so on, ending up "It's time I moved on". "I'm glad to say he took the hint", he said. Macneil arrived in full Highland regalia, very obviously an American, and enthusiastic about the restoration of his castle, in which he lives alone with his wife during the summer months, returning to his home in Maine for the winter. He was steeped in the history of Barra and Kisamul. We had a lively dinner party, with McCormick becoming even mellower under the influence of the drink and gradually growing slightly tipsy — though without its in any way affecting his charm and courtesy. Macneil describes himself as "The Macneil of Barra", but this T. P. McDonald says is inaccurate, the only three entitled to the appelation of "The" being the Pope, the devil and the Chisholm. A letter from home — a pleasant surprise, as I did not recollect having left an address.

JUL. 29. At breakfast Robertson remarked that when he went off in the boat last night to the castle nobody appeared to meet Macneil. He had to walk up the jetty, produced a big key with which he unlocked his gate, and went away in. He had told us that he usually locked his wife in when he left her in the castle. I went ashore at 11 with Ross McLean and some of the others. Tom McDonald and the others turned in the direction of the Presbyterian church, while Ross and I made for the Catholic church, where Mass was at 11.30. 95 per cent of the inhabitants of Barra are Catholic — the dividing line between Protestants and Catholics is said to be at Benbecula — and the church was full. Nice to see the children come demurely up the aisle and genuflect as they moved in to their seats. We had told McCormick we should probably slip out before 12 and go along to the Presbyterian service, and he guided us into a seat near the back, a man in the seat taking a boy on his knee to make room. McCormick as he passed on his way to the pulpit put a booklet in front of each of us, remarking that he did not think it would be too advanced for us: "The Little One's Mass Book", in simple English with pictures on alternate pages. After a short bit in Latin, the rest of the service was in Gaelic. I found it very agreeable to listen to Father McCormick's pleasant voice as he addressed his congregation in conversational tones, though I had no idea what he was talking about. A children's choir in the gallery sang — soft lilting melodies that sounded moving and effective. We left just before 12, but on the way along to the Presbyterian church met Campbell and Anderson, who said the service at Castlebay was at night. Ross McLean suggested to me that we should not trouble to go back to the ship for lunch, saying he would much prefer seeing the island; and I agreed to go back with him to the Catholic church and consult McCormick about means of transport. We encountered two delightful little girls sitting on a wall: Marie McLennan and Marion McDougall. We engaged them in conversation, and they admired our ship; and when we said how much we liked Father McCormick they remarked that Father Kennedy was very nice too. They had been to the early Mass. Though only about 10, they said all the right things, very pleasantly; we thought how nice it would be if city children would converse in such a friendly, courteous way. While Ross went up to the Presbytery, I went to the telephone box and phoned Nancy. Asked her to phone Mrs Burness and tell her her husband was well and happy. Burness has never before had a holiday apart from his wife, and makes a point of communicating with her by postcard every day. On our walk at Colonsay he had gone into the post office to buy stamps, but when he knocked on the door a man appeared and said " She's closed ", so he was unable to send a card from there. On getting to the Presbytery, I was not surprised to find that Ross had got us invited to lunch. A bottle of gin was produced, and some beer from another corner of the room. Father McCormick apologetic about the plain fare — one of the disadvantages of the celibacy of the priesthood, he said, was that they had to rely entirely on their housekeeper. But a plate of hot soup and a slice of roast mutton made an agreeable lunch. Father Kennedy lunched with us, and did the clearing-up. He is a newcomer from Glasgow, and is just learning Gaelic. A jug of milk was provided for me, Father Kennedy explaining that the parishioners were very good in the way of provisions. Whenever he went to Vatersay, for instance, he got a parcel of produce to bring back to the Presbytery. In the afternoon Father McCormick took us round the island in his car, driving at a fast speed along the narrow island road. When another car approached, he did not draw into a passing place, but continued at the same speed until the last moment, when he jammed on his brakes and drew into the side, with an inch to spare between wheels and ditch. But in his own way he seemed to drive skilfully. We passed cottages, and children who saluted or curtsied as we passed. The road wound about among rocky bays, and crossed a peninsula to Traigh Mhor, an enormous stretch of hard sand where the tide goes back for over a mile. This is Barra's airfield, and we saw the BEA office, a hut on the beach. McCormick drove down to the beach, and across the sand at a fast speed. Returning to the road, we turned westwards. The west coast is different from the east: fine sandy beaches with dunes behind, and Atlantic rollers surging in, just like Cornwall. We had to be back at the pier at 3, as the boat was to take us to Macneil's castle. Inside, it is nothing like a castle. Macneil has rebuilt the "great hall", a big, bare, whitewashed room, and in one corner had built himself a little house of two storeys, the castle wall forming the wall of the house on one side and the walls on the other side ordinary house walls. He is making more rooms along the top of the hall, and plans to renovate the tower. He told us that the islanders were law-abiding, particularly where the law of inertia was concerned, and progress had been slow. In order to keep to the dimensions of the old castle, he can only have three rooms in the house, and here he and his wife lived. No doubt his enthusiasm is praiseworthy, but I did not see much point in what he is doing. The boat took us back to the *Pharos* for tea; and at 6 we went ashore to attend the Presbyterian service, in the Seamen's Mission. In contrast to the Catholic service, the congregation totalled 18, including 5 of us. The minister's son, aged 12, played the harmonium, from sol-fa notation, using one hand: a valiant effort, though we should certainly have been better without him. The parish minister, whose name I think was Macleod, preached on Philippians 4,5: a very good sermon, simple, unambitious, and full of that sweet reasonableness which was the subject of his discourse. On the suggestion of T. P. McDonald, who thought discrimination might be dangerous, he had been invited to dine on the *Pharos*.

JUL. 30. We sailed soon after 6. I got up to go on deck and see the east coast of Barra from the sea, but found the island blotted out by mist and rain. Joined the captain on the bridge, where he said that the change in the weather was not surprising, after these two gentlemen had been on board. Among the older school of sailors, he said, it was always regarded as unlucky to have clergymen come on board ship. About 8.15 a promontory with a lighthouse appeared out of the mist: Usinish. We anchored in a lovely bay, and after breakfast went ashore. Lillie at breakfast telling us in his humourless way about an occasion when he was in India and hired an elephant to go and see some old city near Jaipur. He claims to hold a seaman's certificate through having served during one voyage in a ship of the Den Line, which Burness tells me was a small merchant shipping line, now long defunct, operating from Dundee. He was discharged because his ship was not going in the direction he wanted to go. We were put ashore on a shingle beach, to walk a mile along the cliffs to the lighthouse. The keeper suggested we might be able to rejoin the boat from the rocks below. They were covered with wet seaweed, but Ross McLean and I had no difficulty in slithering down into the boat. There we sat, with a grandstand view of our colleagues' descent — amazed at what heavy weather they made of it. Campbell was next to come, and a rope had been strung up for him to hold, while a seaman supported him on each side and he was lowered with every

appearance of acute terror on to the gangplank. Lillie at 79 is
remarkably agile. It never occurs to him that anything might go
wrong, and this must give him complete confidence. I am told that it
was only three years ago that he gave up having the accommodation
ladder put down every morning and going for a swim round the ship
— this became impracticable when the present Diesel-oil *Pharos*
replaced the old one. The captain offered to take me round the ship;
and though I had undertaken this for my own interest it appeared to
have been the right thing to do. Robertson later thanked me for
inspecting the crew's quarters, which he assured me would be much
appreciated. "I've been down several times", he said, "but that's
not the same thing as one of the Commissioners". Meanwhile a
message came that the captain's presence was required on the bridge,
where it was suggested that Lillie might take over the wheel: the first
time a Commissioner had steered the *Pharos*. He seemed to get on
reasonably well, though our wake at times looked somewhat serpen-
tine. Glas Island our last lighthouse excursion before I left the ship at
Stornoway: sad to hear the familiar words "Right, let go, boys", as
the boat came away from the jetty for the last time. At Stornoway
we entertained the harbour master, Captain McLellan, at dinner. He
told a story about a Macbrayne captain named Macpherson who had
been accustomed to navigate very much by rule of thumb. Finding
himself off South Rona in a fog, he shouted to the look-out man to
ask if there was any sign of land. "No land to be seen", was the
answer, "but we can hear ducks". "Ducks?" said Macpherson,
somewhat alarmed. "Tell me, are they walking or are they
swimming?" The *Loch Seaforth* a seething mass of people, but the
cabin quite comfortable.

JUL. 31. Kyle of Lochalsh at 5 — an hour there. As we sailed, I
shaved hurriedly and went up on deck. The sail to Mallaig through
magnificent mountain scenery, finer than any we had seen.

OCT. 1. *Panorama* had an interesting report on Ghana, with
President Nkrumah's pomp and ceremony just as it had been before
independence, and an acrimonious dualogue between the Minister of
Transport and the general secretary of the NUR about a one-day
railway strike scheduled for Wednesday. To my mind, Mr Marples
made a poor showing; his smart-alick tactics foundered on the rock
of Mr Greene's stolid imperturbability.

OCT. 2. Parliament House — the opening of the session: a large
crowd to see the installation of Grant as Lord Justice-Clerk. He has
at last been permitted to appoint himself, after a long delay caused
by the Government's unwillingness to risk an awkward bye-election
in the Woodside division of Glasgow. No opening service in St
Giles', on account of an unseemly squabble between Clyde and Dr

Whitley about whether Dr Warr was to take the service. In requesting the use of the cathedral, "the judges" had asked that the service be conducted by Warr — although he is now retired from being minister of St Giles'. Whitley in reply had said that it was for him as parish minister to conduct it, whereupon "the judges", or Clyde professedly on their behalf, retorted that the cathedral would not be required.

OCT. 4. Had a lot of work to do, and got to bed not much before 12 — but in time to finish reading *The Descent of Venus*, by Douglas Angus, a novel about a professor at an American university, happily married and with a young family, who becomes involved in a disastrous affair with one of his students: a sensual book, but a grim one, for over all the lyrical scenes hangs the threat of impending doom. It is well written, and brilliantly worked out to the inevitable end. The author is an understanding person, and so are his characters; and that is what makes their tragedy so moving and true. It is very harrowing.

OCT. 7. At church the evening service was a service of dedication of the Womens Guild. Mr Reid preached on I Corinthians 15, 9-10. I had thought that as this was a special service he might be a little more interesting, but it was the usual rubbish: a longwinded dissertation on what Paul meant, which made it plain as usual that he had not the remotest understanding of what Paul was getting at. The women got only a casual mention in the last sentence. Counting the collection took a long time, as no one was there to do it but me and the organist's son — who, though a nice young fellow, had no more skill at counting than I.

OCT. 8. St Giles': Lord Normand's funeral service — a surprisingly cheery affair. We sang a hymn beginning "Come, let us join in cheerful song" — something which old Normand would certainly not have done during his lifetime. Dr Whitley conducted the proceedings in a formal manner, with no relation to Normand so far as I could see. These first-name references — "our dear brother Wilfrid" — sound extremely silly.

OCT. 10. Finished reading *The Destruction of Lord Raglan*, by Christopher Hibberd. An interesting, well-documented account of the Crimean War makes it clear that Raglan was merely a scapegoat for the real criminals at home; but it is plain too that this modest, kindly, self-effacing old gentleman was not the man to command in the Crimea.

OCT. 11. A proof before Douglas Johnston: Murray v. British Transport Commission. I had given an Opinion that it was a completely hopeless case, and nothing that happened today caused me to alter that view. The NUR Executive however had in its usual fashion decided unanimously, after hearing counsel's Opinion, that an action should be raised. The pursuer today did not seem much concerned, remarking to me that he had nothing to lose by having a go at it; and he obviously enjoyed his day in the Court of Session. At all events it was a nice easy day. I was amused by the start of a letter from a pursuer which was among the papers I was reading for a consultation: "Dear Sir", he wrote, "I am writing on behalf of my accident".

OCT. 12. With Nancy and the children to the Kings: the Old Vic production of "The Tempest" — an excellent production. "The Tempest" is really a kind of romantic musical comedy, and Alastair Sim as Prospero, aided by two very personable young lovers, effectively emphasised this aspect of it.

OCT. 13. The appointment of Shearer as Lord Advocate was in this morning's paper. It is a good thing I was made a Sheriff last year, for there would not have been much chance of it now. Switched on the television for Mr Macmillan's address to the Conservative Party conference. He was not at his best; and the appropriate comment came from Elizabeth, who after 20 minutes of it remarked, "When is he going to say something that means anything?"

OCT. 14. Elizabeth had been asked by Caroline to a party next Saturday, but yesterday Caroline arrived at the door and according to Elizabeth told her they had asked too many people so that Elizabeth would not be able to come. This seemed odd, and made us think we had been troubling ourselves unnecessarily when we were worried a fortnight ago about being discourteous to Caroline. However Caroline was up again this evening looking for Elizabeth, and phoned later after Elizabeth came home to ask if she would come to the party after all. "All right", said Elizabeth, indifferently — and quite appropriately. But she seems pleased to be going. Sinclair Shaw on the phone told rather an attractive little story about Denise's mother, who died during the summer and who like her husband and daughter was all through her life a great fighter for freedom. Gerald had seen her only once during her last illness, when though very ill she had given him the impression that she did not think much of his beard. He suggested to her that if she really did not like it he would shave it off, but she waved this offer aside, remarking "Je suis pour la liberte".

OCT. 16. A divorce before Milligan — slow progress a nuisance, as it will probably mean my returning a very interesting case out for Friday. I found today's proceedings tedious; Taylor, who appeared for the husband, is better at that kind of thing than I am — he is prepared to go on asking the same question over and over again until he gets a contradictory answer, and I cannot be bothered doing that.

OCT. 17. My Friday case had been dropped, so I was able to sit and listen to Taylor without any anxiety about time.

OCT. 18. The case continued throughout the day: I was still speaking when the court rose.

OCT. 19. Completed my address to the court. As I was also in a Procedure Roll before Migdale, I did not put off time, and had finished before Taylor arrived, with the result that his junior had to reply. As it turned out, I had plenty of time, Migdale being still occupied in reading a judgment. His judgments are usually long: he narrates what each witness has said, then summarises the argument presented by counsel on each side, and in a final sentence says he prefers one side or the other.

OCT. 22. To Browns' bookshop to get tickets for a concert in the Usher Hall featuring Helen Shapiro, the schoolgirl pop singer from the east end of London who has achieved spectacular fame with her gramophone recordings. This is to be Elizabeth's birthday treat, and she is taking 8 of her friends. I was lucky enough to get 9 seats in the middle of the front row of the Grand Tier; the Area is said to be less desirable owing to the enthusiasm of the teenage audiences, which causes them to rise in their seats and howl with delight at the singer, thus interrupting the view of those behind them.

OCT. 23. A jury trial before Milligan. The pursuer, a lad of 17, had to tack weld two plates. A plater named Hollywood struck the plate with a heavy hammer. A particle of slag sprang up from the weld and entered the pursuer's eye, with the result that the eye had to be taken out. It is said that instead of a hammer Hollywood should have used a toggle and wedge — whatever that may be. In any event he should have given the pursuer a warning and taken care that he was clear. I had no precognition from Hollywood, but decided to put him in, and much to my surprise he proceeded to admit that it was all his fault — he had been in too much of a hurry. Grieve conceded that he could not resist an affirmative answer to the Issue, and the jury awarded the pursuer £3500, perhaps on the high side as awards go for loss of an eye. Lord Home was on television in the evening, addressing some merchants' dinner in London on the crisis that has arisen over Cuba. President Kennedy has suddenly discovered that the Russians have put up a rocket-launching site there, and has announced with a great flourish of trumpets that the American navy is now going to stop all ships going to Cuba, including Russian ones, and "turn them back" if they are carrying arms. This, according to American military men, means that if necessary they will sink the ship — so that a critical situation has obviously developed. Lord Home, after remarking that anything said should be such as would help towards a solution of the problem, went on to slang Mr

Kruschev in an amiable, almost disinterested manner — no sort of lead, or recognition of danger, just a mild, kindly sheep ambling along to destruction with the rest of the flock. The unfortunate thing is that everybody else goes down the precipice with him.

OCT. 25. Seeing that nothing could be done about the world crisis, I had yesterday followed my usual practice of not listening to any news on wireless or television, and so was not worried by any of the prevailing alarms and rumours. This morning's paper did not suggest that anything deadly had happened so far. No ship had yet been stopped. The Americans are still uttering their crazy war cries, but Mr Kruschev, in a sensible and lengthy answer to an appeal by Lord Russell, had said he appreciated the dangers of the situation and would try not to be provoked by the Americans into doing anything rash.

OCT. 26. We listened in to a programme which under the unpromising title of Hootenannie gave us half an hour of unalloyed pleasure while three or four young people from Aberdeen sang folk songs, old and new, in a skilful, uninhibited manner, all very delicately done — a contrast to the fulminations of American politicians against Cuba which followed on the News. They have now the extraordinary idea that as the rockets are all set in Cuba for launching against them they should invade Cuba and destroy them — apparently oblivious to the consideration that if they do someone in Cuba might conceivably retaliate by letting a rocket off.

OCT. 28. Communion: Mr Reid preached on Galatians 1, 3-4. In a week which threatened the destruction of civilisation, and at a time when survival still hangs by a thread, he achieved the remarkable feat of not mentioning the matter. Beyond the word " peace " in his text, he made not the slightest reference to the subject, directly or indirectly, in prayers or sermon.

OCT. 29. Pleasantly surprised on opening my paper this morning to find that Mr Kruschev had agreed unreservedly to withdraw Russian rockets from Cuba, and Mr Kennedy on his part was apparently agreeing that Cuba would not be invaded. The correspondence was in remarkably friendly terms, and a violation of Russian air-space over the weekend by American aircraft was dismissed on both sides as merely an unfortunate mistake. Evidently the threat of nuclear destruction has had some effect after all, though it must have been a near thing.

NOV. 16. Motion Roll: Docherty v. Royal Bank of Scotland. The pursuer sent his employee McSherry to the Jamaica Street branch of the bank in Glasgow with a parcel of bank notes. McSherry handed the parcel across the counter to a teller, who counted the money and made out a pay-in slip for £90,995.

McSherry signed this and handed it back, and the teller stamped and initialled the counterfoil and handed it to McSherry. The bank however have credited the pursuer with only £9,995, and say that this was the amount actually paid in. I assumed that their defence to this action for payment of the balance — £81,000 — would be that the teller had made a clerical error in writing out the slip; but it is much more surprising. They aver that after McSherry had gone the teller decided he had made a mistake in counting the money and that it really amounted to £99,995. He altered the pay-in slip to that effect. He then had doubts as to whether he had counted the money correctly, and on counting again found that only £9,995 had been lodged. He altered the pay-in slip to that effect, and on the instruction of the accountant at the branch telephoned the pursuer's place of business and told someone who said he was Mr Docherty that a mistake had been made. The pursuer does not know how much money was in the parcel, but thinks there was more than £20,000.

NOV. 17. Elizabeth's party: eight school friends to tea. Shortly after 5.30 I had to bustle them off to get ready to leave for the Usher Hall. Nancy took three in her car; I took the rest. On arrival at the hall I found that the 6.15 show had been cancelled, all the artists having got stuck in the snow on the way up from England. There was a long queue stretching for some reason or other back into Grindlay Street, but Elizabeth and her friends ignored this and were standing in the entrance. I pushed them through into the vestibule, and joined a small queue of people exchanging their first-house tickets for tickets for the later show, timed to begin at 8.30. All the girls were game to go except Ailsa, who said she definitely could not go — she was going off somewhere on her own. I understood her to say the New Club, but that did not seem likely. It suited me: I did not see how I was to get 9 big girls into one car. The departure of Ailsa — the biggest and heaviest — was a help, and I got the other 8 in all right and motored home. Nancy and Brenda had sat down in the kitchen to have tea from the party left-overs, and were much surprised to see the girls all trooping in again. They proceeded to phone their homes, and all got permission to go to the 8.30 show, except Ann Watt, whose mother is not on the phone, and Enid Blaikie, whose parents were at the Kings Theatre and were to have met her at their car when the concert ended. Ann insisted that her mother knew she might be late, and as regards Enid I said we should all go in to be there by 8 and I should see her parents at the car. The party meanwhile settled in happily again, and ate up most of what foodstuffs were left before we set off again at 7.45. Elizabeth and five of the others went straight to the hall while I walked down Cornwall Street with Enid and her friend Moira to where the

Blaikies' car was parked. No parents were there. Enid suggested we might leave a note, but I wanted to see whether Mr Blaikie would take Enid home after 10, and the three of us got into the car and sat there until Mr Blaikie arrived. He was friendly and helpful, agreed at once that Enid must go to the show, and said it would be no trouble to come back at 10 and take her and Penelope, whose home at Newington was on his route to Bennyrigg. So the two girls ran off to join the others, and I motored home — I had been along to the hall and made sure that the show was to go on. Shortly before 10 I motored back to the hall. There was a solitary man in the vestibule, who when I asked when the show was likely to finish said it would probably be about 11.30 — they had not got started until 9.30. I went through into the back of the hall: packed with teenagers, yelling and clapping their hands at a youth on the platform who was singing to the accompaniment of a jazz band. Holding a microphone in his hands, he sat down on the edge of the platform, where two teenage girls from the audience tried to get hold of his legs amid scenes of wild enthusiasm. I came away almost at once to look for Mr Blaikie, whom I met coming along to the hall. I explained the circumstances, and he took the news very well, merely remarking, " Oh, well, there's plenty of time ". I took him back into the hall, where we saw the second half of the programme for nothing. The audience was the main feature: certainly a sight worth seeing. The performers for the most part had no particular talent, but they were at least full of life — though I was dismayed, particularly when sitting beside Mr Blaikie, to find that a good many of their jokes left much to be desired, for an audience consisting mostly of young girls. Their most objectionable sallies were received with thunderous applause, particularly those of Arthur Worsley, an extremely skilful ventriloquist who had no need of such dubious embellishments. But a great deal that was said necessarily passed unheard or at any rate unnoticed in the general turmoil; and against Helen Shapiro herself, who came on last, there was no ground of complaint. This schoolgirl idol of the teenagers has quite a personality, and looked happy and friendly as she sang her familiar recorded songs. They gave her a fair hearing for her sentimental numbers, but the quick ones were completely drowned by the handclaps of the audience. She might have been singing anything or nothing. But obviously all present were enjoying themselves. The band was good, and the pace never faltered for a moment throughout the hour that Mr Blaikie and I were there. We met the girls at the door, and he went off with Enid and Penelope while I started on a tour round the town with the others. It was freezing hard — a lot of deep rutted snow in the side streets. Elizabeth and I reached home just on midnight.

NOV. 18. To church: ordination of elders. I was ordained, with three others. Mr Reid preached on Acts 14,23. For once, his sermon was altogether to the point: good and sensible. Extraordinary what a difference it makes to his preaching when he has something factual to talk about and is not engaged on his usual task of misinterpreting St Paul.

NOV. 19. The blizzard at the week-end must have been extraordinary for the time of year; on Saturday night all roads into Edinburgh were blocked except the road from Berwick. Soutra Hill is still completely blocked. Shields came up from his home so that I could swear him in as Honorary Sheriff-Substitute to take Donald McLeod's place at Selkirk tomorrow. I administered the oath by the drawing-room fire, in the presence of Nancy, Richard and the two animals.

NOV. 24. T. P. McDonald's: a party to show films he had taken on the *Pharos*. the films gave a fine representation of all the places and highlights of the trip, including the Sheriffs being slung off Dubh Hartach on the derrick. Burness remarked on what a terrible thing it was that he, a marine underwriter, had gone on such a voyage without taking out any cover on himself.

NOV. 26. Papers in a case against Glasgow Corporation had a letter from a witness who says: "I was sitting reading the paper when I heard a dull thud and a groan but I paid no attention to it but about 10 minutes later a knock came to my door (at that time No 7 Halkirk St. Patrick) and when I opened it Danny Graham was all twisted up in agony holding his shoulder and arm. So I told him to come in to see what happened. He said that he had fallen over planks of wood that were laying across his close and that he had dropped his key and some messages he had with him". "My name is James", he adds, "Dan always called me Robert but that was my brother's name. So hoping all is clear any further information from me will be gladly given".

NOV. 30. Gimson told me a story about old Pickard and a block of luxury flats called Tudor Court that was built on Great Western Road in Glasgow between the wars. Pickard bought a piece of waste ground on the opposite side of the road, thinking the builders would want it for a similar block. But the war came, and after the war there did not seem to be the same demand for luxury flats; and no builders wanted his plot of ground. So after taking a good look at the people going in and out of Tudor Court opposite he put up a notice on his vacant plot: "Good site available here for synagogue".

DEC. 6. Kirk Session: an entertaining meeting — going through the list prepared by Mr Gillies of people who had been absent from Communion throughout the year. Consideration had to be given to the question of whether they should be struck off the Roll. Apparently some names come up year after year, and Mr Reid invariably produced some plausible excuse for taking no action. A man had not been at church for 26 years. "Well", said Mr Reid, "he's a merchant seaman and has been quite a lot at sea. We had better give him another chance". Some consternation was caused when Mr Gillies produced a 4-years absentee, and attention was drawn to the fact that about 20 minutes before we had approved her appointment as one of the deacons. Needless to say, she had to be left on. Someone who had gone to England and had been away for 8 years was left on because Mr Reid had promised to keep them on the Roll till they sent for their certificates, and as they had never sent for the certificates he felt he was bound by his promise. Another defaulter was the brother-in-law of one of the elders who was not present tonight, and it was felt that nothing could be done since this elder was absent. A hospital matron who had retired some years ago and gone to live in Banffshire was also left — Mr Reid said he might get in touch with her and see if she would transfer to Grange parish church, near Keith, which he had attended as a boy.

Dec. 16. Elizabeth had been to dancing, and had got off, as she thought, at the wrong bus stop; but on getting down she found that she was at the right stop after all.

Dec. 21. First Division: a case in which the pursuer got an award of £675 for a hernia resulting from an accident. The defenders enrolled a motion for a new trial on the ground that the damages were excessive and lodged a tender of £500, expecting that we would accept and thus save them £175. However, we decided not to give way, and this course was justified by the event. They would not listen to Elliott, attempting to argue the case for the defenders. The Court was in a hilarious mood for their final sitting of the Christmas term. Clyde referred to one of the printed interlocutors dealing with the closing of the Record, from which inadvertently the letter "c" had been omitted. "Lord Guthrie", he read: "The Lord Ordinary loses the Record". Guthrie was amused at this; and the case went on to a speedy conclusion without my being called on. So the defenders' tactics cost them quite a bit more than they had expected to gain.

Dec. 26. It occurred to me that as I had had a good year it might be a nice idea to give £500 to Mrs Thomson, who had her arm taken off in the spin dryer, as some compensation for having failed to get any damages for her. I wrote her right away, and posted off the letter with a cheque for £500.

Dec. 27. A consultation with the egregious Mr Levy, who has come back to ask my advice after employing half a dozen other counsel and finally conducting a debate himself. I told Turnbull, the agent, that I could meet Levy at 1.45 and give him just under an hour. I kept the discussion fairly under control, did not allow Levy to say much, and at 2.40 brought the consultation to an end. "Are you quite happy about the case?" he asked as I was going out, to which I replied cheerfully that I did not regard it as altogether hopeless. The consultation was attended by the elegant beauty whom Levy had with him before and who took quite an intelligent part in the discussion on the rare occasions when she intervened.

DEC. 28. "Emergency Ward 10" on television. I usually go through to the study and do some work while the family have their television serials, *Emergency Ward 10* and *Coronation Street*, but tonight I remained in the family circle. *Emergency Ward 10* is really excellent: quite compelling in its genuine dramatic qualities, and the high standard of its acting and presentation. I got quite worked up about one of the episodes in today's instalment. Another surprise is the radio serial, *The Archers*, which I turned on inadvertently the other morning and was much taken by its wit and character: entirely different from the awful *Mrs Dale's Diary*.

From Mrs G. Thomson:

17 Luath St, Glasgow S.W.1   28/12/62
Dear Mr Stott
I don't know how I can begin to thank you for the very wonderful and much appreciated gift, that you have sent me, you have restored my faith in human nature, and can be sure the money you sent won't be squandered needlessly.
Please convey my sincere thanks to all concerned.
Compliments of the season.
Yours Faithfully

1963

1963: a tolerably successful year, particularly in the Lords. A unanimous verdict in my favour restoring the verdict of a jury had important repercussions in bringing back a degree of sanity into the Court of Session's handling of the doctrine of corroboration. Politics for me took on a new lease of life with the death of Mr Gaitskell. After an anxious moment when it looked as if the Labour members might choose George Brown to be leader of the party, they finally came down in favour of Harold Wilson. The Conservatives too had a stroke of luck. Their plan for fighting an election on support for the Common Market crashed into ruins through the recalcitrousness of General de Gaulle. Needless to say, none of the disasters which were supposed to follow from non-adherence to this anti-communist political and economic bloc actually came about. Meanwhile however an illness had given Mr Macmillan an excuse to resign; and the Conservative inner clique, with great ingenuity, selected as his successor an almost unheard-of Scottish nobleman, Lord Home – an agreeable, simple-minded person with few ideas. I continued to attend church regularly, and entered on my duties as an elder. It fell to me also to act as representative elder in the General Assembly. When first I decided to become a church member, I had done so with the idea that I might become an elder, and sit in the Assembly, where I might stand some chance of being appointed Procurator of the Church. With my practice at its present level, I had now neither time nor need for such an appointment; but as so often happens the achievement I had sought for an oblique motive turned out to be well worth while for its own sake, and I spent a thoroughly enjoyable week attending the Assembly's debates.

JAN. 1. New Year came in without any sound whatever in Midmar Gardens: not a hooter audible. I had to turn on the wireless to find out that midnight was past and the new year begun.

JAN. 3. Motored to town for some consultations. Richard had gone sledging on Blackford Hill, and as I turned the corner into Midmar Avenue I saw a small group of children coming from the hill, Richard among them with his face streaming with blood. As he gave me a cheerful grin, I shook my head at him and motored on, leaving it to Nancy to deal with his injuries when he got home. Papers at Dundas Street concerned one of Mr Levy's numerous litigations, but I was delighted to find that a new junior, Prosser, had brought a lot of light into this obscure matter. He had brought some other papers out to me this morning, with Minutes of Amendment that he had prepared, and they were excellent — he had made his way through the financial jungle with great skill and had all the essentials

72

summarised, so that I had very little to do. Home; where Elizabeth told me that Nancy had phoned the doctor and taken Richard to see him. They returned some time later, having been sent on to the Infirmary, where four stitches had been put in the top of his head. He had been sledging quite a way round the hill, and had walked all the way back carrying his sledge, with a big wound in his head — Dr O'Neill had said it was too big for him to deal with and had at once phoned the Infirmary and told him he was sending in the son of Gordon Stott "the Q.C. He's usually on the other side". So when they got to the Infirmary Richard was expected, and everything laid on ready for him.

JAN. 4. Aberdeen: a commission to take evidence. As there was no train back until 4, I walked up to Union Street to get my hair cut. A hairdresser's in Belmont Street turned out to be a scruffy little place, where the staff consisted of two slatternly-looking girls — hair all over the floor. I thought I might not get much of a haircut, but at any rate I should get it cheap. Both assumptions proved wrong. The girls, besides being cheerful and obliging, were skilled at their job, and the one who attended to me cut my hair very well indeed; and I paid more for it, I think, than I had ever paid for a haircut before: 3/6.

JAN. 5. Finished reading *Auchinleck*, by John Connell. Not a good biography: too long, and cluttered up with lengthy memoranda and contemporary letters. Though sub-titled "A critical biography", the book proceeds on the basis that Auchinleck was always right. No doubt he generally was — he certainly seems to have been persuasive. There is an amusing passage when Churchill sends out Cripps and some high-ranking soldiers to Cairo to tell Auchinleck and his colleagues how wrong they were, and then has to write to one of his soldiers saying that he has heard from the Lord Privy Seal. "I do not wonder everything was so pleasant, considering you seem to have accepted everything they said". I think the trouble was that Auchinleck, though more flexible-minded and a sounder tactician than his successors, was too considerate of other people's feelings and too anxious to persuade them that his was the right course, whereas what was required with Churchill was someone who would say dogmatically what he was going to do and then go his own way without bothering about telegrams from Whitehall. It seems clear enough that when he at last persuaded himself that he should take over the command in the field it was he who stopped Rommel's advance and won the battle for Egypt, Montgomery's victory at Alamein being more or less a follow-up.

JAN. 10. Derby: the Midland Hotel. Walked to the main street. A building marked "Museum and Art Gallery" turned out to be entirely devoted to works of a local artist named Wright; his paintings did not seem to me to show any particular talent. Dined by myself, but afterwards the phone rang: the Portland Cement area manager, Keble. Went down to the lounge and joined him and a scientific colleague, Dr Marshall.

JAN. 11. We were due to leave for Cauldon cement works at 8.45. Keble in a Ford Zephyr was faced with the difficulty which frequently confronts me in the mornings, that the gear lever would not engage. I advised him to put the gear into reverse two or three times, after which it might go into first. He put the gear into reverse rather dubiously, and at once got into first, remarking in tones of pleased surprise, "It works!" The works were hidden in a fold of the hills. We were taken up to the quarry: limestone dug out of the hillside in three perpendicular faces. At the factory we encountered Taylor; he had left Portland House in his car soon after 6 to join us at Cauldon. The most remarkable thing about the interior was the almost complete absence of workmen: an occasional man standing at an electric control was about all. The object of our visit to get an idea of what cement-working machinery is like, particularly as regards moveability; and though it seemed fantastic to regard these enormous machines as moveable one could see that there might be a technical argument to that effect. At dinner Taylor told some anecdotes about Sir James Hope, who has now sold all his mineral-bearing land to the company and seems to have become much attached to Taylor. He is to attend at Oxwellmains to perform the ceremony of lighting the first kiln. He was asked to a cocktail party earlier, but had doubts whether he could come because he would need a pair of new boots. He turned up wearing as usual old shaggy trousers with patches on the knees, and recalling how he had once trysted some dairy maid who failed to turn up at the meeting place so that he got soaked in a storm of rain. "Man", said Hope, "when you get rain above the knees it fairly cools your ardour".

JAN. 12. Reading *The Familiar Faces*, by David Garnett — by a coincidence found a reference to a topic which Nancy and I had been discussing just before I left home: what a mandrake was. I thought it was a kind of dragon, but Nancy said it was a plant, and so apparently it is: white bryony, once used by carters as an appetiser for their horses. Thinking I might as well see the sights, I made for a big tower rising squarely above all the other buildings: Derby Cathedral. A squat little interior, with no transepts, and a clutter of stone memorial slabs along the walls; it almost seems to be tower and nothing else. Trolley bus back to the hotel. As the charge for my room was £3.17.6 per night, I was glad that it was not I who had to pay it.

74

JAN. 13. The milk on the doorstep had frozen solid and pushed off the caps of the bottles, so that there was a little cylinder of frozen milk protruding upwards out of each bottle.

JAN. 17. Grant hearing a debate on the defenders' plea to relevancy. When I arrived, my junior, McNeill, had just sat down after replying to John McCluskey's opening speech for the defenders. McCluskey had got up to reply to him, but seeing me come in and take my place beside McNeill said hastily, "I waive my right of reply", and sat down, thus depriving me of the right to speak. Not having heard what the debate was about, I might not have been able to take part anyhow.

JAN. 19. To the Brotherstons' for supper. William put on his tape recorder to let us hear a recording of wild geese he had made near Heriot — no doubt interesting to bird watchers, but distinctly monotonous, and he seemed to be intending to let it run for half an hour or so. He seemed quite hurt when I suggested that 20 minutes of it might be enough, but cut it off, and set up his magic lantern to show us some bird pictures.

JAN. 23. Hampstead Everyman cinema: "L'Atalante". It starts well enough, with a bride walking with her husband to the barge in which they are to live, and finding it full of cats. But then it all tails away into nothing.

JAN. 24. Bus to Victoria in search of the new Portland House. No difficulty in seeing it: an enormous glass fortress towering into the sky. I had been told to take the lift to the 27th floor — there are separate lifts to the lower range of floors, and three which cannot be stopped before reaching the 14th. Taylor took me for a tour of the building — nobody about except his legal assistant, and Miss Flynn and another Irish girl, but they seemed to be settled in for the evening. Seeing Taylor with his coat on, Partington, the legal assistant, asked hopefully if he was going, to which he merely replied airily, "Oh, I'll be back. Don't go away". We looked into some of the rooms — all differently decorated, as each executive had been given a fixed sum to spend on furnishing his room and left to deal with it as he pleased — then went down to the ground floor to see a working model of a quarry and factory at Shoreham. Taylor then led the way into a lift marked "Lift going up", and pressed a button marked "Basement". The lift began to ascend, and took us up to the 14th floor. "It'll go to the basement from here all right", he said, pressing the button again, and sure enough it did. In the basement was a capacious restaurant, and a coffee room where some teddy boys were finishing coffee: the firm's table-tennis team about to leave for a match. The rest of the basement was occupied by the garage, an enormous underground area broken up by cement pillars, with space for hundreds of cars. Taylor's was one of the few still there, and he motored me to Kings Cross. Taylor had got a sleeper for me on the 10.15 Aberdeen train, which does not normally carry passengers for Edinburgh; he came in with me to the Sleeper Reservation Office and saw me collect the ticket. The window of my sleeper was frozen up, but after some effort I managed to get it open, knocking some icicles off. More icicles formed after the train started, but the carriage was well heated, and with two blankets and my travelling rug I was cosy and comfortable.

FEB. 17. To church for the evening service. Mr Reid preached on Psalms 55,22; even longer than he preaches in the morning, and every bit as bad. It is astonishing that one so reasonable, tactful and understanding in everyday life should preach such extraordinary sermons. He told a nauseating story about little Cathy who was ill with pneumonia, and little Johnny who came and sat beside her for two hours, holding her hand and saying "Breathe, baby, breathe; and in the spring we'll gather dandelions and make posies". So Cathy recovered — a miracle, the doctor said. But what if one waited for the Lord and he did not respond? "Brethren", said Mr Reid, "I do not know the answer to that question".

FEB. 19. Proof in *Rutherford v. Rutherford*. A surprise development at the end of the week, when it was learned that the co-defender, who had attended the consultation at Dundas Street the week before, had committed suicide. Though somewhat quiet at the consultation, he had seemed normal enough.

FEB. 20. Lord Johnston took the case to avizandum. I scored a point over one of the pursuer's watchers who maintained that she could see clearly into the windows opposite because the sun was shining into them. By reference to a plan of Glasgow I was able to confirm that if the witness were right the sun on the evening in question, in July, must have been shining from the north-east. But Douglas did not take the point as I should have liked him to do.

FEB. 21. Mr Shaw rang to say that the Lords had given their decision in *Robertson v. White*, finding unanimously for the appellant and restoring the verdict of the jury.

FEB. 22. Saw in this morning's *Scotsman* that in the Robertson case Guest had said in terms that the Lord President had usurped the function of the jury.

FEB. 23. Elizabeth sat the entrance exam early in the month for the Mount, the Quaker school at York, and a communication arrived this morning to say she had got in.

FEB. 27. Fitzpatrick, the attendant at Parliament House door, told me he had been commiserating yesterday with my client who came for a consultation. He had apparently been asked to come at 3, and coming somewhat before that time had more than an hour and a half to wait before I was free. As the consultation had lasted only about five minutes, Fitzpatrick thought the unfortunate man had had a long wait. But this view, he said, my client had completely repudiated. It had been well worth while, he said. He had had a talk with Mr Stott, and the consultation had been most satisfactory and well worth waiting for. It shows how impressions may differ: I had thought myself it must have seemed anything but satisfactory, particularly as I had got the papers for it only in the course of the day, had no time to look at them, and remembered very little of what the case was about. To Dundas Street for a consultation in *Docherty v. Royal Bank of Scotland*: a lengthy affair. Mr Docherty had arrived in an enormous Bentley, but when I came down the stair after the consultation I found him and his minions clustered round his car vainly attempting to get in. In some extraordinary way — perhaps, as someone suggested, sabotage by secret agents of the Bank — the door locks had stuck, and the key would not turn. I left Joe supervising an effort to break into the car.

MAR. 1. Kissen had remarked in the course of his speech yesterday that he felt rather handicapped in this case by the sympathy which he like everyone else felt for the pursuer; and I observed today that their Lordships would probably feel that despite that handicap he had been able to address them with his usual cogency and force. Left about 5.30 for Jedburgh, where I was to propose the toast of the Jedhart Callants Club at the annual dinner. I had phoned the Jedburgh police about roads, and was told I could get through by the Gala Water road — and indeed that Soutra, which had been blocked for four weeks, was expected to be open from 11 this morning. Ronald McLarty had been dubious about any attempt to take the car to Jedburgh, and had urged me to go by bus to Galashiels and stay overnight. But this did not appear to be necessary — though I took pyjamas, to be on the safe side. The road was clear as far as Middleton, but from then on was rough with hard frozen rutted snow. It seemed safe enough, but made slow going over Middleton Moor. A bad bit south of Stow, when I was slithering about the road in deep ruts among bulges of frozen snow. But on the whole it was a better journey than I had expected. We sat down to dinner promptly at 8. Conversation was not easy: the chairman, on my left, was deaf, and on my right I had the current Jedhart Callant, a youth of few words. The usual interminable song list — mostly songs about Jedhart heroes, and Jedhart qualities of one kind or another — and an accordion player who was good but made rather a noise in what was not a very big room. The toast of the burgh of Jedburgh was proposed by the Provost of Selkirk and replied to by the Provost of

Jedburgh, both of whom had typewritten manuscripts which they read out at length. Then, when we seemed to be coming to the end of the programme, the chairman called for an item which did not appear on it, and a youth got up and gave a long "humorous" recitation. The chairman himself was quite business-like at the start, but as the evening wore on and he had several drinks he became more garrulous and took up a lot of time introducing each item. It was 11.30 when I set off for home. Decided in view of the slowness of the Gala Water route that I might as well try Soutra.

MAR. 2. All through Lauder there were heaps of dirty frozen snow three or four feet high between the houses and the street, but the road continued reasonably clear, even when I came up into the hills. I overtook a police car, which was comforting — indicating as it did that Soutra must be open. They had made a remarkably good job, blasting away 20-foot frozen drifts with gelignite, and then digging a cutting of 2-way-traffic width. The road surface was hard packed frozen snow, and as very little traffic had passed over it it was surprisingly smooth; I had only one noticeable skid, and was able to keep up a steady 30 mph through the cuttings, with snow sides rising to 20 feet-high snow walls along both sides of the road right across the summit plateau. I was home by 1.15.

MAR. 5. Parliament House: I hastily revised 2 more Summonses that Prosser had drawn for Mr Levy. They had wanted them done yesterday, though I got the papers only yesterday morning. I ignored the big bundle of papers that accompanied the drafts, contenting myself with some commonsense revisions and a Note in which I suggested that it would be in Mr Levy's interest to employ senior counsel who could give immediate attention to his affairs. Thereafter I had a jury trial. The employers admitted liability, and had tendered £500. The pursuer was off work for only 4 weeks, with a net loss of £40, but the accident has resulted in permanent paralysis of the deltoid muscle, so that he cannot raise his hand above the shoulder without pain. Despite this, he has continued work, attending hospital for treatment in the evenings. At the moment he is doing work which does not involve the use of his left arm, but the important point is obviously what may happen to him in the future. Accordingly it was arranged at the pre-trial consultation that an amendment should be put on dealing with prejudice to future wage-earning capacity, and the sum sued for would be increased from £1000 to £2000. I was dismayed to find on looking at the papers at the week-end that the amendment had not a word about future loss, so that we had to fight a tender of £500 on pure solatium plus £40. This as it turned out was disastrous. Two excellent doctors gave evidence of the seriousness of the injury, but despite quite a fair charge from Strachan the jury awarded only £440. The verdict was a majority one, 7-5, and apparently the minority would have given him £800. So he was unlucky indeed, paying the penalty for his honesty and determination to continue at work despite a severe disability. Wylie being away at the Glasgow circuit, Croan stepped into his place at short notice and dealt with the situation very tactfully in his opening speech. I was not particularly pleased with my own speech to the jury, but with a proper averment I do not think we should have had any difficulty in beating the tender.

MAR. 6. Finished reading *Prison Screw*, by L. W. Marrow Smith and James Harris. Mr Smith has no very strong views. He gives an interesting, matter-of-fact account of prisons from the unusual angle of a prison officer: a lot of tiresome anecdotes, but much of what he has to say is important and useful. Mr Harris, who presumably put the book in order, seems to have been new to the job, for the writing improves very much as the book proceeds.

MAR. 7. Went through to the National Library and got them to look out a little book of Popular Rhymes and Sayings of the County of Berwick, compiled in 1856 by George Henderson, surgeon at Chirnside; and with the help of this concocted a speech for Berwickshire High School former pupils' dinner, at which at Harald Leslie's instance I am to propose a toast.

MAR. 11. Read *The Shapes of Sleep*, a completely pointless novel by J. B. Priestley. All the stock ingredients: escapes, pursuits, fights, killings, a sinister man and lovely women — the lifeless skeleton of a thriller, with no substance to give it meaning.

MAR. 13. Bought a pair of evening dress trousers. My old ones are still good, but with my present girth I find it all but impossible to get into them. Though last year's measurements were all right otherwise, my waist was an inch more.

MAR. 14. A jury trial: Harvie v. Mitchell Construction Co. The pursuer's real name is Kociszewski. He is a Pole who settled here after the war, when he had been serving in the Polish navy. He is extremely self-confident, and handled R. S. Johnston's cross-examination with pertinacity and skill. The defenders have put in an injudicious Minute of Amendment in which they claim that the pursuer's failure to be employed in tunnelling is because he was an unsatisfactory worker. Unfortunately for them, he has been able to produce a certificate granted him by the defenders themselves in 1954 to the effect that Kociszewski was employed by them as shift boss in a tunnel crew which established a British and European rock tunnelling record.

MAR. 15. Despite a wishy-washy charge from Douglas Johnston, I thought we had a good chance of getting about £2,000 for the pursuer; but to everyone's amazement, including the defenders', the jury found for them by 8 votes to 4. The dinner of the Berwickshire former pupils, at the United Services Club: a surprisingly large company, of both sexes and all ages. The chairman was a teacher, an awful woman with a Cockney-Morningside accent who not only told anecdotes but proceeded to recite at length. On my other side was Dr Mary Collins from the University, a very sensible person, and there was a pleasant, pretty girl opposite, an Earlston girl who is the wife of Fotheringham, a solicitor. Apart from the chairman, the speeches went off successfully — my Berwickshire rhymes going down well. Harald Leslie replied, in what was really a very good little speech. His sentimental passages, so terrible in print, came across not at all badly in his cosy, impromptu style.

MAR. 16. One of the Levy cases came up in the Motion Roll yesterday before the jury trial was resumed. I had received the Summons, but no instructions about yesterday's motion. I hastily moved out, and left Prosser to deal with it.

MAR. 19. Proof in *Docherty v. Royal Bank*. On account of public interest, we had been put into the Second Division court-room, and there was a large attendance throughout the day — mostly, I should think, retired bankers and the like. A queue was waiting for admission before the court sat. The offending teller told the story of his mistake. The notes, he said, were £20 and £5. They were in 10 large bundles, with 10 folds in each. He counted the folds in each bundle, and formed the impression that there was £10,000 in each, although in fact it was only £1,000: 10 folds of £100 each. He was a cool, collected young man, and my cross-examination made no impression on him. I had prepared it carefully, but so far as shaking his evidence was concerned it was a complete failure.

MAR. 20. The case went better today. I got some good answers in cross-examination of the bank manager, and Docherty held his own skilfully in the early stages of Kissen's cross-examination. He was as composed as the bank teller, and gave his evidence in a quiet, matter-of-fact way which took a lot of the force out of Kissen's fulminations. When Kissen remarked that he did not know what a £100 note looked like, and none of the serried ranks of bankers behind him could produce one, Docherty pulled a wad of them from his pocket to show him. I was told afterwards that he had £4,000 on him in banknotes today, and that that was by no means out of the ordinary. Finished reading *Women in Parliament*, by Jean Mann. She seems to me to be hopelessly at sea on all major questions, but as parliamentary gossip it is more sensible than I had expected.

MAR. 21. I adduced two witnesses from Ireland who spoke to handing Docherty £50,000 shortly before the incident at the bank.

One was an accountant who had put Docherty in touch with Vincent McEoin, an architect in Dublin, who gathered £50,000 in cash and brought it to Belfast, where it was handed to Docherty. McEoin was a delightful Irishman, tall, rugged and handsome, apparently a well-known Alpine mountaineer as well as having high professional qualifications. He gave his evidence clearly and convincingly, but trouble arose when Kissen in cross-examination asked him where he got the money from. This question he declined to answer, on the ground that it involved other people; and on his persisting in this refusal when Cameron directed him to answer Cameron told him to stand down and he would be detained in the custody of the court. There was a buzz of excited conversation in the crowded court as I called the next witness, the Irish accountant, and proceeded to lead his evidence. Some time later a note was passed to me from our solicitors to the effect that McEoin would be prepared to write down the source of the money, provided it was disclosed only to judge and counsel. I thought the best course was to ask Cameron to adjourn for ten minutes and hear Kissen and me in private. Kissen would make no concession, and said his clients would want to enquire into any information McEoin provided; but Cameron pointed out that if what McEoin wrote was in the custody of the court it would at least not go out to the public or the press. The clerk of court was sent to give McEoin this information, and came back with the message that McEoin was prepared to do so. The court resumed, McEoin re-entered the box, and wrote a name and address on a piece of paper — somebody in Dublin. Kissen made no impression on this evidence. We had some amusing moments with McSherry, Docherty's manager, who was sent to the bank with a sum of money, admittedly over £9,000, in a zip bag with no other fastening, although to Docherty's knowledge he had just come out of gaol for theft. Docherty explained that he and McSherry had been brought up together, and McSherry had written to him from prison asking for a job when he came out. McSherry said he had been a bit nervous, never having been in a bank before. Kissen showed him one of the teller's metal trays, and asked him if the teller had laid out the money on a tray like that. "It wasn't like that", said McSherry, "it was like a tray you put in the oven". "What do you mean?" Kissen asked. "What did it look like?" "It looked like as if it had been in the oven," said McSherry. Docherty, when questioned by Kissen about an occasion when he had sent to the bank for some money after hours — this was after the incident in controversy, and on the bank's figures of the pay-in the account would have been overdrawn — explained that members of the Harlem Globetrotters basket-ball team, who were playing in Glasgow, had come into the office in the late afternoon and laid a bet of £790 at 6 to 1. They were to be playing in Perth that night, but left one of their number in the office to collect the winnings after the race. Docherty not having enough money on the premises to pay such a bet had had to send down to the bank. Kissen was then passing on to something else when Cameron intervened to ask what had been the upshot of the matter. "The horse was beat", said Docherty. Kissen spent most of the day slinging mud, and though he had not much material for his purpose he seemed to be getting some encouragement from Cameron.

MAR. 22. The Docherty proof was concluded. Kissen fulminated for an hour or so, blackguarding everyone. Cameron seemed to be accepting it, apart from criticism of the Irish witnesses, to which he specifically demurred. I was not hopeful about my own speech, having prepared most of it late last night when I was feeling tired; but as it turned out it was quite effective. Cowie, who was appearing with Kissen for the defenders, told me afterwards that it was the best speech he had ever heard in court. Whether it will make any difference to the result of the case is another matter. If I had to decide the case myself, I should find it quite impossible to say where the truth lies.

AP. 13. An air-mail letter from Paramount, California, from McShane, addressed to "Mr G. G. Stott (who has a wig, and goes into court" — which the Post Office had glossed as "Q.C." In two full pages of closely-typed invective he accuses me of every possible crime, real or imaginary.

AP. 24. Hawick Vacation Court: a petition by the County Mental Health Officer to commit a girl of 17 to Gogarburn mental hospital. Two doctors have certified that she is mentally defective. She was in Gogarburn before, and came out against the doctors' wishes. She was promiscuous and kept bad company, and is going to have a baby; and the doctors do not think she is able to have any proper regard for her own welfare. Last month however she got married to a young bricklayer whom she met by chance in Edinburgh, and he appeared today to oppose the petition. He seemed a sensible young man, and said he knew all about Jean and her behaviour, but he had already improved her quite a bit and was hopeful that he would manage to keep her in order. She was a good baker, and last week she had taken all his clothes and washed and ironed them, which she had never done before. The Mental Health Officer and the woman Children's Officer were both dubious about the marriage, and said they had warned Mr Miller about what he had taken on; but they admitted that they had nothing against Jean since her marriage. It seemed to me that he ought to be given a chance to see what he could do, and that it would be wrong to break up the marriage before it had really got started. Jean's baby is expected at the end of the summer; Mr Miller, who said he did not know whether it was his baby or not, was prepared to take it as his and bring it up accordingly. Mr Bookless would not be persuaded to withdraw his petition, and I accordingly refused it.

AP. 25. Jedburgh Vacation Court. A petition for commital of a 13-year-old girl, Jacqueline Tunnah, to an approved school — rather distressing. The girl's mother went off to America years ago, and no one ever hears of her. Jacqueline has been brought up by her grandmother, but the latter now finds it impossible to manage her. She has left home on two or three occasions, and been picked up by the police, once in Penicuik and once in Lanarkshire. On the second occasion she was brought home she took a dose of pills and powders, and had to have medical treatment. She said she did this because life was not worth living. She got into bad company, and lost her job in a shop on account of being untidy. She got another job in a mill, but left it when she went away to Lanarkshire. It is said that there is now no prospect of her finding employment in the Jedburgh area. I had to put to her the facts in the petition, which she accepted as true; and then asked her if she had anything to say. She said that if she were left at home she would now be able to look after herself better and behave properly. She had been in a remand home for a few days, and realised what she had to do. I felt very sorry for her as she sat there quietly, with big tears coursing down her cheeks, but it seemed that there was no alternative to granting the petition. I assured her — I hope correctly — that she might get on all right when put among the other girls at Dr Guthrie's School at Gilmerton, where the assistant probation officer has found a place for her.

AP. 29. St Boswells: Probation Committee. Mr Angus gives his reports to the accompaniment of a running commentary from Lady Elliot, but generally pays no heed to what she is saying; as he has no sense of humour, the result is sometimes funny. "This young man — " he began. "Well", said Lady Elliot, "he can't be a young man. I see he's 62". "This young man", continued Mr Angus, unperturbed, "has obtained employment as a chef". Another probationer, he thought, would make an excellent farmer. "He is 6 feet 5 inches". "Well, of course", said Lady Elliot, "that's not all the qualification you need for being a farmer. I farm myself, and I know". "He would make an excellent farmer", said Mr Angus, "but he is emotionally unsuitable. He requires a mother figure". After the meeting we all motored to Dingleton Hospital, where after we had been conducted round there was a "seminar" for discussion — mainly on whether the County Council could provide psychiatric clinics and sufficient staff at the hospital to enable them to be worked. Lady Elliot as usual showed herself go-ahead and enthusiastic, though appreciative of her difficultues — "especially now that we have Ratepayers Associations and horrors of that kind to cope with".

MAY 9. Nancy told me that William Muir had been to visit Mr and Mrs Braggins. He turned up here last Friday when I was at Parliament House, saying he had read about my case and wanted to know how it had gone. Nancy had rung me up, and on my advice given him £1 as well as some soup and stew, and sent him on his way. He said he had recently fallen and had a bad leg, and was on his way to Tranent, where he had relatives. He did not of course know the Braggins household, nor they him, but when Nancy heard from them of an old man who came to the door saying he had lost his key and was on the way to Haddington, and had formerly been with the Hudson Bay Company, she had not much doubt who had been there. Mrs Braggins had given him some soup, and a shilling — which would not take him very far on the way to Haddington. He said he was not begging, but would like something to eat on his journey.

MAY 10. Shearer brought me out from the Law Room to the hall to thank me for arranging C. de B. Murray's retiral, a feat which everyone has been aiming at for years. Since becoming Lord Advocate, Shearer hardly ever appears in Parliament Hall, but he had come down from the Crown Office to show me Murray's letter. To Gilmerton, to visit Dr Guthrie's School for Girls. Since sending Jacqueline Tunnah, I have had some unfavourable accounts of the place, and accordingly arranged with the headmistress, Miss McLaren, that she would show me round. I am afraid the reports were right. The building is old-fashioned and institutional; Miss McLaren unlocked doors everywhere we went and locked them again behind us. There is little in the way of intellectual education: just sewing, knitting, housework and laundering. Miss McLaren is young, self-confident and domineering. Whenever we went into a room, the girls had to stand up until she told them to sit. I should not suppose that any independence of mind would meet with much encouragement. I think it would be all right for stupid or halfwitted girls, but I am afraid it is not at all the proper place for poor Jaceuqline. Miss McLaren was careful not to take me to the class-room where "Tunnah", as she called her, was. Mr Reid came up shortly after I got back, to ask if I had heard any complaints about the Cub camp. The Daily Express reporters had got hold of a story that some of the Cubs had been put on bread and water; he said he had reporters at him twice, but told them he knew nothing about it. I assured him that I had heard nothing of it either, and if it were true it had no doubt been a very good thing. Richard told me when he got home that some of the Cubs, including himself, had been put on bread and water for talking during the night. "It was bread and jam really", he said, "and it was much better than the fish".

MAY 17. Cameron was giving judgment in *Docherty v. Royal Bank*. I did not go in to hear it, but I gather that he was very hot against Docherty.

MAY 18. Leith Town Hall: Miss Cameron's dancing display. Elizabeth was in two items. Her dancing has improved, though she still has something of the air of a stranger who has dropped in by chance and condescended to take part in the dance.

MAY 21. Glasgow: Lanarkshire planning inquiry.

MAY 22. Gimson addressed the Commissioner on behalf of the County Council and I followed. Thinking that the best way to get Brand to note my argument was to give him a series of numbered points, I inadvertently caused considerable amusement by announcing that I had 10 points, and then going on to No 11 and No 12. When I announced No 12, Gimson rose to object, amid general laughter, and I then realised what I had done — I had had 10 points originally, and forgot to alter the introductory passage of my address. Gimson remarked afterwards that it had been refreshing to hear a "non-planner" at a planning inquiry, and he hoped they would have me again.

MAY 23. I had returned such work as I had for today, and went across to the Assembly. The highlight of the day's proceedings was the debate on the report of a committee "For clarifying returns to overtures" — actually on whether a statement on the doctrine of baptism should be made a Standing Law of the church. The point seemed to be whether grace and forgiveness were there from the start, for all to accept if they so chose, or whether it was necessary for repentance to come first, after which forgiveness would follow. This was closely and intensely debated, with citations from Calvin and frequent references to Arminianism and suchlike heresies, particularly by a young minister who had been unable to feel sure whether he had truly repented or not. I voted on the side of grace for all, but this was voted down by a substantial majority. It was resolved to commend the statement to the prayerful consideration of ministers and members. The next item on the agenda was the report of the Committee on Huts & Canteens, of which our Mr Reid is convener. He began his address in a hubbub of members' departing or conversing, so that his opening was inaudible. But he went steadily on, and soon had his audience reduced to bored silence, with nobody paying any attention. His report was followed by the report of the committee on Central Africa, which after its success in helping to release Nyasaland from the toils of Federation is now asking to be disbanded. As a parting shot, it asked the Assembly to urge the Government not to grant independence to Southern Rhodesia until it had representative government based on the consent of a majority of the inhabitants of all races. An elder from Hawick rose to dissent, and was with difficulty persuaded to come forward to the microphone, where he slowly and hesitantly affirmed that he had lived in Central Africa and felt that this deliverance was against our kith and kin. He was a distinguished-looking gentleman: no speaker, but obviously sincere. But an overwhelming majority of those present voted him down and adopted the deliverance.

MAY 24. The Assembly were discussing the Iona Community: a lengthy diatribe by a minister who objected to the celebration of St Columba's landing on Iona in 563 because that was not the date of his landing.

MAY 26. To church, where Mr Reid preached on Job 1,9. I saw him on Thursday evening after we both got back from the Assembly, and was relieved to find that his experience had by no means disconcerted him. He apparently had no idea that his report had been anything but a complete success: the audience had been rather small, but he thought they had seemed interested in what he told them.

MAY 29. To the Assembly for the final day's session; I have found the discussions interesting. Professor James Stewart, the Moderator, was excellent — kindly, courteous and firm. He made a distinguished figure as he sat in the Moderator's chair, or more often stood behind the speaker at the microphone, gazing at him with sympathetic interest. I have never seen a chairman stand for so much of the debate as Stewart does.

JUN. 2. Finished reading Nones, by W. H. Auden. I cannot pretend to have understood what these poems are about, but there is an anxious, foreboding air about them which I found rather fascinating.

JUN. 6. To the City Chambers, where I was appearing for George Wimpey & Co. in an appeal against refusal of planning permission for 120 houses on a market garden in Milton Road. Wishart, our expert, is a rambling, unsatisfactory witness, and I did not feel that the case went as well as it should. My cross-examination was completely ineffective.

JUN. 7. Spent most of the morning cross-examining, to no great effect. I got some much-needed encouragement from my people, who were enthusiastic about my speech. "I don't know how you do it", Wishart said. "You pick up every point and fit them all in, everything in perfect order". An amusing incident while I was speaking, and remarked that I was going to make 6 points. I made the 6, and then remembering that I had 2 more added that there were two additional points — whereupon Wishart, remembering what had happened in Glasgow, remarked quite audibly in delighted incredulity ''He's going to do it again!''

JUN. 9. With Richard and Nicholas to Earlston for a motor-cycle scramble: the boys much thrilled by being asked to assist one of the leading contenders, whose machine broke down opposite where they were standing.

JUN. 12. Parliament House: when I was coming away at 3.30, McIlwraith appeared with his small girl, who has just started at St George's. She was lively and friendly, and delighted when I put her in one of the advocates' boxes on the shelf in the lobby. Cameron and Douglas Johnston came past as she was in the box, and entered into conversation with her. As Abbey remarked, she looked very funny sitting up in the box.

JUN. 14. Finished reading *Island in Revolt*, by Charles Foley, a book about Cyprus, very good and very depressing. The author was editor of the local English newspaper, and obviously has no bias except towards decency and common sense. His straightforward, factual account discloses depths of hypocrisy and folly to which one could hardly suppose any government could have sunk. Things were as bad under Foot as under Harding: an indication that personalities are of no account when a policy of oppression is being carried out. The other thing that astonished me was that the British Government had no hand in the ultimate settlement: the Greeks and Turks finally came together and reached an agreement, which they more or less imposed on the unwilling British. A few individuals came out well — including, to my surprise, Barbara Castle, who had the courage to speak the truth and was disowned by Gaitskell forthwith.

JUN. 16. Braid Church: Rev. John B. Logan, minister of Ford and Crichton, on Acts 5,29. It passed the test of a good sermon in so far as it had one thinking hard about what he was saying all the time he was saying it. He was interesting, topical and sensible — not a particularly eloquent preacher, but an attractive, simple person who one felt was a good man himself but willing to make allowances, completely free from self-importance. Some of his best points were made in throwaway asides, and he sometimes could not get the right word or the right conclusion to his idea, but it did not really matter. He was speaking about the Profumo case, the scandal that has blown up in Parliament over the resignation of the Secretary for War because he had to admit that his denial of an affair with a ''call girl'' called Christine Keeler was false; and it was a pleasant relief to hear some Christian charity applied to the problem. Mr Butler appeared on a television programme in the evening, answering questions on the relationship of religion to politics. He skirted round the Profumo case with his usual emotionless skill; but I was more interested in an answer he gave when asked for an example of the church's influence on political affairs. He instanced Central Africa, in which the Church of Scotland had influenced the Government in the direction of independence for Nyasaland. "You mean", asked Kenneth Lindsay, "that if the Church of Scotland had not intervened the Government's policy would have been different?" "Well, I wouldn't go as far as that", said Mr Butler with a gentle smile — but it seems to have been the fact.

JUN. 18. Debate Roll: the simplest possible case, but unfortunately it came out before Walker, and I was sure he would find some reason for depriving us of a jury trial and sending the case for proof. Debates on relevancy before Walker are always completely divorced from reality.

JUN. 19. A meeting with Docherty, to advise him that an appeal was impracticable. As always, he took the bad news calmly and philosophically, making some shrewd comments but not complaining in the slightest about the disaster which had overtaken his case. He is an extremely nice fellow, and I find it very hard to believe that he is a rogue. Finished reading *Pressure Group*, by H. H. Wilson, an account of how a small group of interested backbenchers succeeded in obtaining the introduction of commercial television by a government with no mandate for it and no particular enthusiasm for it either. The author is an American University man, and extremely knowledgeable. He has written a most interesting little book, a factual account free from polemics or emotionalism but with occasional touches of dry humour and concluding with some general observations largely derived from Peregrine Worsthorne, the editorial writer in the *Daily Telegraph*. Throughout the controversy, the author comments, it was apparent that the supporters of commercial television were contemptuous of efforts to uphold cultural or intellectual standards. "The decisive consideration was that it was a great marketing device. They would certainly reject out of hand Worsthorne's insistence that 'the most pressing task of government is to maintain the quality of the national life, the integrity of its institutions and the moral character of its people in face of the quite unprecedented impact of mass prosperity'". The author quotes Worsthorne's comment that traditionally the Conservative Party was "an elaborate organisation for keeping the right kind of people in power at all levels of the national life" — those who "by birth, background, training and station are likely to be endowed with the rare knowledge of how to govern". Now it might almost seem that the Party had become "an elaborate organisation for keeping the wrong people in power". This was the achievement of "the hucksters, who were asked to attract the crowds, but have taken over the show".

JUN. 20. To Jedburgh to instal Paterson as Sheriff. C. de B. Murray was going today to take the hearing in a proof that he heard before his retiral, and I took him with me. He suggested that he should just "slip in" at the back of the court, but at my request he sat with us on the bench, and I made some reference to him before going on to welcome Paterson. I did not say anything very complimentary — remarking that he had had numerous problems to surmount, largely, as he would admit, of his own choosing; but he was most appreciative of what I said, and seemed genuinely touched by the reference made to him. Paterson remarked that he had once been instructed to give a joint Opinion along with me. After many months, as no fee had been received, his wife had taken it up with him, and he took it up with his clerk — only to be told that Sheriff Stott had agreed to forego his fee in this case, so that there was no fee for Paterson either.

JUN. 21. To Duns to instal Paterson. Ailie's father and mother attended, and I took the opportunity to introduce a topical touch, recalling that on one occasion, long before she came to the Bar, I had tried to do her a service. Realising, as we all did now, the temptations to which Members of Parliament were exposed in London, I thought it my duty to try to persuade the electors to stop sending Ailie's father to London and send me instead. The electors had thought otherwise, but Sir Ian had ultimately come round to my way of thinking, on that matter if on no other, and at a subsequent election had decided of his own accord to retire from Parliament and stay at home. Paterson took up this point, suggesting that the result of the West Edinburgh election had been trebly fortunate: for his father-in-law, who had been able to go on being an MP, for me, who had been able to build up my present practice, and for the Sheriffdom, which had been able to get me as its Sheriff — a neat, witty speech. Nancy had called in the painter to patch up one or two strips of paper which had come loose, but as soon as he started today all the paper had come adrift, and it will be necessary to have the whole thing redone — rather a pity, for the hall decoration was the most attractive feature of the house as we bought it.

JUN. 22. *Lift Up Your Hearts* came on the wireless and I was delighted to hear the urgent, distinctive voice of Rev. Werner Pelz, vicar of Lostock, grappling with problems of religion in his wild, honest, realistic way. He is head and shoulders above any other preacher, and what he says is in complete contrast with the sentimental, unconvincing drivel which usually characterises this programme.

JUN. 27. Levy was hanging about during the forenoon, and seized on me when I came out for lunch; but I gave him a telling-off and escaped, and thereafter managed to avoid him.

JUN. 29. Elizabeth's class had been busy conversing in their classroom when the bell rang for prayers yesterday, with the result that they had not heard it and had not turned up; and Elizabeth had had to go to Miss Fleming and apologise on behalf of the class, in her capacity as class captain. This she seems to have found quite enjoyable. The only member of the class who had gone to prayers was Ailsa Wilson, who had as usual arrived late, and gone straight into hall.

JUL. 13. *The Exploration of Outer Space*, by Sir Bernard Lovell. The astronomers seem more firmly committed than ever to the existence of millions of galaxies similar to the Milky Way, all rushing away from us and from one another at a speed of at least 86,000 miles per second — all very mysterious. Richard went off across the wall to spend the night with Gordon Hunt in a tent in the garden.

JUL. 14. To church, where Mr Reid preached on Matthew 21,28. Richard, who had not had much sleep in his tent, went fast asleep during the sermon, and had to be prevented from toppling over in his seat.

JUL. 17. Faculty meeting to consider the provisions of a new Bill about intestate succession. Several youthful members of Faculty who appeared to be knowledgeable about agricultural and landowning problems orated on these matters at some length; and as I was feeling drowsy anyhow I more or less went to sleep.

AUG. 1. Newquay. The house we have taken for the month on the Pentire peninsula is in a lovely situation on the hillside, looking out over the Gannel to Crantock sands. A big wild garden — the very place for Richard to play at being a Commando. The livestock consists of three pet bantams.

AUG. 4. St Michaels, the English church: an elderly clergyman who appears to be permanent chaplain to the Mission to Seamen. He did not preach a sermon in any proper sense of the word — God was not mentioned. But he rambled on, telling anecdote after anecdote, each more pointless than the last. There seemed no reason why he should ever come to a conclusion, and in a sense he never did; but he did at last stop. I thought the children would be fed up, but they seem to have been rather amused. Richard and I bathed, getting some good runs. Richard has mastered the art of surfing, and generally comes at least as far up the beach as I can get.

AUG. 5. To the town to get some flowers for Nancy — thinking, mistakenly, that this was our wedding anniversary.

AUG. 11. To St Columb Minor for Matins. The vicar, Rev. J. E. Holland, preached a short, sensible sermon about the rich young man who wanted to know what he had to do to inherit eternal life. Richard was much disappointed, and I also, by not being allowed to bathe. The beach patrols at Fistral now whistle in anyone who attempts to bathe when a red flag is flying; and as it flew throughout the day Fistral's merits as a surfing beach were lost. The tide was going out, and no doubt there was some undertow, but with a little care surfing need not have been dangerous, and they had had the flag flying even in the morning when the tide was flowing. Newquay's popularity, one would think, must suffer when its best bathing beach is closed to bathers throughout a fine Sunday in August.

AUG. 12. Mawgan Porth: Nancy, Richard and I bathed. Bathing at Mawgan Porth was just as I remembered it: rather a mix-up of waves, so that one got a good run only occasionally, but then it was very good — a triple wave which brought me right up the beach. As the tide was well out, Nancy was a little apprehensive about bathing there — a lot of pits, and some seaweed.

AUG. 13. The ferry to Trethellen is operated just as it was when I first crossed 30 years ago: a big rowing-boat, with a powerful man to row against the current. The present boatman was a friendly, chatty man, who had bought the ferry from the previous owner.

AUG. 15. A sail down the Fal. The helmsman gave us information about points of interest through a loud-speaker, but this was confined to a minimum, and quite interesting: no persistent talk for the sake of talking, and no music or other nuisance of that kind. Falmouth seemed a cheapjack place, but we were lucky enough to come on an Olde English tea-shop, and going up a stair found ourselves in a different world: a quiet little tea-room with a table in a lovely bow window, giving a magnificent view over the harbour. An excellent tea of homemade scones and cakes, still warm from the baking.

AUG. 16. Elizabeth has been sending postcards to herself, from places we have visited. From Restormel she wrote: "This is not a very good castle for exploring but the view from the top is wonderful. The moat is now grass, a good place for small children". At Falmouth she said: "Very quiet here compared to street. We had a lovely journey by boat from Truro to Falmouth but towards the end it rained heavily. We found a nice little tea-shop and had tea opposite a big window and were able to see the boats".

AUG. 22. To the garage at Tower Road and left my wheel to have the tyre repaired; shortly after we got here it started to lose 2 lb per day. We bathed in a good sea and lovely sunshine — surprised to find a red flag being run up just after we came in, and the beach guard whistling everyone in: a ridiculous precaution when the tide was flowing and conditions for surfing perfect. To Tower Road to collect my wheel. They said the valve had been faulty, and repair charge was sixpence.

AUG. 23. Finished reading *Night and Darkness Who is Here?* by Pamela Hansford Johnson — hard to understand how an intelligent, sensitive author came to write such drivel.

AUG. 25. I am not bothering to read any daily papers during this holiday, and so save a lot of time for other reading.

AUG. 27. We all motored to Lostwithiel, and went by rail to Fowey: a diesel car, well filled. The line descended the wooded valley of the Fowey river: lovely views across the water to wooded slopes on the other side, with the little church of St Winnow at the water's edge. Three big ships loading clay at a dock near the mouth of the estuary: an Irish ship, a Danish one and a Dutch one. There is surprisingly little to see in Fowey. The streets are narrow, and shut off by buildings from any view of the sea except at a few points where there is an opening. No beaches, no paths by the water side: just like walking along a sultry close in a city. Nancy, Richard and I went down a lane to a little pier and were ferried across in a motor-boat to Polruan: 3½d each way, 2d for children. Elizabeth was writing a postcard to herself: "This is where the ferry at Fowey goes to. It is very interesting to watch it. It is able to hold six cars. I wandered round the town of Fowey by myself". The ferry she refers to is a pontoon, driven by a motor boat lashed alongside it, which crosses to Bodinnick. She wrote also a card to Isobel, which begins: "Fowey is not as busy as it looks, in fact it is not busy at all". For supper tonight I had fried fish from the fish-and-chip shop. Richard had expressed a desire for chips, and as it proved impossible to buy chips without fish he bought a fish supper for 2/6 and we took it home, where he ate the chips and I the fish.

AUG. 29. Breakfast before 8, too early for the gulls, who come down in the garden every morning when we put out breakfast remains and devour everything in a few seconds, squawking and wrangling over a kipper or a bacon rind.

AUG. 30. High tea at Newcastle, in the Central Station: a nice meal in the tea-room. There had been some idea that if the journey from Stratford to Edinburgh proved too much we might find a seaside boarding house at Whitley Bay or Seahouses, but in the prevailing weather conditions an evening at the seaside held no attractions, and as the children, like myself, were all in favour of pressing on home we did so. The children were still indefatigably collecting the names of places we passed through, and bus destinations, for which I had promised to pay at the rate of 1d each. They took it in turn to look out for these, while the other slept; and Richard was still noting Tranent and Haddington as we passed through. Finished reading *Dialogues of Alfred North Whitehead*, reported by Lucien Price. I had expected these to be heavy going, but the conversations are about everything except philosophy and make easy reading. The author himself is an enterprising, knowledgeable conversationalist, and although in the nature of things there is a good deal of repetition it affords a steady flow of interesting ideas and reflections.

SEPT. 5. Trade Union Congress on television. They are an extremely dull lot; Alexander Kitson of the Scottish Horse and Motor Men, though not exactly pleasant, brought a touch of reality into the discussion.

SEPT. 7. Finished reading *Acrobat Admits*, by Alfred Grossman, a remarkable novel by reason of the author's skill in portraying characters by means of extremely varied dialogue which brings each person vividly to life. It is written with wit and knowledge, all completely uninhibited, and the mood changes with complete naturalness from wild hilarity to illuminating discussion of the problem of evil or the American way of life. The author always sees both sides of a question, and both are brilliantly presented in delightful, entertaining dialogue. I could not help thinking it was rather spoiled by the odd, violent ending, so remote from the wise, witty urbanity of the rest of the book. All in all, however, it is a novel that transcends criticism.

SEPT. 11. The Liberal Party conference was being televised. They were a lot younger than the TUC, and the speakers earnest and eloquent, but rather remote from practical everyday life. To the parcels office on Waverley Bridge to see about sending off Elizabeth's trunk to school. Two or three youths behind the counter wandered about in an aimless manner, sticking labels on with a big brush. Eventually I secured a form, from which it appeared that a rail ticket had to be produced. The man had handed me the whole book of forms, in a metal clasp, and in order to keep my place in the queue I kept possession of this, taking it down with me to the station while I bought the ticket. When I got back to the parcels office, they did not seem much further on, and the temporary absence of the book appeared to have passed unnoticed. The man in charge was unable to tell me whether the trunk would be collected on Monday or not. It is the Edinburgh Autumn Holiday, and no one had told him whether the men were to be out or not. It is only when one has to transact any business with the railway that one comes to think that Dr Beeching is probably right and the only thing to do is to close the whole system down.

SEPT. 12. Motored with Nancy and Miss Sutcliffe to Queensferry, where the new bridge has now joined up with its approaches both north and south. Only the central span remains to be completed.

SEPT. 13. North Berwick. Tea at our usual place: a good plain tea at 9/11 for the five of us.

SEPT. 18. Motored Elizabeth to Waverley for the train to York. Susan Orr, another new girl, rather scared and woebegone, and Elizabeth quite in her element cheering Susan up.

SEPT. 21. Bellingham Show. A speedy journey home in the dusk. I gave a lift to two soldiers who are in camp in Redesdale, and having not even a canteen there wanted to go across and sample the pleasures of Jedburgh on their night out. I do not think they would find much there, but they expressed appreciation of the Scottish countryside coming down from Carter Bar — which was new to them.

SEPT. 22. Wakened in the middle of the night by laughing at a funny dream. I was showing two women on the top of a bus a copy of a Record in a case in which the pursuer was claiming damages for having been attacked by a general while on the defender's farm. The defences, drawn by Bellamy Cay, bore that persons on the defender's farm were liable to suffer from visions and hallucinations, and it was believed and averred that the general who was allowed to have attacked the pursuer was a vision or hallucination of that character. It turned out however that " general " had been a typist's misreading of a word in the draft Summons, the actual word being " gannet ".

SEPT. 23. A letter from Elizabeth. "Latin is *terrible* and I hardly know a thing compared to everyone else. We have tests every day for Latin and learning vocabs is *awful*. I think daddy's way was much better". Occasional bright spots, such as "a smashing film on Saturday evening called 'The Importance of Being Ernest'".

SEPT. 26. Another long letter from Elizabeth, much more hopeful.

SEPT. 27. Another letter from Elizabeth, quite chatty. She seems to be settling in reasonably well after all.

SEPT. 28. The first of a new series of *That Was the Week That Was* — mostly rubbish. The star was Sir Cyril Osborne, who had no doubt been chosen as outstanding example of a boneheaded Tory MP, but whose sincerity and downrightedness enabled him to rout Bernard Levin, while denouncing the programme as sex-obsessed. "You've been fooling around with sex the whole evening", he retorted to a suggestion by Levin of some obsession on his part.

OCT. 1. Parliament House: the opening of the session. The judges and the St Giles authorities having settled their differences by an invitation from Dr Whitley to attend today, we processed across

94

to the service. It was unusually stimulating, not to say entertaining. For one thing, the choir were attractively dressed — no hats, instead of the awful blue bonnets they used to wear; and for another Dr Whitley mounted the pulpit, whence he was generally audible. Dr Warr was allowed to read the lesson, and someone with a sense of humour, presumably Dr Whitley, had allocated to him a passage from the New English version in which we were warned of the dangers of being puffed up and conceited, and thinking we were of some consequence when that was mere hypocrisy. The point was emphasised by the singing of Chesterton's hymn, in which we asked to be delivered from sleep and from damnation — "From all that terror teaches, From lies of tongue and pen, From all the easy speeches That comfort cruel men" — and, referring to the "walls of gold" that "entomb us, The swords of scorn divide", asked: "Take not thy thunder from us, But take away our pride". Finally, in the retiring procession down the aisle, when Warr stopped opposite the Lord President and made his usual genuflection to him, Whitley coming immediately behind strode past looking neither to right nor left. Proof in *Purdon's Curator v. Boyd.* Cole-Hamilton, Miss Purdon's curator, was called to speak formally to the assignation of her claim in return for a payment by insurers of £12,500. I did not ask him any questions; and Bobby Johnston, appearing for the pursuers, told me afterwards that he had been waiting with interest to hear if I was going to ask Cole-Hamilton if he regarded £12,500 as reasonable compensation for his ward's injuries. Cole-Hamilton's reply, he said, was going to have been: "I did not apply my mind to that at all, but I took your opinion as leading counsel and you advised that it was the proper figure" — a reference to an Opinion on quantum that I gave to the other side at the start of the litigation, long before I came into it for the defender's insurance company.

OCT. 2. A curious situation arose when Johnston called Wilson, the driver of the car involved in the collision. He said that he had had tuberculosis, and had been advised to put all problems out of his mind — with the result that he had forgotten all about the accident. The only thing he remembered, oddly enough, was that he had put his indicator out. My left eye had begun to be sore, so after going round by Midmar Drive with Nancy and the dog I went straight to bed. I had not been asleep for more than 10 minutes when I was wakened by the ringing of the phone at my bedside, and had to answer a call from Farquharson. But this had been enough to clear the trouble, and I was able to get up right away.

OCT. 4. Procedure Roll before Strachan: Watson v. Edinburgh & Dumfriesshire Dairy Co. The pursuer was employed to deliver milk in Juniper Green. On a morning in February he collected four empty bottles from the back door of a house. On the way back to the van he slipped and fell. The bottles broke, and he got quite a severe injury. He says the defenders should have provided him with a crate or basket. This was a simple case, but it was complicated by an averment which I had unfortunately omitted to delete: that the defenders should have known that because of the number of deliveries he had to make he would require to hurry. As it was nowhere averred that he was hurrying, Caplan — who appeared for the defenders — seized on this as likely to cause confusion to a jury, and therefore to justify ordering a proof. Strachan was obviously taking the point seriously, and nothing could be done but to ask leave to delete the averment. As Caplain wanted time to answer this amendment, the case was continued: an unfortunate result for which I must accept responsibility. Consultations in the afternoon. Ian Stewart was with me, and remarked that he was always amused at my consultations because the first ten minutes were occupied in cross-examination of my client during which I gradually got him to the point where he admitted he had no case. Stewart said he had often wondered whether it would reach the stage of our saying, "Very well then, we can't go on with it". But it has always been possible to find some way out.

OCT. 6. To church, where Mr Reid preached on Luke 4,18-19. Richard, who timed him, said he preached for 25 minutes; but I found the time passed quickly while I was reading the first four or five chapters of the New English version of the New Testament. I had not realised before that Ruth, besides being the heroine of a pleasing little anecdote, fitted into the whole biblical scheme, being the great-grandmother of David. This appeared from the genealogy in Matthew I, where it was interesting to observe that Jesus' descent from Abraham was traced through Joseph, albeit that Joseph was supposed not to be his father. It was evident that he regarded the family as belonging to Judea, and his explanation of their being in Nazareth was that they went there to get out of any danger from the king.

OCT. 7. Parliament House: two consultations. I decided to go down to Macvitties and have herring for lunch.

OCT. 8. Farquharson called for me, to take me to Dunbar cement works. The factory was tidy and well organised, and even emptier than the one in Derbyshire: no workman in sight except two men sweeping the floor. The manager had been brought up from England, and liked the sailing and shooting in East Lothian, but there was not much hunting. The quarry superintendent was more impressive, and knew very clearly what he was talking about. He took us in a jeep to his office, perched high above the great limestone cut, and showed us how it worked: drift on top, then the upper limestone, then sand-stone which had to be discarded, with shale below, and the lower limestone below that — a railway line at each level of limestone. Finished reading *Tragedy in Dedham*, by Francis Russell, a verbose account of the Sacco-Vanzetti case. The case attained to world wide notoriety because of the popular impression that the accused had been framed on the ground that they were anarchists, but in reality it seems to have been a typical case of mistaken identity, Vanzetti being almost certainly innocent of the murder for which he and Sacco were executed, and Sacco possibly innocent of it. There does not seem to have been deliberate injustice. The most striking part of the story is the personality of the two workmen concerned, and the almost lyrical quality of the letters which they wrote to friends and supporters, in strange, ungrammatical English but full of poetry and charm right up to the end.

OCT. 10. House of Lords. Since I was last there, Lord Kilmuir has been replaced as Lord Chancellor by the former Attorney-General, Manningham-Buller — now Lord Dilhorne. He has no great reputation for sagacity, but he grasped my point quite early and stuck to it manfully throughout the day, unimpressed by any qualifications or refinements. It was pointed out to me beforehand by my opponent, Gimson, that our petition of appeal applies only to the Inner House interlocutor and we have no appeal against the Lord Ordinary, so that technically Hunter's decision against us cannot be dealt with. I had no responsibility for this, as I did not get the petition to revise, and indeed had had a discussion with my junior when he was drafting it and pointed out to him that it must include the Outer House interlocutor. As I had no idea how to deal with this problem, I thought it best to say nothing about it. Wyndham Theatre: "Oh What a Lovely War": troups of pierrots either in their own garb or dressed up as soldiers, politicians and the like, singing the 1914-18 songs, while one of them acting the part of Sir Douglas Haig gives utterance to the actual nonsense which Haig talked about the Western Front offensives — no great subtlety about it, but witty and entertaining in its own grim way, and it was nice to hear the songs. Looked into a cafe in the Strand and had a glass of milk, at the price of 1/-, no doubt to recompense the proprietor for keeping open after 11 o'clock at night.

OCT. 11. Finished reading *The A6 Murder*, by Louis Blom-Cooper, a short critique of the recent trial of James Hanratty. The author is critical of the limits placed on the Court's powers of investigation in a criminal trial, which he suggests are calculated to conceal the truth rather than bring it to light. What, he asks, on the assumption that Hanratty was guilty, was an urban criminal like

Hanratty doing in a Buckinghamshire cornfield on the evening when he came on his victim and the victim's lady friend and forced himself on their attention? He thinks that behind the apparent purposelessness of the crime there must have been a lot more that would have been very important for understanding it if it had been anyone's business to pursue the necessary enquiries. He favours the continental system of judicial investigation which would have gone into all these collateral aspects. It is not clear that this would be altogether an improvement, but the author deals with it in a very interesting way, and makes some incidental criticisms of criminal law which are obviously sound.

Oct 12. Home in time for an excerpt from Mr Butler's winding-up speech at the Conservative party conference, which should not I think enhance his chances of succeeding Mr Macmillan as party leader. He was stilted and unconvincing, like a schoolboy reading an essay; but it seems likely that he will evolve as successor to Macmillan when the latter retires, as he now has to do on account of illness.

Oct. 15. A jury trial before Lord Walker: Walker v. Thomson. The pursuer was executor of a will made by an old man, John Thomson, in his lawyer's office, in which he left the residue of his estate to Mr Walker and his two sisters. None of the three was related to the testator, but like him they belonged to the Christian Brethren, and had befriended him after his wife died, one of the sisters having taken him into her home until a vacancy should occur in the Christian Brethren's eventide home at Newton Stewart. Soon after Mr Thomson was admitted to the eventide home he became violent, standing in the doorway and refusing to allow the door to be shut, and striking with his walking-stick at anyone who tried to reason with him. Finally he barricaded himself into his room and proceeded to turn on the taps in the wash-basin with the plug in, so that the room was flooded. He was removed to the Crichton Royal Mental Hospital, where he remained from January 1962 until his death in April. He was about 85, and suffering from senile dementia. He misidentified nurses and female patients as being his wife. He thought a man was hiding in a cupboard in his room, and that he was receiving visits from Harry Lauder. In March his brother Andrew, with whom he had had no dealings for years, turned up with two other people and a printed will form which he had filled up so as to provide for the bequest of the residue of the estate to Andrew's two daughters. This will he got John to sign, and it was witnessed by his two companions. The action has been brought by Mr Walker as executor under the 1961 will, for reduction of the will made in March 1962, on the ground that at that date the testator was

98

mentally incapable of making a proper will. Doctors at the Crichton Royal gave evidence of severe mental derangement; but O'Brien, who was defending, scored a point with one of them who had applied various tests, such as to ask the patient to name the reigning monarch — he had said "George". "At least", said O'Brien, "he was clear about who the Prime Minister was, which is more than most of us can say at present". The pursuer made an excellent impression. Asked how he had got into close friendship with John Thomson, he replied, "Well, it may be difficult for you to understand, but it is a fact that we spent many very happy and profitable hours together reading the Scriptures".

OCT. 16. O'Brien made a much better speech than mine, so I was much relieved when the jury returned a verdict for the pursuer by a majority of 10 to 2.

OCT. 22. Mr Wilson on television: about Lord Home's appointment as Prime Minister. He stood up well to some vicious questioning; but Lord Home, with his courteous, unflurried manner and apparent air of simplicity, may be a formidable opponent. The fact that he is so completely unknown may be in his favour with people who do not realise his connection with the Government's failures.

NOV. 1. To York, to visit Elizabeth. At Bishop Auckland the Victoria Grill supplied a meal of bacon and egg, tea, and bread and butter — the bill for the three of us only 10/-. The cutlery was marked with the name of some hotel, and the teapot according to the legend on it had belonged to Johannesburg Turf Club.

NOV. 2. I had thought Elizabeth would want some good meals to make up for the school food, but one of the surprises she had for us was a complete change in her attitude towards school food, which she now regards as excellent and is apparently able to get as much of as she likes. So far from regarding today's meals as a special treat, she seemed to be looking forward to getting back to school feeding. In other respects she seems to have settled in happily, and liked her bedroom, where the eight occupants, of varying ages, had interesting conversation every night before going to sleep. She wanted to take us round the school, saying that it was in order for us to come and see it at any time. She went at a great rate, and it was a thorough tour. It seemed to be usual for a girl to take parents round; we encountered one or two others similarly engaged. There were five girls in her classroom, but she made no attempt to introduce them and simply demonstrated the classroom as if the girls were not there — though from a description Elizabeth had given I recognised one of them as the girl she has chosen as her special friend. Elizabeth says she is very clever. The girls have a lot of freedom at weekends, but can go out only in pairs, so that unless one has someone willing to make up a pair one has to stay in. The girls seem free to go about the school as they please, and I liked the friendly, informal way in which they all seemed to do so. Altogether I was favourably impressed by the school.

NOV. 3. To the Quaker meeting-house for Elizabeth and Barbara Jane. No hymns or addresses at these meetings; the company sits in silence, broken occasionally when someone feels called on to speak. Elizabeth says that Miss Blake, her headmistress, is a usual speaker, but today there had been something much more unusual: one of the boys from Bootham School, who attend as well as the girls from the Mount, had spoken. There is a record that a Bootham boy has spoken before, but a long time ago. The meeting ends when two old gentlemen sitting in front turn to one another and shake hands — which is not done until a decent time has elapsed since anyone has spoken. A run in the car to Bridlington. On the way back I had to stop the car to allow Barbara Jane to get out and be sick. The critical moment arrived when we were rounding a corner, so that in the excitement to let BJ out Elizabeth opened the door and fell out. She picked herself up, none the worse, and when BJ had recovered somewhat we proceeded. The girls seemed to think we could come to the Sunday evening meeting in the school hall — more like an ordinary service, but I was impressed by how silent the silences were. Miss Blake, announcing the hymns, might have been a stock symbol for headmistress of a Quaker school; slim and neat, with a soft, friendly but precise voice, and a long neck which drooped as she sat in prayerful silence. A middle-aged man in a well-cut business suit spoke for 15 minutes on beauty in relation to religion: interesting and sensible. He was an official of the Yorkshire Insurance Co.

NOV. 13. On television tonight an interesting programme on the Beatles, a skiffle group from Liverpool whose progress round the country is marked by enormous crowds of hysterical teenagers and children.

NOV. 14. Lord Cameron remarked that he was still smarting under a rebuke I had given him the other day — I had told him when I happened to meet him on the day after the jury trial in *Leith v. Glasgow Corporation* that it was his fault that the boy got such a small award. He said he was very sorry.

NOV. 25. Women Artists' exhibition. The exhibitor we most admired was Louise Annand, who paints marvellous seascapes, invariably disfigured by some foreign object in the foreground. This year she runs true to form, with two pictures which would have been most attractive if they had not been spoiled by this curious trait: in one case by large brown blobs supposed to be spray, and in the other case by what appears to be a large red wheelless vehicle constituting a startling eyesore right in the middle foreground of a fine picture of mountain and sea.

NOV. 26. Surprised to see in this morning's paper that Kissen had been appointed to the bench, to fill the vacancy caused by Sorn's retiral and Migdale's moving up into the Inner House. Kissen should make a good judge, but no one so far as I heard had expected that he would be appointed under a Tory Government.

DEC. 1. North Morningside Church: Rev. Archibald T. Black, the assistant minister, on Matthew 11,3. He seemed very young — thin, dark, frail-looking — but he preached an eloquent, dramatic and scholarly sermon. With experience, I should expect him to become a very fine preacher; he faced up to the problems.

DEC. 2. Finished reading *The Bronte Story*, by Margaret Lane, an interesting, moving account of the life of Charlotte Bronte, from the horror of her early days at the school for Daughters of the Clergy — which she survived, though it killed her two sisters — to the brief moment of happiness before her own untimely death. The author quotes a striking poem of Charlotte's written when she had fallen in love with the master of the college in Brussels where she studied and taught:

"He was mute as the grave, and stood stirless as a tower;
At last I looked up and saw I prayed to stone:
I asked help of that which to help had no power,
I sought love where love was utterly unknown".

DEC. 3. Jury trial before Cameron. Although Bennett tried to get the case withdrawn, Cameron refused the motion and charged the jury strongly in the pursuer's favour. The operation of the machinery was complicated, and the explanation of its working — mostly through Bennett: I did not know much about it — had taken up a lot of time. The jury found for the pursuer by 10 to 2. The assessment of damages, £6,000 is very much on the high side: the pursuer had a broken leg, but is fit for work as a wages clerk, and the net loss of wages is only slightly over £600. We may be able to hold it, but Cameron will be able to use this as an example to me of what happens when he refrains from telling a jury that their award should be well within the sum sued for.

DEC. 6. Brand told us that on Tuesday, when the Second Division had one of its comparatively rare sittings — all the work nowadays being commandeered by Clyde for the First Division — the sitting of the court was much delayed because Mackintosh after taking part in the ceremony of Kissen's installation had absent-mindedly put on his hat and coat and gone home.

DEC. 7. Finished reading *Newman's Way*, by Sean O'Faolain, a biography of Cardinal Newman written in a coy, allusive style that is almost unreadable: a page of mush to every sentence of fact. Newman's life would provide material for an interesting book, but this is not the book.

DEC. 10. A retainer from a firm of publicans in Glasgow in connection with a local veto poll. Scotland told me they had said they wanted the best counsel available, and after what he called very full enquiry among Glasgow solicitors had decided that I answered to that description.

DEC. 13. The Dumfriesshire by-election result: the Solicitor-General had only just succeeded in finding a seat he could hold. David Anderson had scraped through by the skin of his teeth, the Labour candidate coming a good second, and Liberal and Scots Nat candidates losing their deposits. We saw all four on television the other night: David, though lively as usual, and smiling happily at his questioner's ignorance, was hardly a convincing candidate, and the Labour man seemed gloomy and morose, with a rasping Glasgow accent — though I have heard that privately he is very amusing. The two deposit-losers seemed much the best of the four.

DEC. 14. Finished reading *Bobby Locke on Golf*, by A. D. Locke. A lively, confident personality is usually interesting when writing on his own subject — this book is no exception.

DEC. 15. Mayfield North church: Rev. James A. Whyte, professor of Practical Theology at St Andrews, on John 1, 26-7. He is quite a young man, and preached an interesting, thoughtful sermon.

DEC. 17. Proof before Wheatley: the main question whether the pursuer's admitted tuberculosis is complicated by pneumoconiosis, or the X-ray markings found on his lungs are due to a deposit of iron oxide which is inert and causes no damage. As the pursuer was a welder employed by constructional engineers, and not exposed to silica, it seems likely that the second is the true explanation, in which event the case must fail. It has been made more difficult by my having practically no information. I had to put Green into the witness box to speak to efficiency of respirators without any precognition or statement of any kind from the solicitors. Luckily I had looked out for my own purposes some volumes of evidence from old pneumoconiosis cases and was able to examine Green from the notes of his evidence. The preparation of the rest of the case has been equally defective; it was a pleasant surprise that the evidence went as well as it did.

DEC. 19. I had to cross-examine the defenders' medical experts, and as there seemed no prospect of winning the case I rather enjoyed myself. The medical problems, about tuberculosis and siderosis and mixed-dust pneumoconiosis, are very interesting, particularly in connection with some recent post-mortem examinations which seem to show that iron oxide in the lung was not as harmless as all the experts have thought. The evidence concluded about 3, and Wheatley suggested that I might prefer to put off starting my speech until tomorrow. But I thought I might as well make a start, and addressed him extempore for the next hour on medical questions. My only note for this part of the speech was: "Does he have pn? Dust which he has inhaled contributed to his disability?" I was glad to find that from this text I was able to present an orderly and perfectly competent argument.

DEC. 21. Portobello: Nancy and I went to Ross's to change a queer pair of slippers that Mrs Braggins had got me for Christmas. The pair we exchanged them for was almost equally queer, but at least was a better fit. The children had gone down to the sea-front with the dog, but when we were walking along the High Street the dog appeared by itself and joined us. We walked down with it to the Promenade, where it dashed away at full speed in the direction of Tower Street, where it had last seen the children. Despite its whippet-like appearance, it has sheepdog instincts and likes to keep its party together.

DEC. 23. Finished reading *The Fate of Admiral Kolchak*, by Peter Fleming, the story of how a misguided Russian patriot was led up the garden path to his death by the allied powers which for reasons of their own had decided to intervene in the war against the Bolsheviks. An interesting book.

DEC. 24. Miss Mitchell came across with a Christmas present for the cat: some slices of cold turkey, wrapped in cellophane. The cat arrived home just after she came, and spent the time of her visit in busily trying to open its parcel — which it succeeded in doing and starting on its turkey before she left.

DEC. 25. "The Gold Rush" on television. Amazing how effectively it comes over after so many years; the comedians of those days really knew how to create a situation.

DEC. 29. I was on duty at church, and went back for the evening service. No need for me to have gone — plenty of people to take the collection, and enough to stand at the draughty door and welcome the 48 who attended. But despite Mr Reid's appalling preaching I rather like the evening service. During the sermon I continued reading the New English Bible. I am now on Mark, who seems particularly taken up with miracles and marvels: a simple-minded writer compared to Matthew.

DEC. 30. All to the Lyceum to see "The Fol-de-Rols": an extremely good show, bright, colourful, entertaining. Denny Willis and Charlie Stewart both very funny in a pleasant, friendly way. Finished reading *The Fire Next Time*, by James Baldwin. Though uncompromising in his condemnation of Americans, he has written a thoughtful little book: hardly a page that does not suggest some new, interesting idea.

DEC. 31. The children had decided to wait up for the New Year — Nancy and I putting off our lights so as not to attract any neighbours in to celebrate with us, and leaving the children in the drawing-room with one of their favourite television programmes, a terrible Glasgow comedy series called "The Adventures of Francie and Josie". We were in bed in time to hear Big Ben chiming midnight.

1964

1964. The General Election on 15th October resulted in a Labour majority of 4 – sufficient to bring about the replacement of Sir Alex Douglas-Home's Conservative administration by a Labour one under Mr Wilson, and incidentally to put me in the Government as Lord Advocate. Though I should have been sorry to see the Conservatives back in office, I was not greatly concerned with the result on personal grounds, feeling that although I should quite like to be Lord Advocate it would not matter greatly if I were not. I took no steps to press my claims or communicate with anyone who might be concerned. If I had realised beforehand how pleasant and interesting the work would be I might not have been so indifferent. The Lord Advocate's salary was £5,000, so that acceptance of office involved a considerable financial sacrifice – to a great extent offset by the tax concession whereby arrears of fees were free of tax after the cessation of the employment. It was ironical that whereas as a young junior at the Bar I had imagined that some day I might be a Law Officer and pictured it as a means of providing me with an income and giving me something to do, now that the ambition had been achieved, at the expense of cutting my income by half, I welcomed it as giving me something of a holiday. One would have had to be a slow worker to be unable to get through the work of the Crown Office between 9 in the morning and 4 in the afternoon; and so, when in Edinburgh, I had my evenings free – a great change from the normal life of a busy counsel. Much the more interesting part of the work was done in London, on one or two days each week to coincide with the meetings of the Legislation Committee of the Cabinet. William Ross, the Secretary of State, was an obstinate man, but I liked his enthusiasm and genuineness, and was able to work in well with him and the Scottish Office team. Of the Under-Secretaries, Dr Dickson Mabon was so far the outstanding success. I found the Minister of Housing, R. H. S. Crossman, a particularly agreeable person to work with. The Lord Chancellor, Gardiner, was a different character; his attitude to day-to-day problems of government would not have supported the public view of him as an enthusiast for progress and reform. The Government on taking office was faced at once with a serious economic crisis. With a strong majority and the firm prospect of five years in office, the Government could no doubt have afforded to let the pound go and rebuild the British economic structure without reference to foreign interests, but it was thought, no doubt rightly, that devaluation was impossible without a further crisis of confidence sufficient to topple the Government, and measures had to be taken to restore the exchange position *directly contrary to fundamental Labour policy. With the help of massive financial assistance from international bankers, the policy succeeded in its object, but at the expense of having to pay ransom to the financiers in the form of interest rates even higher than under the Conservatives.*

JAN. 3. Letter to Ian Fraser, congratulating him on appointment to the bench, to fill the vacancy caused by Patrick's retiral and Wheatley's consequent promotion to the Second Division.

From Lord Fraser

20 Moray Place, Edinburgh 3 4th Jan 1964
Dear Gordon,
Thank you very much for your letter and good wishes, which I very much appreciate. I owe a great deal to you, as I am well aware, for having encouraged me to stand for election as Dean and for then having organised support at the election. Without your encouragement I would never have gone forward as a candidate. . .

JAN. 8. A case in Procedure Roll before Hunter. He followed the argument with close attention throughout, asking very pertinent questions of both sides.

JAN. 9. A jury trial before Douglas Johnston. The pursuer was working on the catwalk of the Forth road bridge during the operation of spinning the cable upon which the bridge is suspended. One night in November 1961 the pursuer slipped on the catwalk and fell, injuring his kneecap. The action against his employers was based on two grounds: that the foothold on the catwalk was unsafe in frosty weather, and that the lighting was inadequate. The more important ground appeared to be the first, but though the pursuer maintained that it was frosty he insisted in the witness-box — as, to do him justice, he had said at a consultation three weeks ago — that the condition of the catwalk had nothing to do with his accident. There was however evidence that one of the two lights where the pursuer was working was not operating, and on that account Johnston refused a motion by Ian Robertson, at the end of the pursuer's case, to have it withdrawn from the jury. Nobody had bothered much about the lighting case, least of all the defenders' precognoscers, so that I had no difficulty in getting from one of their witnesses in cross-examination that it was quite likely that one of the lights was out and it was essential for safety that both should be operating at each working point. I had had difficulty in getting the pursuer to agree in the witness-box that the faulty light had anything to do with his accident either. Ian Robertson's young daughter, home on holiday from St Leonard's school, listened to the case throughout the day, and on my asking her after the jury had retired how she would have decided it she said she would allow the pursuer the wages he had lost, and that was all. The jury must have taken much the same view, as they found for the pursuer and awarded him £500 — there being an agreed wage loss of £405. I thought he had done as well as he deserved.

JAN. 10. Mr Shaw, discussing yesterday's case, was amused to hear that as we were leaving the court Robertson had complained to me about the vagueness of the pursuer's pleadings. It had not appeared to him from the Record that lighting was in any way important, and he was sure I had nothing to do with the framing of such an imprecise Record. On this I made no comment. I think that the pursuer's success was due to the failure of the defence to adapt themselves to the situation as it developed at the trial; they put in witnesses to speak to matters which were no longer a live issue, and so gave me opportunities for cross-examination.

JAN. 11. *Androcles and the Lion* on television. Robert Newton stood out majestically from the rest of the cast — mostly American, though Jean Simmons made an ornamental Lavinia.

JAN. 13. Finished reading *The Lesser Infortune*, by Rayner Heppenstall, a kindly, unassuming novel about a writer conscripted into the army during the war. Nothing much happens: the conscript's whole service is in this country, and he never sees any fighting. But it all rings true, and one feels one has a thorough acquaintance with the casually introduced people whom the writer knows and meets with. A likeable book. Had to go down to the church hall for a meeting of the Scouts' parents group, into which I have been inveigled by the scoutmaster: 2 hours rambling discussion of means of raising money, a complete waste of time, though no doubt necessary. It would have been much easier to write out a cheque for the sum involved, which was not large.

JAN. 14. A lot of work requiring attention, but after supper I wanted to see University Challenge on television, and then there was a lengthy telephone conversation with Sinclair Shaw, who had rung up from Aberdour to seek to persuade me to let my name go forward for the office of Dean of Faculty, vacant through Ian Fraser's appointment to the bench. He had discussed this with James Leechman, and got James to find out what support was likely. The idea had passed vaguely through my mind, but I had never regarded it as a practical possibility, and in any event was not at all sure I wanted to be Dean and become involved in the tedious round of social functions and official engagements in which the Dean has to take part. At present I am more interested in anything that will reduce the volume of my work rather than something that would increase it, particularly as it would mean resigning my Sheriffdom. It has the advantage of being an almost certain passport to judgeship. I did not give him much encouragement, though I said that if anybody wanted to make enquiries about prospects I should take no objection. I had made up my mind to take no part in pre-election discussions this time, since I had no real concern about who was to be Dean and thought I had done sufficient in getting Fraser elected on the last occasion. When this had been disposed of, and I had just settled by the fire to do some work, Kate appeared, wanting to talk at length about George and the boys. I eventually retreated to the study, but did not get much done before she left and I returned to the drawing-room to see a programme on television about the recent disaster to a cruising liner. The programme lasted from 10 to 10.45, by which time it was not worth while doing anything except go to bed. So the day ended with all my work still to be done.

JAN. 15. Parliament House. Leaving home before the rush hour, I was in by 8.30 and got a lot of work done before the court sat. Spoke to Leechman, and told him I did not want to be Dean. He made rather a halfhearted attempt to persuade me to the contrary, and said he would make some tentative enquiries. He came to me later in the day and said that although enquiry had elicited a good measure of support he did not think it would be enough. I had said to him that if either of us were to be Dean he had really the better claim, but that I did not honestly think he would have any more chance of being elected than I had. John McCluskey approached me later, and apparently had come to the same conclusion as Leechman. I was very glad.

JAN. 16. Isabel Sinclair expressed regret that I had not consented to stand, saying she had found a good deal of support for me — though, she agreed, probably not enough to get me in. Alex Thomson, it appears, will be elected without opposition — Emslie, who had been suggested by some people, having now decided to act as Thomson's proposer, no doubt with the idea that the office will come to him next time. Finished reading *Red Curtain Up*, by Beryl Grey, an account of her visit to Russia to dance with the Bolshoi Ballet: a plain, unvarnished account confined almost entirely to ballet and ballet performers. Within these limits she gives a favourable impression of the country and its friendly, hospitable people.

JAN. 21. A proof before Lord Fraser: an action of damages arising out of an accident in December 1951. The pursuer consulted a solicitor named Richmond King soon after his accident, but Mr King proved extremely dilatory. The pursuer not having got legal aid eventually went to his Member of Parliament, and in the end legal aid was allowed; but Mr King still did nothing about it. An attempt by the pursuer to consult Dan McKay apparently failed because someone at McKay's office took the view that as the pursuer was being advised by Mr King they should not interfere. In 1961 the pursuer went to the Legal Dispensary, and was referred to Nightingale & Bell. By then Mr King was in hospital, and had lost all the pursuer's papers. He has since died. Nightingale & Bell therefore started off afresh. Since the accident happened before the Limitation Act of 1954, there was no question of his claim's being barred; and in fact the evidence today came out remarkably clearly. The pursuer's main case however is based on a section of the Building Regulations which provides that an excavation into which a person is liable to fall more than $6\frac{1}{2}$ feet shall be provided with a barrier, and it was impossible to prove that the excavation was more than $6\frac{1}{2}$ feet deep. The pursuer would say only that it was about $6\frac{1}{2}$ feet, and the defenders produced some plans which they maintained showed it was rather less. I had to argue that the distance the pursuer had to fall was the depth of the excavation plus the distance up from the ground to the step of the crane — which together would have meant a fall of more than $6\frac{1}{2}$ feet. But whether Fraser will accept this argument remains to be seen. There was a subsidiary case based on the failure of the crane-driver to warn the pursuer that the door opened outwards. The pursuer said in the witness-box that he knew it opened outwards; so that case did not get far. As the pursuer has been able to work very little since the accident, the damages had reached a colossal sum — the figures when we worked them out exceeded by a substantial margin the £5000 we have sued for. But it is another matter to say that the pursuer will get any of it. A message from London that we had won Kelly v. Cornhill Insurance Co.; the Lords have overturned the First Division by 3 votes to 2.

JAN. 24. A Faculty meeting. Alex Thomson was elected Dean without opposition. Wilton attended the meeting, despite his age: 101.

JAN. 31. *Cameron v. Woodall-Duckham* a loser — Fraser found for the defenders on the ground that the excavation had to be $6\frac{1}{2}$ feet deep.

FEB. 1. Richard and I with the dog to Blackford Glen. We saw a big fox scrambling over the top of the cliff.

FEB. 9. Nancy has a cold, and stayed in bed for breakfast. I fried an egg for myself along with the bacon, and was surprised to find hoe easy it was. Remarkable how as soon as the egg is broken into the frying-pan it congeals into shape.

FEB. 10. St Boswells: a meeting of the Probation Committee. I wanted to see Miss Honeyman about Jacqueline Tunnah, who I thought must be about due for release from Dr Guthrie's and for whom I might have to do something in order to get her back to some sensible work after a wasted year. Miss Honeyman told me however that for the past four months she had been in Dingleton Hospital, where she is having psychiatric treatment and has been given a chance to help with the other patients: an occupation that should suit her — she seems to want to go in for nursing. Mr Angus reported on current cases with his usual rich vein of unconscious humour, starting with Patrick Wilson who had stolen a quantity of Beatle postcards from Woolworths. George Rait, we were told, "suffers from a woman-dominated house". He would, said Mr Angus, make an excellent soldier. "He has plenty of aggression". Thomas Stevenson was "a typical street hooligan". "A loud-mouthed youth who does a great deal of boasting". He was small-sized and the apple of his mother's eye. With Malcolm Fraser, on the other hand, "his mother is the only stable element in the household". His father was keen on physical punishment, though Malcolm was not the kind of boy who required beating. "Understanding is what he needs". Mr Angus however thought that things were improving as the father had given up addressing Malcolm — now aged 15 — as "Boy". Then there was James Douglas, whose father and mother were divorced 14 years ago, before James was born, and who lives with his mother and Mr Davidson — known as "the lodger" though he is the father of James and three younger brothers, all of whom apparently do not know that "the lodger" is their father. "But why doesn't he marry her?" asked one of the ladies. "Because he doesn't want to", said Mr Angus. "He is an old age pensioner, aged 67". Piet Eisten Matuscyzk was on probation for sending indecent messages by telephone from a call box. "He approached twelve telephone operators in the Earlston area", said Mr Angus. Thomas Mowgray was attending Dingleton Hospital, where Dr Jones had devised a set-up as nearly natural as could be obtained, so that Mowgrey — aged 19 — would be forced into association with girls of his own age. Margaret Blaikie was in a house where her material needs were well catered for, but Mr Angus was trying to get Mrs Blaikie to see that ranting and raving at Margaret was no use. Alexander Smith's parents kept telling Mr Angus he must do something about him, but would not let him place him in accommodation away from home. Douglas James had turned out to be a natural rugby player, and now that he had moved to Galashiels was finding companions of his own age — one of the main problems when he had been living at Maxpoffle. His mother however thought the games might be too rough for him. Charles Wilkie, who was rather undersized and as a farmworker had found great difficulty in the stacking season because he could not reach up to the stacks, had been found work with horses, and had turned out to be a natural jockey, particularly over the sticks. "Any punters present please note", remarked Provost McCallum. Mr Angus had been to see Alexander Hinchelwood, who had said practically nothing, but his mother "garbled on endlessly", so that there was "rather a chaotic atmosphere". The farmer who owned the cottages in which they lived had not been "fully aware that he had two ex-Approved-School boys" there. He had mistaken Mr Angus for the insurance man.

FEB. 23. Church: the prospect of a half-hour sermon from Mr Reid does not perturb me now that I have settled in to read the New English Bible. I am halfway through Luke, whose picture of Jesus — intolerant, outspoken, ready to flare up on the least provocation — is as remote as can be imagined from "Gentle Jesus meek and mild" of the children's hymn. He may have gone around doing good, but if Luke is right he certainly went round being as rude and unpleasant as he possibly could to all the respectable citizens, hostile or friendly.

FEB. 29. On my television appearance last night, Mrs Cook said they had been surprised that I had just been myself: a remark that puzzled me, since there had always been three others with me — until I realised that she meant I had been just the same as I usually am at home.

MAR. 1. Motored to Waverley to meet Nancy and Richard. They had been to Bootham, for which Richard sat the entrance exam, and had seen round the school. Richard seemed much taken with it, but I doubt if he would be happy at a boarding-school, with its day-long discipline and lack of freedom to roam about; and the outdoor activities that they favour at Bootham — gardening, and tramps over the moors — would be a poor substitute for his football and gun-fighting.

MAR. 5. A jury trial before Cameron. The pursuer was 75, and had been crossing the Gallowgate in Glasgow when he was run down by the defenders' lorry. He was deaf, but once he got accustomed to being there seemed able to hear my questions and those put by Cowie for the defenders. He treated us both with equal friendliness and courtesy, without the least trace of antagonism to defending counsel, and answered every question with complete frankness — to an alarming extent when I came to ask him about his injuries. He had had a broken arm, but in answer to my question as to whether it was a painful injury assured me that it had never been painful at all. He had not the slightest trouble with it, and was able to get about and look after himself as well as he had ever done. In my address I remarked to the jury that I did not often have to ask a jury to disregard what was said by my own client, particularly such an honest and straightforward one as I had today, but on the matter of damages I advised them to pay more attention to the doctor's evidence than to the pursuer's. We had a tender of £100 to beat, and in the end recovered £300: damages of £500, with a 40 per cent deduction for contributory negligence. The old man was delighted, all the more when I told him that it was all his own doing — he had won the case for himself.

MAR. 7. At Harthill I was hailed in the dusk by three nurses wanting to go to Bangour. I asked about Jock Milne, who is surgeon in charge. They told me he did not like fat people. If someone appeared at the hospital wanting treatment who was fat without any medical reason for it — " he can tell at once by looking them over " — he told him or her to go home and come back when they had lost 1½ stone.

MAR. 8. With Richard to church, where Mr Reid preached on John 18,37. I came across an odd passage in Luke's account of the Last Supper, when Jesus says to the disciples that things will be different now, and they had better sell their belongings in order to equip themselves with swords. Somebody says they have two swords already, whereupon Jesus rather impatiently dismisses the subject — all very mysterious.

MAR. 10. I had been appointed with another elder to visit the Women's Guild on behalf of the Kirk Session. A Bible Society missionary spoke for an hour on the work of the society in Indonesia; and though he occasionally dropped an interesting remark it seemed to me to go mostly to show the utter absurdity of foreign missions: what kindly, innocent people were the ignorant natives in the Indonesian jungle, and how we were straining every effort to put Bibles into their hands, presumably so as to convert them into something else. After speaking of the poverty and malnutrition among Indonesians, he went on to stress the importance of getting Bibles into their hands. A single Testament in the hands of one educated Indonesian, who had been a Moslem, had brought him to the mission asking to be baptised, and he had asked at the same time whether he could bring 26 others. All the lecturer's ideas seemed remote from reality — I cannot imagine what he supposed he was achieving. It seemed to go down well enough with his audience.

MAR. 12. A Faculty meeting. Under the Dean's business-like chairmanship, the Faculty covered a lot of ground in 1½ hours.

MAR. 13. A consultation at 3 with some people from Dundee who wanted to be advised about the proper way of running a gaming house for roulette and chemin de fer.

MAR. 14. With Nancy to Watsons for the last of a series of concerts to inaugurate their newly-built music school. The guest celebrity was Christopher Elton, a former pupil, who played with great vigour and brilliance. His *Allegro Barbaro*, by Bartok, was unexpectedly attractive and exciting.

MAR. 17. A divorce proof before Douglas Johnston. The pursuer divorced her first husband before she was 20, on the ground of cruelty, and is seeking to divorce her second husband on similar grounds. The substantial defence is that the cruelty was condoned by the pursuer's spending nights with the defender right up to last month. Despite the fact that Alastair Johnston was on the other side, evidence went through with commendable rapidity. In the evening I had a programme on television on the Quorn hunt. This was brilliantly photographed, and brought out not only the absurdity of the pastime but also its lunatic fascination. Finished reading *The Complete Stories of Herman Melville*. The trouble about these is that they are not stories at all. The author writes well, and creates an effective build-up, and then the whole thing fizzles out.

MAR. 19. Alastair led a remarkable collection of witnesses, practically all of whom had criminal records. The evidence if believed falls a long way short of proving cohabitation — proof of which depends on evidence of a housebreaker friend of the defender's and the wife of a similar character who keeps a " boarding house " in Grove Street. Douglas Johnston seemed to think he had seen the witness before, and questioned her closely about whether she had given evidence on some other occasion. In reply to his question as to what kind of boarding house she kept, she said that it was an " ordinary " one.

MAR. 20. Douglas ill with flu, so that the hearing was off. He must have caught it from the boarding-house keeper, who had failed to turn up on the excuse that she had influenza, and had to be forcibly brought to court in a car sent by the defender's solicitor.

MAR. 24. Finished reading *Alps and Elephants*, by Sir Gavin de Beer, a short treatise on Hannibal's route across the Alps. The author is most enthusiastic, and contemptuous of all those who have put forward alternative theories; but despite his diligence in unearthing every clue it is all rather dry reading.

MAR. 25. Hawick. Before the trial, I dealt with two boys, charged with stealing 24 picture postcards from Woolworths. They had both been on probation as the result of previous offences, but there was a message from Mr Angus to the effect that he hoped to be able to do something with them and asked that they be admonished on this new charge so that probation treatment could continue. Accordingly I gave them a talking-to and sent them away. When I arrived home, I had a note to type which I had prepared at Hawick while the jury were out. It seems to be a fallacy that a judge's job is necessarily an easy one: I found these two days quite exhausting, though I enjoyed the trial and felt in complete command of it throughout.

MAR. 26. I was abreast of all current work by the time I left Parliament House. Lunched at the Wee Windaes: the usual very good lunch, for 6/6.

MAR. 30 Finished reading *Dulce Domum*, a family memoir of Dr George Moberley, Bishop of Salisbury, by his daughter, published in 1911. Dr Moberley had 15 children, and they were an extremely happy family. Their religion was deep and genuine, and in their fervent belief in a life to come death meant little to them; they faced it, like everything else, with cheerfulness and confidence. Their journals and letters sometimes read a little like Beachcomber, in their extreme simplicity; but when one laughs at them it is rather an envious laughter, for theirs was a good life in every sense of the word. It is refreshing to read a book like this, where everyone is happy and friendly, and companionship intelligent and understanding.

MAR. 31. The children getting new bicycles at the cycle shop. The proprietor died recently, and the business is being carried on in a haphazard way by his widow, who obviously was much cheered by selling two cycles. A very attractive girl said "Goodnight" to us at the end of the Scottish Television programme for today.

AP. 1. Had arranged to call for Idy Young and Alexis and bring them through for a day at the Zoo. We were coming down into Harthill at an easy 45 mph when a policeman stepped out and held up his hand, telling me that I had just passed through a radar speed check. The policemen were all very friendly. I thought it wise to describe myself as "Sheriff", adding as if correcting myself that they had better put me down as "Advocate", which would not sound so bad. They told me, after a short conference among themselves, that on this occasion they would give me a warning, so as to avoid any undesirable publicity. I thanked them warmly, and resumed the journey. At the Zoo we walked round the park and visited the aquarium. The keeper told me they fed the fish on nothing but horse flesh, and had much the best record of any aquarium for keeping fish.

AP. 4. The new Forth Road Bridge now all joined up with its great suspension span across the Firth.

AP. 5. A queue of teenagers camping out on the pavement for two nights to buy tickets for the Beatles' show later in the month. They stretched right along the side of the Regal cinema and the whole length of Semple Street, lying on the pavement three or four deep, in coats and blankets and sleeping-bags. The box office was supposed to open at 2 pm today, but the manager after consultation with the police, who were present in some force along the line of the crowd, had brought the long vigil to an end by opening the box office at 2 o'clock this morning.

AP. 10. Finished reading *The Love-Lives of Charles Dickens*, by C. G. L. du Cann. The author starts with the astonishing assertion that Dickens as a man was much more interesting than any of his writings, but does nothing to prove it: pages of padding to an occasional grain of fact, if fact it is — a model of how such a book should not be written.

AP. 13. Richard and Elizabeth had devised a new way of making money: a gaming saloon which they set up in the dining-room, with homemade versions of the "amusements" from St Annes and Blackpool. They proceeded to invite all the neighbouring children to come and play, and for once in a way their enterprise succeeded, in quite a remarkable degree: at one time they had 10 children taking part, and their profits from morning and afternoon sessions amounted to 16/- of which they had announced that they were to give a share to "charity". I was worried about some of the children who had been asked in, and went round to the Lowsons' to enquire whether the two girls, whom Richard had invited, had lost anything. They would not say how much they had spent, but had won some chocolates and were quite satisfied, so I did not press repayment of their outlays. In evening to the church for the Scout Group Committee: its main purpose to discuss arrangements for the jumble sale. This went on for nearly two hours. I felt I could not stand any more of it, and left as they were going on to the next item on the agenda.

AP. 14. As I was crossing George IV Bridge to get a bus, a car stopped at the traffic lights with a pretty girl in it and a driver who I thought was Caplan. Thinking he would give me a lift down to Princes Street, I opened the door of the car and proceeded to get in, only to find that it was not Caplan. He was evidently quite pleased to give me a lift — though he may not have been so pleased afterwards if he found I had made a slight dent in his bowler, which was lying on the back seat. After supper we all motored to the Gateway to see "The Lady Vanishes". Seeing this old thriller again after many years, I found it great fun. Analysed in cold blood, the plot would be nonsense, but it is so delightfully built up, with tension, humour, excitement and amusing characterisation, that the plot does not matter in the slightest. We all enjoyed it. Finished reading *Exploring English Character*, by Geoffrey Gorer, an interesting book based on a questionnaire submitted to 10,000 readers of the "People" newspaper: convincing documentation of what English people think and do. Those who regard living with "in-laws" as a major drawback in marriage apparently include their own parents under the definition of "in-laws".

AP. 19. A television production of *Hamlet* from Elsinore castle made full use of the Castle's spacious rooms and battlements: an exciting, lively production of this marvellously timeless play.

AP. 24. Selkirk: the burgh extension enquiry. I was annoyed at finding that the heating at Selkirk court had gone off this week for the "summer", but I had an electric radiator put on the bench beside me, with the result that I was really rather too hot.

AP. 26. Hopetoun House opening under the Gardens scheme. A grassy avenue bedecked with daffodils, and daffodils scattered through the trees making a very attractive setting for the enormous mansion. The rooms are surprisingly small, with no impression of spaciousness — not even an entrance hall, only a little stair winding up to a tiny landing beyond which rooms opened out of one another. The best feature of the house was its paintings: a veritable picture gallery of old masters, with fine ornamental ceilings and cornices.

AP. 27. Symington: the Probation Committee. Lady Elliot presided, and when Miss Honeyman started to give the first case report, in a low, mumbling voice, looked round the company and said "Can you all hear?" Getting a vague murmur in reply, she said, "Will you speak up, dear?" Miss Honeyman proceeded in a rather more audible tone. Mr Angus was his usual inimitable self. Victor Karminsky, whose father Mr Angus told us was "hypersensitive about law and order", had committed 17 offences of stealing women's clothing. He was now attending Dingleton Hospital once a week, and there they were getting him used to mixing with feminine company. Robert Wilson broke into his own house at Corby and stole a lot of furniture. "He maintains", said Mr Angus, "that it is all his". His employers had given him a mobile caravan to drive and live in, and Mr Angus had visited him there on Saturday and found him lying in his bed dead drunk. He could not waken him, and was therefore unable to tell us anything about his present attitude. George Black's father was "much indulged in his own youth", and felt that everyone should continue to indulge him. He had been employed by British Railways, but they had dismissed him because they could never locate him — he was never on duty. There were constant battles between him and George about which programme to watch on television. George, who was working, put the sixpences in the meter, but father insisted they should have his show. Father had a car, and George had to buy him an occasional gallon of petrol to let him run it. Fraser Montgomery had also been found in bed by Mr Angus when he went to see him on Saturday. He refused to go to his work, because he suffered from an obsession that he could work only as a plasterer. He had been dismissed from his apprenticeship, but refused to take any job other than plastering. Margret Krull had arrived from Germany speaking no English and had been sent straight to a primary school where she learned nothing, being unable to follow what was happening. She had pled guilty of theft by finding — a purse with £4.15 and two dance tickets in it, which she had found in a cafe. She maintained that in Germany a finder of such things was allowed to keep them if they did not have on them the owner's name and address. Carried away with this case, Mr Angus told us that Richard Smith was a boy who lived in Germany — "I'm sorry, lived in Jedburgh". He lived with his married sister, and his relationship with his brother-in-law was such that there was likely to be " a head-on collision ". James Tranter was bigamously married to a lady down in London, but had deserted his bigamous wife and was missing. His lawful wife had been concerned as to whether he had gone off with the bigamous wife, but had been reassured on finding that she had gone off with someone else. " Has he not been had up for bigamy?" Lady Elliot asked. "Oh, no ", said Mr Angus, " this was committed in England". "But you can be had up for bigamy in England, can't you?" said Lady Elliot, apparently unconvinced. Douglas Flett had failed to pass the Merchant Navy examination, and had been "so disgusted that he wanted out of the district ". Andrew Forrest, on being locked out one night by his parents, had thereupon broken into a mobile shop "as a gesture". Andrew Maxwell, a man of 56, was being treated at Dingleton. "Although they say 'responding to treatment'", Mr Angus remarked, "the view of Dingleton Hospital is that there is no progress". His two brothers live with him, but had their meals separately and would not speak to him. Someone remarked that that was rather a shame. "Oh, well", said Mr Angus, "he is slightly deformed. He is untidy, he doesn't make the effort to keep himself as clean as he might be". Dealing with the case of Betty Simpson, Miss Honeyman mentioned that her sister Mary was engaged. Several of the ladies, who apparently knew Mary, at once protested, saying she was already married. "We know that", said Mr Angus, "but Dingleton Hospital are of the opinion that this man is a much better influence on Mary than her own husband. He is most solicitous ". Some members of the committee having expressed dubiety, Mr Angus reassured them — Dingleton, he said, were so much impressed by this man that they wanted to encourage the relationship. David Bruce had been living with his parents, but his grandmother arrived at the house and took David back by the scruff of the neck. Now he was back with his mother, but the grandmother refused to give him his working clothes. She had been maintaining also another probationer, Andrew

Montgomery, but unfortunately he had been reported to the police for breaking into a church. Finally Mr Angus reported rather proudly on his success with James Jamieson, who had been committed to his after-care after serving 7 years preventive detention in England. His case was very satisfactory, due to his relationship with his landlady. Her own husband had deserted her, and he found it rather novel to be required to help in the household. "He takes the three young children out and about". The air of fantasy which pervades these reports was continued by Mr Kyle, reporting on attendance by himself and Provost McCallum at a meeting to set up a working party for the promotion of a central council of probation committees. The meeting, he said, had been a shambles, as everybody wanted on the working party except Provost McCallum, who had the greatest difficulty in keeping off it. Lunch was provided, and thereafter we all motored to Loaningdale Approved School. The boys conducted us round. I had a very intelligent little boy of 13, from Glasgow. The headmaster explained to us later that his object was to make the boys feel it was their school, not something thrust on them by those above, and so far as my boy was concerned he had apparently succeeded: the boy seemed proud of his approved school, and spoke highly of it in practically every respect — including the food, which was "fabulous". After tea we had a discussion in the headmaster's room. There is a school meeting held three times a week for discussion of school affairs, and a court once a week run by the boys for punishment of offenders. They are given every opportunity to develop a sense of responsibility, and I imagine it is quite a success. But as there are only 18 boys, and a staff of 9 full time and 2 part time it seems hopelessly uneconomic. They have their pick of delinquent boys, and select those "most likely to respond" — who I suppose are easier to deal with. Still, it was encouraging as an indication of what might be done if taken up on a bigger scale. I had expected Lady Elliot to monopolise the discussion as usual, but instead she went fast asleep, waking at 4.30 to say how interesting it had been and how grateful we were to the headmaster for answering our questions in such an excellent way.

AP. 29. Dingleton Hospital: Dr Maxwell Jones taking a seminar of young social-study students. I asked him about Jacqueline Tunnah, and he suggested we should go along to the ward and see her. We were interviewed by the sister in charge, a youngish woman, in her own way obviously just as much of a tartar as the headmistress of Dr Guthrie's School. She was very much on Jacqueline's side, and strongly disapproved both of the school and of me for sending Jacqueline there. Speaking to me more in sorrow than in anger, she did not dissemble her views. It was plain that Jacqueline's interests were fully safeguarded so long as she was in charge of her — which seems likely to be the position for some months. Jacqueline was working elsewhere in the hospital, doing hairdressing — her present employment; and though the sister seemed at first to think I might see her she came to the conclusion that the sight of me might arouse unpleasant recollections and had best be avoided. I did not mind so long as she was in good hands and there was no likelihood of her being sent back to Dr Guthrie's. Obviously that would not happen if the Sister had any say in the matter. Jones had told me that the head-mistress of Dr Guthrie's had been invited to come and see them at Dingleton; and if she does I think the meeting between her and the Sister in charge of Jacqueline will be worth seeing.

MAY 5. First Division: the defenders' reclaiming motion in *Macdonald v. North British Steel Foundry*. They are attacking Johnston's award on the ground that there is no evidence for the claim for loss of wages.

MAY 6. Clyde had his "extempore" judgment prepared, and read it when I sat down. As I had expected, fear of the House of Lords — whose judgment they could see hanging over their heads as soon as I came in on the pursuer's side — frightened them off from overturning Johnston's decision; Clyde delivered a ridiculous judgment to the effect that Emslie was right in his argument but they would with great hesitation refrain from giving effect to it. Emslie was much annoyed — with some reason in view of the complete contradiction between what they said and what they did. I was amused to see on looking at the notes of my speech to Johnston that I had taken the view the defenders had been pressing on the Division, and thinking there was no evidence of wage loss dur to pneumo-coniosis had not asked Johnston to award the pursuer his loss of wages. He was a long time in issuing his judgment, and there is a rumour that meantime he had lost his notes of the argument, which would account for his having awarded me more than I asked for.

MAY 15. The Zoological Society's annual report has an interesting paragraph about 6 racoons donated during the year. 5 escaped during their first night in the racoon enclosure. One was found sleeping in the hollow of a tree in the enclosure — it was not known why that particular one had elected to remain. Nothing was heard of the others, apart from one which was shot near Cupar. Thje report goes on to say that it is not surprising that a racoon should travel the distance between Edinburgh and Cupar, but it can only be conjectured how it crossed the Forth. "Whether it boarded a stationary lorry, or crossed by the railway or the new road bridge, or swam the river, or stowed away on a ferry, the journey for this little American mammal must have been an adventurous one".

JUN. 1. Finished reading *The Night the Old Nostalgia Burned Down*, by Frank Sullivan. The piece which gives the book its title is a dead-pan take-off of the "I remember" school of writing — very funny — but many of the other pieces are no more than rather ordinary examples of that school. Some proverbs are amusing: " A fool and his money rush in where angels fear to tread ". " Sleeping dogs make strange bedfellows ".

JUN. 8. Finished reading *Mary of Modena*, by Carola Oman. This biography of James II's queen gave me a new idea of the Stewart monarchs. Charles II emerges in a favourable light, and even James, despite his pigheadedness, comes off not too badly in comparison with the dry, cynical, uninspiring William of Orange. But the real heroine is Mary herself — not only a ravishing beauty, as appears from the portraits, but friendly, intelligent, loyal, with a good sense of humour and completely free from malice or rancour. This excellent biography is well written, scholarly, and full of agreeable little touches which make it interesting to read.

JUN. 20. Ian Ritchie phoned with a problem for a Glasgow correspondent whose client was in Barlinnie awaiting trial on a charge of robbery. Someone had obtained a warrant from a Sheriff to shave off the beard which the prisoner had grown, in order that he might attend an identification parade. This seemed an extraordinary proposition, and I at once went up to the Crown Office in search of Bowen. Bowen however was not in today, and I was told that Lionel Gordon had gone over to see the Procurator-Fiscal. I tracked them down in a coffee bar in the Lawnmarket, and Gordon said he would phone Glasgow and see what was happening. He told me later that they had indeed got a warrant and had decided to go ahead with it; and as the shaving was scheduled for 11 a.m. this morning there was nothing that could be done — except a possible action of damages later on.

JUN. 22. Finished reading *Last and First in Burma*, by Maurice Collis, an account of the Japanese invasion and what followed. An interesting book, fairminded and perceptive: to some extent an attempt to rehabilitate the reputation of Sir Reginald Dorman-Smith, the Governor, who seems to have the right idea most of the time, if perhaps ineffective in putting it across.

JUN. 23. A jury trial before Douglas Johnston. The pursuer, a lady of 57, had been a passenger in a car which was run into by the defender's car. Liability was admitted, and the action defended on a tender of £500. The pursuer as a result of the fright developed an anxiety depression, and is unable to cope with everyday life. At the time of the accident she was running a small sweetie-shop, which she had built up by her own efforts; but this was in any event about to be closed in the course of a Corporation development scheme, and it was not possible to establish any financial loss resulting from the accident. The claim was therefore a solatium one. The pursuer's main champion was her panel doctor, Dr Wohl; and as soon as he appeared in the witness box and gave his qualifications as MD of the University of Bologna I realised that he was the doctor who once got a large award for a tram-driver client of mine by saying that the only cure for his anxiety state was a "big shock of happiness". Today he was even more extravagant, arguing with Robert Reid, and complaining about his attitude, scorning his suggestion that if anything much had been wrong with Mrs Harley he would have sent her to a specialist. "A specialist? Who? Name him. Name your specialist that I was to send her to. I am not a crossing-sweeper". I thought he rather overdid it, and Douglas had to beg him to answer questions briefly and without so much emotion; but much of what he said was supported in rather different terms by our two experts, and even the defender's experts had to agree that the pursuer's anxiety state, though mild and likely to cure itself when the case had been disposed of, was genuine. I handled them tactfully. Douglas said nothing of consequence, not even urging the jury to be moderate; and they almost went too far, awarding the pursuer £2500 — every effort had been made last night to get the pursuer to accept an offer increased to £600.

From Mrs Mary Harley:

52, Westwood Road, Pollokshaws, Glasgow S3. 25th June 1964
Dear Mr Stott,
No doubt like ourselves you would be delighted to hear Tuesday's result, and I sincerely hope that there will be no snags within the next seven days.
Although I was not present in court my family assure me, that the award was gained through your splendid efficiency, and for that I am very grateful, and wish to thank you very much indeed.
Wishing you good health & happiness.
I remain
Yours very sincerely

JUN. 27. Finished reading *Wellington at War 1794-1815*, a selection of Wellington's letters. The editor's literary talents are not equal to Wellington's, but the letters themselves are very good: vigorous, decided, obviously written by someone who has plenty of confidence in his own judgment and good reason for having it. He is courteous and fair to everybody, but the recipient of the letter can never have been in the slightest doubt as to where its writer stands.

JUN. 28. A film on television: "Rancho Notorious". This old Western was head and shoulders above most of the films one sees nowadays: a good story, beautifully done, with significance in every shot. It avoided the weakness of so many films where an incident is thrown in to give a thrill or a laugh, when it adds nothing to the development of the story. Everything helped in the build-up to the inevitable climax.

JUN. 29. Glasgow. Lunch with Mr Reo Stakis prior to a discussion about the rules for gaming at his new Casino Chevalier — joined by his manager and his head croupier, who has been brought from France at a salary of £6000 and proved lively and entertaining. I rather liked them all: straightforward, singleminded people of surprising simplicity. Our discussion round the roulette table ended shortly before 4.

JUN. 30. On television tonight *World In Action* presented Senator Goldwater. There is a grim fascination about him, and the obvious sincerity with which he holds his childishly simple opinions make him so much more dangerous. The trouble is that he gives honest and fervent expression to all the worst and most jingo instincts of the average American, and on that account is obviously well placed to win support.

JUL. 2. A jury trial before Milligan: the pursuer an elderly man who was clocking out at the end of the day when he was knocked down by the press of other workers in the queue behind him and broke his ankle. He blames the defenders in so far as they provided only one board from which 180 workers had to take their tokens, passing through a narrow passage between a railway and a wall of the building. The defenders have lodged a series of photographs which strongly support the pursuer's view that there was quite a scrum at the clocking-out board; and the defence apparently is that nothing could have been done to prevent it. The pursuer turned out to be extraordinarily stupid, denying matters which were obvious, including his own photograph in the crowd, and insisting that he never went into any part of the queue which was in the slightest degree dangerous. Naturally he found it difficult to explain how he met with the accident. I think however that despite the pursuer we may have enough to win his case for him. Keith's funeral at the Crematorium at 4 — a surprisingly small attendance. No doubt at the age of 71 Keith had outlived the generation of those who knew him.

JUL. 3. Milligan charged very much against us, making fun of the pursuer and his case. I was not sure that this would go down well with the jury, and thought we should probably get a verdict of some sort. In the end the jury found unanimously for the pursuer and assessed damages at £200, but found him 70 per cent to blame, so that he gets £60. This I thought a sensible verdict: quite as much as the pursuer deserved.

JUL. 5. Mayfield South church: the minister, Rev. Ian Mactaggart, on John 3,21. He spoke in a rough, Highland-sounding voice, but preached a good sermon, brief but compelling. The church is like a gaudily whitewashed barn.

JUL. 6. Train to Dundee, where as chairman of the Lighthouse Commissioners I was to attend the opening of Dundee Harbour Board's "tidal model", a scale model of the Tay estuary with depths and shoals, and electric machinery which reproduces the movement of tides and rivers and the action of the waves. No seats — we stood around on the floor while being addressed by the chairman, who was inaudible, and by Lord Rochdale, who might as well have been. The best part of the proceedings was the refreshments. I saw two men leaving as soon as I had my cup of tea, and hurried after them to their car. They acceded to my request for a lift, and though they did it grudgingly, and did not address another word to me on the journey into town, I did not mind that. The new bridge pillars have now got about a third of the way over the Firth.

JUL. 8. Margaret Pike to supper: she seems devoted to the memory of her late husband. They must have been a peculiar pair, and it seems to have been lucky for other possible mates that they were married to one another.

JUL. 9. After tea I began to feel unwell, and retired to bed. Got up at 9, feeling better, and had sausages for supper before starting work.

JUL. 12. With Nancy to church. Rev. R. S. McNicol, a chaplain from India, preached on I Samuel 17, the story of David and Goliath: a short, chatty, easy-to-listen-to sermon. He seemed to have no idea what a wily bird David was, and accepted at its face value the ridiculous excuse he gave Saul for not wearing the armour Saul wanted to give him: that he "had not proved it". It is obvious that armour was useless for David's unprofessional fighting methods, and that all David required was to be free to run sufficiently well to keep clear of Goliath's weapons while he slung stones at him from a catapult. David clearly knew what he was doing, as he seems to have done all his life, and was not greatly concerned with the acceptability of the means he used provided he got results. In the afternoon with Nancy and Richard to Islington to see kart racing: not particularly interesting, little motors following one another round a track, keeping the same position relative to one another except on the rare occasion when there was passing.

JUL. 14. A proof before Walker. The pursuer proved far too

124

honest to be able to make a case before Walker, and it was hardly surprising that both defenders decided to lead no evidence. Knowing that Walker never listens to what counsel says at a hearing on evidence, I had nothing prepared, and contented myself with reading the pursuer's case from the Record and waffling away for half an hour. The judgment, assoilzing both defenders, was clearly right.

JUL. 15. Watsons boys' dramatic entertainment: extracts from Shakespeare's plays, performed with great aplomb. Battle scenes from *Henry IV* were particularly well done, and we were much impressed by Sir John Falstaff: a boy named Tulloch.

JUL. 16. Television programme on the nomination of Senator Goldwater at the Republican convention: a short interview with him, displaying as usual his courtesy and the quiet reasonableness with which he propounds his insane policies. It all seems simple to him, and so he genuinely conveys the impression that the achievement of his idea of total victory over Russia and the Communists should present no difficulty.

JUL. 17. Gullane: a round of golf — Nancy playing much better again, having recovered from the effects of tuition at evening classes.

JUL. 18. A 50-miles speed limit is in operation now at weekends. So far as I can see, its main effect is to make passing more difficult, and possibly more dangerous.

JUL. 22. To Waverley to meet Elizabeth off the train from York. She is enthusiastic about the school, and came home with an unusually good report.

JUL. 23. *Pharos* at Greenock. We started our sail down the Clyde in lovely sunshine, and anchored off Holy Island. The tide was too low for the boat to get in to the landing stage, and a search had to be made for another landing place among the rocks. After going in twice and encountering underwater rocks, Mr Fraser got the boat nicely in. It is delightful to watch and listen to him handling the boat, with a quiet, crisp order to the man at the engine, the order repeated back, and no fuss or comment. We were met by the principal lightkeeper, and a supernumerary who is taking the place of one of the assistants, at present on holiday. Ross McLean asked him if he liked Holy Island, to which he replied in the affirmative. "It's better than work", he said. He had been a greenkeeper at Dunbar golf course, and worked for a short time in the cement factory. As guest for dinner we had a doctor from the local hospital, McClure. He had been a surgeon for the British Army on the Rhine, the doctors who had passed him for this having according to him failed to observe that he had a wooden leg. After McClure left, about 11, there was a learned discussion in the after cabin about the whereabouts of Robert Bruce's heart, and the possible effect of tides on the result of the battle of Bannockburn. The ship was sailing for the Isle of Man at midnight.

JUL. 24. Woke before 6, not long before we came to anchor in Ramsey Bay, not far from the end of a long pier. Read for a while, then slept for half an hour, to find on awakening again that we seemed to have moved. No sign of the pier, merely a stretch of low sandy cliffs. The explanation appeared when I came up on deck, and saw the pier on the port side instead of the starboard side where my cabin is, the ship having merely swung round at her moorings. A couple of miles farther out we could see a ship with one very tall mast: Radio Caroline, the pirate wireless station which transmits pop music and advertising material throughout the day. Being outside the 3-mile limit, the operators are immune from prosecution under the Wireless Telegraphy Acts, but they have the disadvantage that on coming to Ramsey for victualling they have to go through the same procedure with Custom House and passports as persons entering the country from abroad. We went ashore in the boat — cars waiting to take us to Point of Ayre. In addition to the main lighthouse, which is about ¼ mile back from the sea, there is another small lighthouse, erected only about 10 years ago, at the edge of the water. The story circulating among the Commissioners was that when first built the main lighthouse had been at the water's edge but the land had gradually built up between the lighthouse and the sea. Ross McLean and I found this difficult to believe: the beach rose steeply, and there were no obvious signs of silting. On our way back, the cars at McLean's direction made for the village of Andreas, where he had arranged with the drivers that the cars would " break down" outside the local bar. The next " breakdown" was at a better place: a magnificent hotel, the Grand Island, in a fine situation overlooking Ramsey Bay. To the ship for lunch. There is always a choice of port or marsala, and instead of my usual glass of port I decided to try some marsala. It tasted much the same as the port; but it turned out that by mistake the port had been put into the marsala decanter, so that it was port I had had after all. After lunch we were again ferried ashore, where cars were waiting to take us to Manghold Head and back to Ramsey. The tide had gone down too far to make it possible to embark at the harbour, and we were told we should be going back from the pier. Alastair Robertson informed the man at the turnstile that we were exempt from pier dues under the Merchant Shipping Act. At dinner we entertained the Governor of the island. His ADC, a motor agent in private life, gave me an interesting account of how the island is run. Despite the strongly conservative views evidently held by most of our guests, I got the impression that there is a lot to be said for small autonomous communities of this kind. I reverted to port as my drink but then found that owing to an over-correction one of the port decanters had been filled with marsala, so it was marsala that I was drinking. It still seemed to taste much the same as port.

JUL. 25. Mull of Galloway. Alastair Robertson and I went down to the fog signal, halfway down the cliff, joined by Ross McLean and the indefatigable Lillie, who was today celebrating his 80th birthday. Watt, as commodore of the day, presented him with a silver gilt model of the Bell Rock lighthouse. As we came through the tide race round the Mull, I went forward to the bridge, and stayed there with Captain Campbell for the voyage to Campbeltown Loch — Davaar Island, to which we went off in the boat. At low water Davaar is joined to the mainland by a ridge of shingle, and Ross McLean suggested to me that we might forgo tea on the ship and walk to Campbeltown along the loch side — stopping at the cemetery, where Ross wanted to look at the grave of his wife's parents. He had instructions from her to book a lair for herself and him, and for some reason thought this should be done through an ornamental sculptor. The sculptor's house had been Mrs McLean's parents' home 20 years ago. We were shown into the front parlour, which was obviously used only by visitors; and to Ross's delighted surprise the furniture and decoration was exactly the same: Victorian red plush. Even the red cloth on the table, he thought, was the same. The sculptor informed Ross, as I had expected, that the person to see about the lairs was the cemetery keeper. Lillie at dinner tonight explained to me at some length how a memorandum by him was the origin of the present system of National Insurance, and how in spite of efforts he had made he had never had from Lord Beveridge any public recognition of the part his memorandum had played in the introduction of the Beveridge scheme. He thought that now that Beveridge was dead he ought to take it up again with the authorities. One of our guests told an anecdote about how a country minister encountered in Edinburgh Dr Warr, who had been at College with him and was then minister of St Giles and Dean of the Thistle. Dr Warr greeted him and asked what charge he was in. "Cove and Kilcreggan", said the minister. "And what charge are you in?" After dinner Lillie persuaded three of the others to join him in a game of shuffle-board. He is keen on the game, and takes it with dead seriousness. The others were keen that he should win, particularly on his birthday, but he made it difficult for them: whenever they had arranged to knock one of his side's counters into a scoring position he would make some blunder and knock it out again. Scoring was therefore slow, and the game lasted a long time before they at last succeeded in letting Lillie and his partner win. I congratulated him on his victory when he came into the saloon. '' It's a game you've got to play constructively'', he explained.

JUL. 26. *Pharos* does not sail on Sundays, and remained tied up at Campbeltown — quite a number of people coming along the pier to look at us. Alastair Robertson said that one of the bystanders asked him if this was a millionaire's yacht. We attended the service at Castlehill church: a lot of young people, including a party from a Youth yachting club in Glasgow. During lunch the Procurator-Fiscal, a lively young man named Stewart, said he would lend his car if Alex Thomson would drive it to the lighthouse at the Mull of Kintyre — it was not on the list for visiting this time. Our road soon began climbing steeply along the edge of the mountain, and came across the watershed to a notice stating the road was unsuitable for cars. Immediately afterwards the lighthouse came into sight, directly beneath us. The road descended 1200 feet in about a mile, in a series of terrifying hairpin bends, each with a sheer drop at the end of it down to the Atlantic — the road narrow, and nothing resembling a passing place. Alex, despite his lack of acquaintance with the car's controls, handled it magnificently; I was profoundly thankful that he had to drive and not I. In the lighthouse courtyard we found a milestone recording that it was 16 miles 1030 yards to Campbeltown: also the Youth yachting party, who had come down in a jeep and two other vehicles. I remarked that they had never been so near to Ireland. ''Never been so near to death'', said one of the girls. Alex drove us up the precipice as skilfully as he had brought us down, and back to Campbeltown. The sabbath is not as strictly observed as it is farther north — I had noticed that the putting green had been open. At dinner we entertained the captain, with Mr Fraser and the chief engineer. There was a gale warning out, and Ross McLean was worried about his yacht *Kelana*, which with his daughter Christine and four friends had passed through the Crinan Canal on Saturday and was making northwards to rendezvous with us at Bunessan on Tuesday night. Mr Fraser assured us that from all appearances the gale would be 48 hours late.

JUL. 27. Pladda. The wind freshened while we were on the island, and as the boat was at the ship's ladder it was one minute on the crest of a wave and next away down in the trough, so that one had to choose the right moment to jump. T. P. McDonald and Alex Thomson had chosen slightly wrong, and got one leg soaked. ''I know'', said Alex cheerfully, ''that those lads think this is nothing, but I would say it was damned rough''. Lillie came on and off the boat with complete equanimity. The officers had been dubious about landing at Turnberry, where there is no shelter in a south-west wind, but Mr Fraser with his usual skill steered the boat round the rocks, through a tumble of waves, and brought it in to the jetty at the first go-off. Our next landing was at Sanda. Just below the lighthouse is the bow of an American liberty ship — all that is left of the ship which ran aground there shortly after the war, carrying a large number of GIs and five or six of their brides. It must have been an extraordinary piece of folly — the light was shining directly above — but it was a Saturday night and some kind of junketing was going on. All on board were rescued. We liked this island: much nicer than Pladda. We were to tie up for the night in Proaig Bay. The weather forecast was very wet, with gales everywhere, making Ross McLean worried about his yacht. About 10 he announced that he was going to bed. "I'm hot, and bored, and worried", he said to me. I was in my bunk before 11; and it was nice to lie there, in perfect comfort, with a gale roaring round the ship, and everything calm and peaceful within.

JUL. 28. Our assistant steward, when he came to shut my porthole at 6.15, agreed with me about the excellence of Proaig Bay as an anchorage. "You can tell from the polished table in the dining saloon", he said. "Nothing's moved on it". T. P. McDonald told us about evidence given by Lord Ardwall in an action challenging the will of the late Sheriff Thom on the ground of mental incapacity. Ardwall, then Andrew Jamieson, had called on the Sheriff not long before his death, and his conversation had been perfectly rational. "He offered me a dram". McArthur's Point: a stone stairway up to the cliff where the lighthouse stands, like an Edinburgh tenement stair, but much steeper and narrower. Luckily the railing was on the side towards which the wind was blowing. No road to the lighthouse: the lightkeeper said they had only once in his time had visitors coming by land. This is a desolate part of Islay. The lightkeeper told us that in a recent count 280 stags were counted. The wind had freshened to an extent to alarm Douglas Campbell. He tried to sit down and descend the stair seated, but this was not a good plan, and he stuck altogether until the lightkeeper pushed past those behind Campbell and went to his assistance — all unnecessary, for there was no difficulty in getting down in the ordinary way. I stood in the shelter of the cliff at the top while the fuss was going on, and ran down when those in front had got to the foot. It seemed mild under the cliff: honeysuckle and fuchsia among the bracken. At Turnberry Mr Fraser had been able to turn the boat before taking us out, but at McArthur's Head we had to back out into the waves. A big wave broke over the stern, and those on the port side got wet. Lillie, who was nearest the stern, had the old waterproof he wears at all the landings, but his clothes got a wetting, and I had to change my jacket and trousers after getting on board. I remarked to Mr Fraser that he must have done it on purpose because I had said to him yesterday that I had never even got my feet wet at a landing. Skerryvore, which was to have been our next port of call, was out of the question, landing being impossible in any kind of wind, much less a gale such as today's. The captain had heard that the waves were breaking up to the lighthouse door, which in a rock station like Skerryvore is a long way above the rock. So we headed for Bunessan, but at McLean's instigation the captain agreed to take the ship along the south coast of Mull and look into some anchorages — Erraid, and another that Ross called the Tinker's Hole — to see if there was any sign of *Kelana*. Once out of the shelter of Colonsay we got the full force of the south-west gale, and when John appeared to announce lunch he suggested that I could wait for 10 or 20 minutes, when we might be in "quieter waters"; but in new-found enthusiasm for stormy weather I went along to lunch. MacGrory, I observed, was giving rather perfunctory answers to Campbell's remarks about the kinds of vegetables mentioned in Sir Walter Scott's novels. It did not surprise me when he hastily left the table; and a few moments later I retired to my cabin. It has been my experience that I am never seasick when lying down. So far from being in quieter waters, we seemed to be in wilder ones. At one point, when the ship rolled through 90 degrees, there was a crash from the direction of the saloon, followed on two occasions by the sound of breaking crockery. Presumably we were rounding the south-west corner of Mull. Not long after, things quietened down. I sat up, and proceeded on deck. We had rounded the Ross of Mull, and were sailing eastwards in quite sheltered conditions. Ross McLean was now in excellent fettle, having had a radio-telephone message that his wife had got through to Bunessam on the phone and confirmed that there was a yacht in the anshorage answering to the description of *Kelana*. I stood on the bridge with him and the captain as we sailed into the loch; and the captain, who was scanning the anchorage ahead with his glasses said "There she is", as a yacht came into view. Ross however after looking through his binoculars observed that it was not *Kelana*. There was an anxious moment as we continued up the inlet until the captain remarked "There's another mast coming up behind the rock"; and this was indeed *Kelana*. "I can't think why they've anchored her so far in", said Ross, much relieved to find his yacht safe and sound. He invited us all aboard. I should much have preferred to go ashore and have a good walk, but could hardly say "No" when everyone else accepted — except T. P. McDonald, who had had a nasty blow on the head when thrown to the floor of the dining saloon shortly after I had left it. *Kelana* was beautifully fitted up but very small; it passes my comprehension how five people could sail it for long distances with any comfort, much less enjoyment. They had got as far as Mull on Sunday, and put into Erraid; but on hearing a gale warning, which would have made Erraid an unsuitable anchorage, they at once came out, and sailed full speed round the Ross of Mull to Bunessan. At the moment, the only people on board were McLean's daughter, Christine, and a retired company director named Arbuthnott. Arbuthnott's nephew and his wife had gone ashore, and the fifth member of the crew, Christine's boyfriend, had left the yacht and gone home. It was however uncertain whether he had got off the island, as *King George V* had had its sailing cancelled on account of the storm, and no one knew whether the ferry was operating from Craignure. The *Pharos* boat brought a young couple from the other yacht: a nephew of Arbuthnott's called Donaldson and his wife. The yachts had sailed together from Crinan, the Donaldsons having as their crew a married couple who had proved a serious liability: the husband had been so sick that he had gone into a coma, and lain help-less on the deck. With some difficulty, they had got him ashore on arrival at Bunessan. The crew from both yachts all piled into the boat with us, to join us on *Pharos* for tea. I was feeling hungry, and ate several slices of bread and butter, some shortbread, and three chocolate biscuits, and as a consequence did not feel as comfortable as I should have liked for the next hour or so. The girls had been offered a bath, and went off enthusiastically to baths which had been prepared for them. We left them on deck trying the shuffleboard while we went off to *Fingal*, which had meanwhile arrived from Oban: a new ship launched this year. As I am to sail in *Fingal* tomorrow, I made a point of introducing myself to the steward, Mr Spence, an old fellow in a blue tail coat and black bow tie. Emslie and Grieve had come out in *Fingal*, and came back with us in the boat. Grieve remarked on the absence of birds in this part of Mull: a consequence of there being no trees, only the grey rocks and grass which make the landscape so unusual and to my mind attractive. The yachting party had returned to their yachts. Emslie was taking over my cabin, and we shared it while dressing for dinner. I was surprised that he would not use the shaver, preferring an old-fashioned safety razor. After dinner the yachting party returned. The girls had changed into dresses, and made a colourful picture on the after deck, where they proceeded to play shuffleboard with Lillie. The presence of ladies on the *Pharos* is something of an innovation: Ross said that nothing like this would have been conceivable in Wakelin's time. Soon after 11 I went off in the *Fingal*'s boat. I have a comfortable stateroom, and being the only guest have Mr Spence all to myself. He offered me coffee, and as he seemed anxious to do something for me I got him to make me a cup of tea; and so to bed with tea and buscuits, at 11.30.

131

JUL. 29. I did not hear *Pharos* when she sailed at 1 am for Cape Wrath. *Fingal* sailed at 6.45. I got up about 7, and went up on the bridge. Breakfast at 8.30: an excellent breakfast. Went up on the bridge again as soon as I had finished. We passed Duart Castle, where Ross McLean's wife had been spending the night with Sir Charles and Lady Maclean. Though a flag was flying from the ramparts, and our captain had someone standing by the ship's flag ready to dip it if we got a salute from the shore, there was no indication that anyone saw us. I stayed on the bridge until we had passed Lismore, then went down to the engine room. Mr Strachan, the chief engineer, had asked me during yesterday's inspection to come down if I liked today, and see the engines operating, and though I was not particularly interested I thought I had better go — the chief engineer of the *Pharos*, when he came to dinner the other night with the officers, had expressed special appreciation of my visit to the engine room two years ago, saying he remembered me very well on that account. Mr Strachan seemed pleased to see me, and showed me not only the engine room but the steering gear, which was interesting. By the time I came up on deck, we were coming into Oban Bay, tying up at the Lighthouse Commissioners' pier. I did not see any vehicle on the quay, and wondered how I was to get myself and my luggage round to the station. I had no doubt that something would be arranged, and the solution was simple, Captain McEachern remarking that they would send a boat round. Mr Spence insisted on making me another cup of tea; and a boat was then lowered, and I had my last sail of the present trip, across the bay to the station pier. The bay seemed to be full of jellyfish. A seaman carried my bags across to the station, and one of the ship's officers came with me as far as the luggage office, where I said goodbye. No dining-car on the train, so I was quite thankful for Mr Spence's tea and cake.

SEPT. 14. Glasgow Sheriff Court. I was appearing for four officials of the Casino Chevalier, charged with unlawful gaming: roulette which is alleged to have been unlawful in respect that the chances were not equally favourable to all players.

SEPT. 18. Continuation of the casino case: a second charge relating to two fruit machines played by two policemen who got admission to the casino by giving a false name. I argued that this did not mean that the machines were in a place to which the public had access, for access must be obtained legally. I was able to cite a curious case in the English Courts, in which Lord Goddard had held that the public did not have access to a public house, because the proprietor had a right to refuse admission.

SEPT. 29 Motored to Jedburgh to receive the nominations of the four candidates. Steel, the Liberal, seemed a nice fellow. The

Scottish Nationalist, Anthony Kerr — a middle-aged man with a big black moustache — did not know about Yetholm Show next Saturday, but his agent put him right about that and said he would have to be there. I liked the agent: a frank, unassuming farmer type. In between the candidates I discussed election affairs with Dale.

OCT. 1. Court of Session service in St Giles. Dr Whitley had it all to himself, and having gained his point went the length of making a slight bow to the Lord President on his way out. This I thought unfortunate: but he has greatly improved the choir by abolishing their ugly three-cornered hats. They now have no hats, and seemed a very pretty lot of girls. A jury trial before Milligan. The pursuer, it seemed to me, would have had quite a good case if his record had not been so deplorable. He had been off work for three years as a result of what was no more than a bruise on his knee. All the medical evidence was dead against him, and he had to admit under cross-examination that he had been in prison for housebreaking, and had been fined for defrauding the Ministry of National Insurance. His claim looked as if it might be worth about £10 instead of the £2000 which was claimed, and I thought it unlikely that the jury would give him anything.

OCT. 2. Verdict unanimous for the defenders.

OCT. 3. Yetholm Show. Ronald McLarty had asked us to Heiton for a meal after the show. In the showground we encountered the Nationalist candidate. Ronald took us to visit the two old ladies who live in the farmhouse behind his cottage. While we were chatting, a small harvest mouse came out from the side of the wall. The ladies were much alarmed, and rushed shrieking out of the room. I succeeded in catching the mouse. Having a glass of sherry in one hand and the mouse in the other, I was unable to keep hold of it, but eventually managed to chase it out of the door. This enlivened our visit.

OCT. 4. A new serial on BBC television: *The Count of Monte Cristo*, with Alan Badel outstanding in an excellent production.

OCT. 6. Shearer installed as a judge; he has appointed himself to fill the vacancy caused by Lord Mackintosh's resignation. A little man in a velveteen jacket got up after the judges had taken their seats and said he wanted to protest at the way in which Sheriffs were neglected in favour of political appointments. Shearer has chosen to take the judicial title of Lord Avonside, rejecting his own perfectly euphonious surname. A jury trial before Kissen: the pursuer suing in respect of the death of his son, who was gassed in a boiler pipe in Colvilles' works. The defenders admitted liability and tendered £200. The deceased was 20 at the date of his death, and seems to have been a good, hard-working lad, but the difficulty was that the

133

pursuer had often been separated from his wife, the lad's mother, and at the time when his son was killed was serving a prison sentence. Reid appeared for the defenders, and brought out every conceivable point to the pursuer's detriment, including fights with his son, and a criminal record stretching back over 20 years. In my speech to the jury I explained that the only parent entitled to sue was the father, and although the law had now been changed to allow a mother to sue the alteration did not apply as regards accidents occurring before the passing of the amending Act. The jury had obviously been impressed by this, and after deliberating for half the afternoon came back to ask to what extent they could have regard to the wife's position. Kissen at first ruled that they could have no regard to it, but I argued in the jury's absence that they could have regard to any loss the pursuer had suffered through being deprived of what the son was doing in pursuance of the father's obligations to support the mother. This allowed them to give some expression to their apparent sympathy with Mrs Osborne, who had so far been reconciled with her husband as to come and give evidence on his behalf, and who indeed made a very good impression. The jury awarded £300: a satisfactory result not so much because I felt satisfaction at beating the tender as because of feeling that Reid's tactics were not very commendable. He even fought against payment of a funeral account of £56, paid mostly out of insurance to which both father and mother had contributed. Scout Group committee tonight; but feeling that I could not endure wasting two hours at their drivelling discussion I wrote Mrs Jones apologising for absence on the plea of election work, and asking her to put my resignation before the committee so that they could appoint someone who would give proper attention to the Committee's work.

OCT. 8. Paterson phoned to say he had dealt with an appeal about a postal vote, by a "Lady" who had gone to Mull to help in looking after an invalid sister, and had written appealing against the Registration Officer's decision on the curious ground that if votes such as hers were to be disallowed it would be impossible for the Conservatives to get back. I seem to have the election much in my mind just now, for when I was intending to ask a witness in today's case whether the pursuer had complained about headaches before the accident I asked instead whether he had ever complained about them "before the election". This made the jury laugh.

OCT. 11. Peebles, to dine with Mr K. V. K. Sandaran, Chief Election Commissioner of India, and three of his colleagues. They are in this country to study the conduct of an election, and seemed sagacious, fairminded people, particularly Mr Sandaran, who was Law Secretary to the Government of India from 1948 to 1958. All were Hindus, and I had been given an elaborate leaflet of "personal notes", including the visitors' diet. Mr Sandaran was "normal European diet", but two of the others were "not beef". One was stated to be "soft drinks only", but another was "not a teetotaller". We had some difficulty in getting rid of the head waiter, who claimed to have seen me on television and was expansive about his political views — Conservative — and his admiration for his native city of Venice.

OCT. 12. Glasgow. Middleton gave judgment in the casino case: a considered judgment, which dealt efficiently and fairly with all the points. He held, as was inevitable, that as the bank was offered only on every second spin of the wheel the Club was bound to have an advantage over the other players who had to share alternate spins. My purpose in going today was to make a plea for M. Beysson. Under the rules of the croupiers' association, any conviction would have been disastrous for him, since a conviction would mean that he could no longer work as a croupier in French casinos. I read out a letter in French, that had been obtained from the association, and asked Middleton to grant an absolute discharge so that no conviction be recorded. At first he seemed doubtful, but obviously he thought highly of M. Beysson, and it did not require much persuasion to get him to accede to my motion. To Comiston Road to deliver Communion cards. Miss Richardson had been much impressed by a call from the Liberal candidate, but would have to vote Conservatice as she had joined the Association and paid her subscription. She was scornful of Miss McLeay, who has a Liberal poster in her window, and told me it had aroused a lot of ill-feeling.

OCT. 13. The Prime Minister tonight wound up the series of television broadcasts, making his usual propaganda points against Labour in rather a pedestrian manner. Nancy thought Sir Alec was pretty formidable. She detests him, and has become violently anti-Conservative and pro-Wilson, and gloomy at the idea she had that the Tories will get back for another five years. Though sharing her views about Wilson and the Tories, I think it is a very open question.

OCT. 15. Motored to South Morningside School to vote, then set off for Jedburgh, to go round my polling stations. The chief constable met me at Jedburgh, and for the rest of the day accompanied me on a tour of the constituency in a police Jaguar, driven by a competent young constable who has won several awards at flower shows for his chrysanthemums. High tea at Kelso. McCallum assured me that I had already visited far more polling stations than were usually visited; but as he agreed that those in charge liked to see the Returning Officer, and feel that some interest was being taken in them, we stopped at Heiton, Eckford and Crailing on our way back to Jedburgh.

OCT. 16. Up soon after 6.30 to get to Jedburgh for opening of the boxes. I sat on the platform and worked on some Records, adjudicating now and again on batches of doubtful papers. On each occasion I had the candidates and their agents up, and unanimity was reached. I allowed all the papers where voters had merely used the wrong mark or put the cross in a wrong position. One voter had written "Socialism" across his paper. When the count ended, it was found that Donaldson had 18,924 votes to Steel's 17,185. Donaldson in moving the vote of thanks made a pointed reference to Murray and Kerr as having fought a very clean contest, adding that he said nothing about any other candidate. Steel ignored this, and merely referred, as he was well entitled to do, to the big swing to the Liberals which had reduced the Tory majority to a very small figure. I had heard nothing of the progress of the election generally, but on getting home learned from Nancy that the Tories had held some very marginal constituencies. The result was a Labour majority of 4. On this slender margin Sir Alec Douglas Home had gone to Buckingham Palace to resign, and Mr Wilson became Prime Minister. In a television interview, Sir Alec seemed a different man: pleasant, relaxed, amiable, answering questions frankly and sensibly. Nothing about his tenure of office has become him so much as his manner on leaving it. He seemed positively likeable, and not nearly as stupid as he has appeared.

OCT. 17. Hamilton carnival. Home at 8.30, finding Nancy annoyed at me after a conversation on the telephone earlier in the evening with William Ross from London — who has been appointed Secretary of State for Scotland. He had been extremely vague, but had referred to a paragraph in this morning's *Scotsman* where it had been said that likely names for the new Law Officers were Mr Gordon Stott and Mr I. M. Robertson. Luckily I had read this out to Nancy, so that she knew what Ross was talking about; she said very sensibly that she supposed this was conjectural. Ross had agreed, and asked if he could "use" my name. Nancy had said she supposed so, but he would have to ask me. He suggested I should ring him at his home in Ayr after 10. He said he had discussed the position with the new Lord Chancellow, Lord Gardiner, but he knew nothing about it, and it was left to Ross to make suggestions. He had had no hesitation in suggesting my name. Nancy was depressed at the idea of my resigning the Sheriffdom and becoming Lord Advocate, particularly in the circumstances of the present Parliament; but in spite of the difficulties I am rather looking forward to it. It is nice to think that it is apparently to be offered me without my having done the slightest thing to push my claims or contact anybody in authority.

OCT. 18. Phoned James Leechman to see if he would be agreeable to becoming Solicitor-General, and found he was. A lot of stuff had come in: and I am aiming to get it all disposed of before I have to give up private practice, as I require to do if I am appointed to be a law officer. Nancy was worried about my appointment, much more inclined to weep than rejoice over the possibility of being the wife of the Lord Advocate — an ironical situation when there must be dozens of people worrying themselves sick at the thought that they may not succeed in getting a post in the Government.

OCT. 20. Mr Gordon phoned in the evening to say I was to go to London tomorrow to be sworn in as a member of the Privy Council. A sleeper was booked for me on the 10.05 train to St Pancras — all that was obtainable, as the Motor Show opens in London tomorrow.

From Mr Sinclair Shaw:

Aberdour 20 Octr 1964   9.45 pm
Dear Gordon
Denise and I heard the good news on TV at 9.15 and we send to you, and to Nancy, our warmest good wishes and congratulations. I have no doubt whatsoever that you will make a first-rate Lord Advocate and I send you my best wishes for a long, happy, and successful reign. It is a great happiness to me to see such *true* Socialists as you, James Leechman, George Willis and Willie Ross in office — and all the damned humbugs defeated! You make a formidable quartet, more than capable of crushing the Tories — but for me the prospect is most alarming because I feel certain that if, from now on, I dare to raise my voice publicly, I will at once be banished to St Kilda, at the very least! With all good wishes
P.S. I am so very glad that you have James as your colleague — and not the blooming bore or the hellish humbug!!

OCT. 21. To the Lord Advocate's office. J. H. Gibson, my principal legal assistant, greeted me and took me to meet the other five advocates who work there, then left me in my room: a big, comfortable room with a pleasant outlook over the green quadrangle of Deans Yard. At 11.40 a car came to take me to the Privy Council Office. A number of prospective Counsellors went through a rehearsal of the ceremony. I had some sympathy with Mr Pannell, the Minister of Works, who thought it was a lot of balderdash, but the officials took it all seriously, and were so amiable and courteous that one could not think of hurting their feelings by voicing any criticism. At Buckingham Palace the Queen received us in the Bow Room. She was simply dressed in blue, and looked neat and pleasant:

an attractive picture against a background of windows and garden. The oath dealt with various matters, including resistance to potentates and prelates; and the whole rigmarole had to be gone through again, as three of the potential Councillors — Benn, Pannell and Robinson, the Minister of Health — had to be allowed to affirm. The Queen remarked that it was not often that she had such a big increase in her Privy Council, and she was glad to see that the new Councillors included a number of ladies. Having said this, she pressed a little bell on her desk, and we made our way out. Miss Howat, the efficient private secretary who attends to my requirements, had booked a sleeper for me, but at my suggestion changed this for a seat on the 7.50 plane. I had the same driver all day, an elegant lady of public-school type who discussed my appointment with me, and questioned me amiably on my family and interests. She drove me dexterously to Heathrow. At home Nancy told me that after I had left last night the phone, according to Richard, had rung steadily. We had told him not to answer, and he also left the door unanswered when there was a ring at the bell. Undeterred by this, a party of men had come into the house, and on shouting up to Richard learned that I had gone to the station. The party, presumably pressmen, had indicated that they would go and look for me. Of course it would never have occurred to them that I was going by St Pancras, so I had a lucky escape; and as my appointment by now will be stale news I may escape their attentions altogether.

OCT. 22. Parliament House. I had to get together a team of Advocates Depute: Ewan Stewart, King Murray, McCluskey and McNeill. Feeling there might be some difficulty about Stewart's appearing by himself — the only one of the four who is a QC — I mentioned the matter to the Dean, who said he did not think there should be any difficulty. Clyde, it was arranged, would see me when the Court rose for lunch. He assured me he would give me every assistance, though on the one point I mentioned — the senior Depute appearing alone — he was not forthcoming. He thought the Dean might have something to say about it; and I, taking this as a suggestion and knowing already the Dean's general view, said I should certainly speak to the Dean about it. O'Brien agreed to take on the post of Home Depute, completing the Crown Office team. At 4 the Dean came up — helpful and cooperative, but it was obvious that as soon as I had told Clyde what I wanted Clyde had gone straight to the Dean himself and tried to stir up trouble. It was obvious that cooperation with Clyde was to be impossible. I am glad that that has been made clear, for I shall be much happier going my own way, fighting him if necessary and otherwise ignoring him. When I went through to see Gordon, I actually found Clyde with him. In the

Crown Office, on my own ground, I could take a stronger line, and when he said that my proposal would be used as a lever by organisations like the Coal Board told him that I could not accept for one moment that there was any analogy between the Crown Office and the Coal Board. Though keeping friendly, I made no concession, merely indicating that we should keep what he had said in mind, and showing him to the door. To the church for a Session meeting. Mr Reid congratulated me on my appointment as Advocate Depute — an error at once corrected by several members.

OCT. 23. A memo from the Attorney-General on the question of prosecuting someone in London for the reset of one of Prince Charles' school exercise books, stolen from Gordonstoun. It appears that this contains essays on political matters, the monarchy and the like, and American newspapers were offering a high price for it. The police had skilfully got it back. The English law officers had advised against proceedings, and I agreed with them.

OCT. 26. We had the television on to see Mr Wilson exhorting the nation to face the economic crisis caused by an adverse balance of payments. He did it as well as anyone, but I have always thought that this balance-of-payments problem is entirely artificial, and that if we got into payments difficulties foreign countries would simply go on sending goods to us, at a lower price.

OCT. 27. Legislation Committee, efficiently conducted by Bowden in his capacity of Lord President of the Council. The Lord Chancellor, despite his reputation for reforming zeal, struck me as a cold fish.

OCT. 28. I had some vacancies to fill in the ranks of junior counsel to Government departments, and thought it reasonable to offer them to the retiring Tory Deputes.

From Miss Isabel Sinclair:

Advocates' Library, Edinburgh 1. 28th October, 1964.
Dear Gordon,
Thank-you for your letter. My delay in acknowledging it arose mainly from my difficulty in deciphering it — indeed at one point I felt that your injunction to treat it as confidential was unnecessary and that it would remain your secret alone!
I very deeply appreciate your writing to me as you have done, and I am honoured by your confidence.
I know that had you considered me suitable for a post as a Depute neither my sex nor any opposition would have deterred you in making the appointment. May I say that I completely agree with your (unvoiced) opinion that it would not have been a good appointment. I have no doubt that I could have made an equally poor showing with many we have had! But such an outre appointment could only be

139

justified if I had been going to make an outstandingly good showing. This would not have been so. I cannot think of one of the men you have appointed with whom I could successfully compete in the field of criminal law, and this is really the only criterion. (I think you have a splendid team and this seems to be the general opinion in P.H. — I have heard no criticism at all.)

Let me assure you still further — in case you have any lurking feeling, however baseless, that you should have put me on the list as "grace and favour" to an Aged Party Member. I don't really think I would have liked it very much. Or rather, I would have liked being appointed, but not really enjoyed doing the work . . . which is, after all, what matters. No, it is not my kind of job. It is one example of your good sense that you recognised that: and another that you should not have fallen over backwards to appoint me for the wrong reasons.

You mention certain matters in which you feel that my experience as a Reporter to the Court would be of value. I would be very happy indeed to be of use in such enquiries. I think I could perhaps really contribute something positive to this kind of work — not merely do it not less badly than someone else. I have a fairly wide experience of committees and of public-speaking and this might also be useful in certain types of investigation.

It is more than kind of you to say that you would consider me a suitable candidate for a Sheriff-Substitute's post, and I am very much complimented. You will, of course, appreciate that as a married woman I am restricted geographically (and perhaps, from my husband's point of view, in other ways) from giving the unconditional whoop of joyful acceptance that I would otherwise accord to any such suggestion. Had there existed the proposed Children's Courts (what *did* happen to that idea?) or had there been, in Glasgow or Edinburgh, courts dealing with domestic and family matters, then I do think that I would be at least a likely candidate for such an appointment. But unless you create a special Court for me (vide — Lord Gibson!) I may have to remain unseated.

But, as you say, all this is for the future: and I am very happy to leave the matter with you, knowing, as I now do from your kind and warm letter, that you will have me in mind for any suitable opening, and perhaps even allow me the privilege of discussing things with you more fully when the time comes.

Forgive this long letter: but I wanted you to know that I wholly understood your position and, as you invited, to give you some idea of my own. I think you know that, jobs and status aside, I shall be only too happy to serve your administration in any way that I usefully can.

Again my thank-yous: and my affectionate good wishes.

Yours sincerely

NOV. 3. Legislation Committee: Protection against Eviction

Bill, a standstill measure designed to preserve occupiers' position until the Government is able to introduce its main Rents Bill. I had been gravely disturbed about its terms: instead of defining "occupier" by reference to tenancies it included a wide definition taking in "residents", which would extend to whole classes — hotel guests, domestic servants and so on — who had never been protected by any Rents Act. So yesterday I set James Leechman the task of finding a formula which would give effect to what seemed to be the purpose of the Bill without trespassing into fields where the Government would be exposing itself to ridicule. Bowden summed up the result of the proceedings by saying that the Bill would have to go back to the Minister for consultation with the Law Officers. I got hold of Elwyn Jones, who agreed to a meeting some time today while I was in London. At the meeting, somewhat to my surprise, I found that I really took charge — the old story of the country of the blind in which the one-eyed man was king. Elwyn Jones knew nothing about Rent Restriction, nor did any of the others, so my limited knowledge of the subject gave me the advantage. Crossman and his advisers were amenable, and I had no difficulty in obtaining agreement to a complete re-drafting of the main clause. It was left to the Treasury draftsmen to put our ideas into proper form, but they have been given Leechman's draft to work on. I encountered Woodburn when coming from the cafeteria and assured him that — contrary to what had appeared in one of the Sunday papers — I had no desire to have him removed to the Lords to provide a seat for me. I told him that apart from disinclination to have him leave the Commons I had no wish to sit for a county constituency, with the necessity of attending every week at some village or other to keep one's constituents happy. He told me that that would not be a good reason for turning down East Stirlingshire, which was the easiest constituency in Scotland to work. His people never expected him to be there, and if they saw him there felt he ought to be in London attending to his public duties.

NOV. 4. Car to the airport. My driver — Miss Reilly, I think — has a manner very like Biddy's, and chatted throughout the journey about her father's Guernseys, and cats that came into the dairy, and grey squirrels which ate her walnuts, and her fondness for the Dutch school of painting: most entertaining.

NOV. 5. In the office Leechman took the opportunity of telling me that as soon as I left Clyde had been up conferring with Gordon — no doubt Gordon told him the coast was clear. It suits me better that he should come up when I am not there than adopt what most people would consider the more courteous course, but no doubt it is a good reason for treating Gordon with discretion.

NOV. 6. Home Affairs Committee. I encountered Griffiths in the vestibule, and out of courtesy to him as elder statesman said I would rely on him to show me the way to the meeting. He proceeded to lead me into the wrong building altogether, from which we were rescued by a civil servant. The Committee is presided over by the Chancellor of the Duchy of Lancaster, Douglas Houghton. Though reputed to be a knowledgeable person, he was anything but a good chairman, talking a lot and failing to keep any proper grip on the proceedings. We spent 40 minutes in a rambling discussion on the Gas Bill, which Bowden would have disposed of in 5; so there was little time left to deal with homicide. Soskice said there was a case pending in the English courts where the accused was almost certain to be convicted of capital murder, with no mitigating circumstances, and although he was prepared to do his duty in exercising his discretion under the prerogative of mercy he would find it extremely distasteful. More important, he thought it would be shameful if a Labour Government had been responsible for hanging a man when Parliament was prepared to abolish hanging. He accordingly was most anxious that Parliament should have an opportunity of voting on the question of abolition in time to avert such a situation. Soskice thought the Bill should be as simple as possible, but he had been persuaded by a memorandum from the Lord Chancellor that the Bill should include a provision to abolish the defence of diminished responsibility, introduced into the law of England by the Homicide Act of 1957. Gardiner's reason seemed to be that this defence was no longer necessary if capital punishment was abolished. It did not seem to have occurred to him that it would be much easier to get a plea to manslaughter than murder, particularly when a murder conviction automatically carried a sentence of imprisonment for life. Elwyn Jones had not had a copy of the memorandum. Neither of course had I — but it seemed extraordinary that the Chancellor was proposing an important change in the criminal law without even troubling to send his own law officer a memo of his reasons. It did not matter to me what they did provided they were not to interfere with the common law of Scotland. I intervened to ask for an assurance that they were intending only to repeal the 1957 statute, without affecting the Scottish position, and this was given. Crossman came across to ask if he could show me the revised form of the Eviction Bill. I said I should come and see him as 12.30, and had a word about this with Elwyn Jones. I told Mitchell what had happened, and asked him to come round with me to the Ministry of Housing. It now appeared however that the civil servants had got busy, and that there must have been phone calls between Deans Yard and the Ministry to the effect that I had no business to advise anyone but the

Scottish Office. Nobody from Deans Yard had ever set foot in the Ministry of Housing before. I was in no way concerned about that, but Crossman had evidently taken fright, and after assuring me that our talk was informal and that he realised I could not in any way advise him officially said he had asked me to come in order to show me the result of our efforts and to thank me for my share in them. I had to apologise to Mitchell for wasting his time on a pointless errand.

NOV. 9. Norah gave me a cutting from the *Daily Record* about Caroline McNaughton. I am not on good terms with the *Record*, since someone from that paper rang me up last night shortly after 11, when Nancy and I were in bed, and wanted to know whether I had had a letter from McInnes, the Glasgow MP, about a constituent who had been found dead in his cell. The reporter said he had been asked by his Glasgow office to get in touch with me about this. I told him to give his Glasgow office my compliments and tell them to go to the devil. I am usually courteous in dealing with press enquiries, but not after 11 at night. With no briefs to work on, it looks as if I may have a lot of evenings free; and though there is a Legislation Committee in London tomorrow I have arranged for Leechman to attend in my place.

NOV. 10. Gordon had left out for me a file about the efforts made by Noble to get rid of Robert Gibson from the chairmanship of the Land Court. He had three meetings with him, and got him nearly to the point of offering his resignation, but at the last moment he always shied away on some trivial pretext. The Civil Service people, after recording the final meeting, had minuted: "What do we do now?" — to which Shearer had replied in one word: "Pray!" Gibson has ceased to take an active part in the work of his court. He either does not come, or he comes and sleeps — probably more in the public interest than any active participation by him in the court's judgments.

NOV. 12. Noticing in the Minute of the Legislation Committee that they were short of Bills to submit to private members successful in the ballot, I drafted a note for the Scottish Office suggesting a Bill to make an employer liable for failure to provide safe plant, thus restoring the law of Scotland to what it had been before the Lords held that it was a good defence for the employer to show that he had got the plant from a reputable supplier.

NOV. 13. Home Affairs Committee. The Lord Chancellor outlined his proposals for a Law Reform Commission. I do not think he has a clear idea of what he wants. He is proposing a high-powered Commission of 5, with status equivalent to High Court judges, but as an example of what they might do he mentioned the need to tidy up the law of waterways, contained in a multitude of different statutes: a task, it seemed to me, more for consolidation draftsmen than for a high-up judicial commission. Soskice in a lengthy criticism said he would prefer to take advice — on criminal law, for instance — from his own officials than from any commission of judges, however distinguished. A sensible contribution from Jay, the President of the Board of Trade, and Niaill MacDermot, Financial Secretary to the Treasury. I supported what Bowden had been saying about some special committee of the House to deal with this type of legislation — otherwise the Commission would be a source of delay rather than expedition. Gardiner, when this point had been put by Bowden, waved it aside, saying there would be no possibility of legislation this session, perhaps not for 3 to 5 years. To me this seemed absolute nonsense. To Kings Cross for the 3 o'clock train to York.

NOV. 14. To the Mount of meet Miss Blake. Elizabeth wanted to see *Goldfinger*, one of the famous series of thrillers about the secret service agent James Bond. It was surprisingly good, with a number of ravishing blondes for Bond to disport himself with. One of the advantages of having an entirely promiscuous hero is that the film can dispense with the girl friends as it goes along, and two exceptionally attractive ones are bumped off before Honor Blackman appears. When the wildly exciting climax is past, and Bond on his way to Washington to receive the congratulations of the President, the scriptwriters have another surprise in store: a depressurised plane crashing headlong towards the ground, and Miss Blackman saying to Bond " You can't do it ", as he strives desperately to retain control. In accordance with the film's customary flouting of Hollywood convention, she is quite right. The plane does crash, thus giving the producers the opportunity for a final, ingenious, semi-ironical twist, completely in character with the rest.

NOV. 15. Dringhouses church. A young clergyman preached on Isaiah 26,3: simple to the point of naivety. I doubt if many of his hearers would accept from him as self-evident that if they had faith to tell a tree in Dringhouses churchyard to remove itself into the sea it would do so.

NOV. 16. Motored to town for the animals, and released them in my room. They were rather excited, and I had to retreat to the Crown Agent's room to phone St Andrews House in response to an urgent call. I spoke to Ross, but all he wanted was to inform me that he had been unable to secure that the Lord Advocate should get the same salary as the Solicitor-General for England. I assured the Secretary of State that while appreciating his people's efforts I was not unduly worried. Noticed that half the cases in the Court of Session programme for the week were cases that had been mine; and it was nice to think that I could spend a peaceful, lazy evening instead of having to set to work to prepare for tomorrow.

NOV. 19. A visit from an official from London, who came to "brief" Leechman and myself on security. After a lot of rubbish about the activities of Russian spies, he gave us various pieces of "advice", including an instruction that classified papers should not be read by Ministers in public transport. As practically all our papers are "classified", this would mean that we could not read the agenda for next day's meeting when on the train to London. When I taxed him with this, he attempted to support it, then had to climb down to the extent of agreeing that we could read the papers in the train provided that no one was looking over our shoulder.

NOV. 24. Legislation Committee: a Bill to make it illegal to recover compensation for damage or destruction carried out in the course of war operations. This arises out of actions by several subsidiaries of Burmah Oil, who have claims of about £100 million for damage to oil installations in Burmah, destroyed by General Alexander in order to deny them to the Japanese. I had to enter a caveat against a phrase in the Bill to the effect that any action in respect of that type of damage should abate. This meaningless phrase seems to have originated from Gibson, who had the notion that it would enable the Clerk of Session to decline, in defiance of the House of Lords order, to fix a diet of proof. A more serious difficulty arose when Gardiner proceeded to attack the policy of the Bill, as retrospective legislation, and suggested that, as the Government were already being criticised for breaking agreements in imposing import levies, the proper course would be to postpone this Bill until next session. This absurd proposal was effectively answered by Elwyn Jones, but Bowden said it would obviously have to go to Cabinet. The more I see of Gardiner, the less his judgment impresses me; but I am perhaps prejudiced on account of his cavalier treatment of my proposal to restore the law of master and servant to what it was before *Davie*'s case. As this is a United Kingdom matter, I had agreed with Gibson that he should consult the Lord Chancellor's department; and he has a letter back saying that the Lord Chancellor thought that the decision in *Davie* accorded with principle and commonsense, and that as no case had been made for altering it he hoped that the Lord Advocate would not proceed with his proposal. Admittedly Gibson's letter had been lukewarm, but I should have thought the Lord Chancellor would have enquired what the case for his colleague's proposal was before concluding that it was unsupportable. The Chancellor had suffered defeat on diminished responsibility, and concurred with Soskice and Elwyn Jones in a Minute to the effect that the doctrine should be retained.

145

NOV. 25. Buckingham Palace: the Queen's sherry party for the middle tier of Ministers and their wives. Willis was there, and I was interested to find that he had come to share my suspicions about the Lord Chancellor and his half-baked ideas. The Duke of Edinburgh recognised my tie and started to speak about lighthouses: a lively, uninhibited conversationalist. The Queen was engaged in talk with Mr and Mrs Willey about white fish, regarding which the Queen observed that something always appeared in the Speech from the Throne. One of the court officials remarked on seeing me admiring a Vermeer painting in the ante-room that there were also some fine Cuyps, and took me to see them. At the House we had supper in the cafeteria. The House was coming to the end of a debate on the National Insurance Bill, and seemed much more alive than when the last Government was in office, no doubt to some extent because it is a new Parliament but also I think because of a feeling that something is being done.

NOV. 26. The Committee stage of the Protection from Eviction Bill. I heard the Prime Minister answer his questions. His answers were clever and amusing, but he seemed to be trying to score over the Opposition rather than answer the questions. I began to see why it is that he makes himself so much disliked in Conservative circles. The debate on the Bill was pretty miserable. Labour members, particularly lawyers like Harold Lever and Sydney Silverman, did not seem to realise that they were now on the Government side, with a Bill to be got through, and wasted a lot of time debating with Conservatives and attempting to answer them, with arguments which were not always sound and in any event could have been put more briefly and effectively by a Parliamentary Secretary. Sir John Hobson led for the opposition. When anything controversial came up, Boyd Carpenter took over; and though I do not like him I had to admit to myself that he made a good speech. Progress was slow — Rowe, the English parliamentary draftsman, remarked to me that it was the kind of thing that almost made one despair of democracy.

NOV. 27. Home Affairs Committee: a proposal by Wedgwood Benn for a Bill to ratify an international convention which would do away with "pirate" broadcasting from ships such as Radio Caroline. Crossman pointed out that Radio Caroline was highly popular among young people; and the Committee gradually came round to the view that though we had to ratify the convention we need not be in any great hurry about it.

DEC. 1. Lunch which Ross was giving to the Moderator of the General Assembly. Noble was one of the guests, and in a few words he had with me expressed the view that it was not a good thing that the Lord Advocate should be a Member. I replied that I was aware there was some difference of opinion about that.

DEC. 2. The Lord President in course of conversation remarked that Gardiner, when chairman of the Bar Council, had a reputation for simply blocking everything. He does not know Gardiner, but apparently did not like what he had heard of him — Clyde and I may have something in common after all.

From Esme Carlisle:

7 Abingdon Gardens W8 2nd December 1964
Dear Sir,
With reference to your advertisement in today's "Times" I have a comfortable bedroom which I would be prepared to let on the conditions you mention. This is a large flat in an Edwardian block on the corner of Abingdon Villas & Allen Street, between High St. Kensington & Cromwell Rd. It is 5 minutes or less from High St. Kensington Underground station, & the buses.
It really is quiet. Abingdon Villas is a quiet road, but your bedroom would be at the back of the flat overlooking small gardens and you would have no traffic. I come from Cumberland and am accustomed to the country, and do not find this noisy. . . . I am a widow with a daughter at school in London, & we live very quietly. I do not have anyone else in the flat. I would of course provide breakfast if required.
Yours truly

DEC. 3. A summons to attend the Cabinet — Burmah Oil. Gardiner made his objection, quite moderately. I told them when the case was likely to come on, and the awkward position I should be in if I had to explain away a further delay of 12 months for which there seemed to be no explanation, once the necessity for retroactive legislation was accepted. Wilson made a nice reference to me, remarking that they had not been accustomed to receive from a Lord Advocate so definite a ruling presented with such brevity and speed. The feeling of the meeting was clearly in our favour, and Wilson summed it up by suggesting that our proposal be accepted and authority given for introducing the Bill forthwith. An interesting experience — I was grateful to the Lord Chancellor for giving me the opportunity of appearing at Cabinet. Ross seems to have been having difficulties with his civil servants, who under Noble's regime has been in the habit of taking decisions themselves without much reference to the Secretary of State, and had been trying to continue on the same lines. He appreciated my own difficulties with the Lord President, and obviously knew all about him. I gathered that he was not enthusiastic about Gardiner.

147

DEC. 6. To church, where Mr Reid preached on Mark 1,2. We had a visit from him last night, to ask my advice about a magazine called *Parade* which is sold along with other periodicals in shops attached to canteens and huts for soldiers in Germany, for which Mr Reid's committee is responsible. A deaconess who had gone out to work in the huts had resigned to come home on the ground that the sale of this magazine was equivalent to distribution of pornographic literature, and her complaint has now come to the attention of the Committee on Temperance and Morals. Mr Reid had bought a copy of *Parade*, and brought it for me to see. Consisting as it does mainly of photographs of naked women, I could see that *Parade* might not meet with the approval of all the members of the General Assembly, and though Mr Reid himself did not seem to see much wrong with it — nor did I — I advised not to attempt to defend the magazine, nor to put forward the argument which he proposed, that to stop selling it would mean a loss of revenue of £2000 per annum. I thought it would be possible to say, without considering the magazine on its merits, that it would be presumptuous for Mr Reid or his Committee to set themselves up as censors, and if this was one of the magazines normally on sale in such places — which are run by a variety of organisations — it was not for them to adjudicate on what was really a matter of taste. Whether he will get away with that remains to be seen.

DEC. 7. London: a committee to consider the proposals for a Law Reform Commission. Starting off with a reference to 20 years as the likely period for the Commission to reach a conclusion, the Chancellor came to the opposite extreme, urging that they should present an annual report. A car at 6.15 to take me to the airport. On account of a strong wind at Turnhouse, we were diverted to Renfrew. As we came down to land, there was the most extraordinary buffeting and tossing. The plane was thrown about, all over the place. I did not as it happened find this particularly alarming, even when the air hostess seated across from me remarked to her neighbour that we were having to brake more than usual because the runway at Renfrew was none too long; she said it was worse coming in to Gibraltar. I joined the Edinburgh bus — "Miss World", a Dorset girl, was in the seat behind with a male escort.

DEC. 8. We put on the Here and Now programme on STV to see Miss World being interviewed. She had smeared herself with lipstick and make-up so as to be positively grotesque. Last night she had been pleasant to look at, if not particularly pretty.

DEC. 9. I had given James Leechman a Minute drafted by Haddow about Scottish aspects of a proposed Bill on rent control, and this morning he brought it back, remarking that it read like a memo from Glasgow Property Owners Protection Association. This was the view I had formed, but the only ministerial reaction was a feeble Minute by Willis, that the proposal to increase rents to one-and-a-half times the gross annual value should be deferred until each house became vacant. I sat down and in 10 minutes drafted a Minute saying that in my view the policy inferences from Haddow's Minute were totally unacceptable, and that there could be no question of increasing rents of low-grade houses. I had a couple of letters to dictate to Miss Black, and was starting the first — to Dalgetty — when she said, "Is that about Government advances to defray revenue deficits of the New Towns?" I said it was, and she said she had had Miss Howat on the phone last night to say that Gibson had seen a letter from Dalgetty asking my views about these advances, and thought I should do nothing about it until it was seen whether the English people wanted to take the opinion of their Law Officers on the matter, which concerns New Towns in England as well as Scotland. I would not accept this, saying I had been asked for my opinion and it was immaterial to me whether the English people wanted to consult the Attorney-General or not. They could do so if they pleased — as they had, without consulting us, on a question of "hot pursuit". Gordon was called in, and suggested I should phone Gibson, but I demurred to this too, and in the end it was agreed that Miss Black would send Gibson a copy of my letter to Dalgetty. Shortly after, I had Dalgetty on the phone to say he had heard that Gibson had been saying something about it, but the fact was that the English people had no desire to have their position raised, no one having queried the English payments. So I was justified in my view that Gibson should be content to mind his own business and let the English mind theirs. It is rather fun to have to take decisions over the heads of these officials.

DEC. 14. A lengthy communication from Frieda Hohenner-Parker about her communings with the spirit world. She had learned that Sir Alec Douglas-Home gassed himself in his car March 14th, 1964 and Mr Butler did the same about 2 weeks later. Both were substituted by Pseudos. Dalgetty came to discuss the legality of payments made by Glasgow Corporation to Councillors to cover their telephone rentals. This payment was first made out of the rating account, and was challenged by the Auditor and disallowed by the previous Secretary of State. The Corporation asked for a Stated Case to the Court of Session, and meantime decided to make the payments out of the Common Good. These payments have now in turn been challenged by the Auditor, and Dalgetty is advising Ross to disallow them, so that another Stated Case can be taken at the same time. So far as I can see, the Council has a much wider discretion in regard to payments out of the Common Good, and though the First Division might well agree with the Auditor I cannot believe that it is illegal to apply the Common Good towards maintaining an efficient means of communication with Councillors. The Auditor has come to the extraordinary conclusion that there is "sufficient reason for doubt" — as to whether a payment which would be illegal from the rating account may be made out of the Common Good — for the payment to be considered contrary to law.

DEC. 17. James had been at a Rents meeting, and seems to have formed the same impression of the Lord Chancellor as I had. "That man gives me the creeps", he said.

DEC. 18. Owing to a derailment, trains to London were being diverted; and at 10 o'clock, when the Cabinet meeting was due to begin, the train was crawling through Cambridge station. I enjoyed the diversion, and was pleased that the train was so late that there was no question of attending the meeting and hence no need to hurry. Miss Howat had been on the telephone to the station, and phoned my apologies to the Cabinet office. To the House at 12.30 for a meal — a welcome one, since I had had no breakfast. Car to the airport. Ross was getting a plane to Glasgow, and pulled my leg about the Cabinet meeting — everyone at the meeting demanding "Where is the Lord Advocate? Why is he not here?"

DEC. 19. Kissen complaining of judges' salaries — the momey meant nothing to him, but when his friends in industry asked him what he was getting, and he told them, they thought it was chicken feed, and his standing was affected. Surprising what a silly ass Kissen is in some ways.

DEC. 20. To church: the children's Christmas gift service. Apart from having no children's address, the service was the same as usual. Mr Reid preached on John 1, vv.1&14.

1965

To everyone's surprise, including their own, the Labour Government continued in office throughout 1965; and I spent an interesting, agreeable and comparatively leisurely year in the office of Lord Advocate. Except in so far as one might want to get anything done, life as a member of the Government was very pleasant. I was increasingly impressed by the Prime Minister. Always friendly and unpretentious, not in the least pompous, he seemed to know what he wanted to do, and how to set about doing it. If one avenue seemed to be closed, he tried some other way. Without interfering in the day-to-day work of his Ministers, he kept a close watch on what was going on. Everyone accepted that in case of dispute his was the final decision. I thought he would perhaps be even more effective if he were prepared to admit occasionally that he might have been wrong. Most of the Government's leading members were well on top of their jobs – in many cases, head and shoulders above their Tory predecessors. The ablest with whom I was concerned was Niaill MacDermot, the Treasury representative on the Legislation and Home Affairs committees. In the midst of day and night debates on the Finance Bill, he would come to the committee in the morning with a complete understanding of the matters to be discussed and all the relevant facts at his finger ends. I liked Douglas Jay, the President of the Board of Trade, and Peart, the Minister of Agriculture, whose lighthearted approach to public affairs appealed to me. My work did not involve meeting many celebrities. Of those few whom I encountered, much the most delightful was the Queen, by whom, somewhat to my surprise, I found myself completely captivated: an extraordinarily nice, friendly person, lively, vivacious, eager to converse on any topic with candour, wit and a great sense of fun. If, as was rumoured, the Prime Minister regarded an audience with the Queen as more of a pleasure than a duty it was easy to understand why. The Government were assisted by one extraneous event: a "rebellion" against the Crown by the whites of Southern Rhodesia. This was a challenge just up Mr Wilson's street. He had a more difficult problem to deal with in Vietnam, where support for America's anti-Communist war was far from palatable to many of his own supporters. I myself was all for the Vietcong, and would have been happy to see the Americans thrown out and the unfortunate people of Vietnam left to live their lives in peace, under a Communist Government or otherwise. Mr Wilson may have felt that the wiser course was to continue to treat the Americans as allies in the hope of gradually influencing them in the direction of a more sensible policy. The comparatively leisured life of a Lord Advocate

*left me more time for recreation; and my reading included nine
volumes of Anthony Trollope.*

JAN. 4. A letter from the Minister of Works, by virtue of a warrant
under Her Majesty's Royal Sign Manual, asking whether I wished to
be supplied with a quarter of a doe from the Royal Parks for my
personal use, at a charge of £1.

JAN. 7. Sir Alec Douglas-Home had written me with a query
from one of his constituents, a solicitor named Liddell. With his
usual naivety, Sir Alec had sent on Liddell's letter in its entirety,
although it concluded: "Glad you did so well. I hope we trounce the
lot properly next time".

JAN. 12. London: Stag House, to pay a call on John Taylor. I
told him I had given his name to the Prime Minister as a useful
person for the Government to call on if they wanted the services of a
business tycoon.

JAN. 15. Home Affairs Committee. I sat next to Dr Mabon, an
extremely perky, self-confident little chap, who intervened on every
topic with complete assurance, whether it had anything to do with
the Scottish Office or not, and was not in the least abashed by
attempts to discourage him.

JAN. 19. Legislation Committee: the Law Reform Commission
Bill. In the Scottish section "Minister" is defined as "the Lord
Advocate and the Secretary of State", and I thought it reasonable to
explain that I was consulting with the Secretary of State with a view
to ensuring that the day-to-day operation of the Scottish Commission would be for the Lord Advocate to deal with. Mabon did not
seem to have been briefed on this point, and said he expected that
would be agreed; the civil servant behind him, however — a man
named Pottinger — at once got him to retract, and explain that he
could not commit the Secretary of State.

JAN. 20. A meeting of the Scottish Ministers, at which the
legislation programme was discussed. The Scottish Office paper
included a paragraph on law reform, and I had taken the opportunity
of proposing to amend this by including corroboration in personal
injury cases and the right of a workman to sue for injury caused by
defective plant. I explained that I was concerned that law reform
should include measures that were of some assistance to the ordinary
litigant, not merely trustees or lawyers. Despite the lukewarm
attitude of my own officials and the Secretary of State's I had no
difficulty in getting approval for the suggestion that both my
proposals could be offered to private members with an indication of
Government backing if that were obtained. After the officials left, I
stayed on with Ross and the Under-Secretaries while they discussed

other matters. Like other Labour politicians, they suffered from long-windedness and lack of appreciation of what was relevant, and though it was all very friendly and useful enough a lot of time was wasted. When the meeting seemed about to finish, Lawson, the Scottish Whip, raised a question about a letter sent to him when Ross had visited his constituency, which he had not regarded as a significantly cordial invitation to be present. As in fact he had been present, the complaint seemed pointless, but this footling matter was pursued for another half-hour. Throughout the meeting I was again impressed by Mabon, who did not intervene unless he had something to say and then said it effectively. To the House at 5 for a meeting of Ministers on the Parliamentary Commissioner, which spent the whole hour which the meeting occupied in discussing the single point of whether complaints to the Ombudsman should be channelled through MPs, and could only come to the conclusion that they were unable to decide. Houghton's handling of the meeting was lamentable. The main controversy was between Wedgwood Benn and Robinson, on the one hand, who thought all complaints should come through MPs, and Bowden and Soskice on the other, who thought the citizen should have direct access. Jay intervened occasionally to observe that the whole idea was absurd. I said nothing. Went in to hear the debate on the Science and Technology Bill. They were discussing research: interesting in an academic, unrealistic kind of way. Sir Harry Legge-Bourke drew attention to the danger of land-drainage schemes, which in one area had resulted in the destruction of a type of sphagnum moss found nowhere else in the British Isles.

JAN. 21. The flight north exceptionally pleasant, with lovely views of snowy country. The captain made a curious mistake, announcing over the loud-speaker that we should arrive at Glasgow on time and land at Renfrew at 4.20. A stewardess was hastily sent forward to remind him that we were supposed to be making for Edinburgh.

JAN. 22. News that Gordon Walker had failed to hold Leyton, where a vacancy had been made for him by putting Sorensen, the sitting Labour member, in the Lords. A swing of 8% to the Conservatives in a seat which had been Labour for 30 years makes things difficult for the Government.

JAN. 26. An American film on television, about the war which the Americans are trying to carry on in Vietnam against the Communists, with lukewarm support from Vietnamese. It was to the film's credit that it showed conclusively the futility of the war, and a realisation that there was no possibility of obtaining any intelligible success.

JAN. 27. To Juniper Green to call on Robert Gibson. I had phoned and invited myself to tea, he having ignored a letter asking him to come and see me. Enquiry at the Land Court had elicited the fact that the clerk had not seen its chairman since September; but Robert, when I had hauled him up from a semi-recumbent position on the sofa, seemed remarkably spry, though very tubby; about as thick as he is long. His memory for names is failing, but otherwise he was the same as usual: endless anecdotes to show how superior he was in all respects to his contemporaries at school, at University, and in the law, and how Cooper had conspired against him to prevent him from reaping the full fruits of his position. From time to time I tried to bring the conversation round to the problems of the Land Court, but with indifferent success. He was willing to discuss his successor, and seemed to think Leechman would be a good choice, but showed no inclination to retire. He thought there was some pensions question to be cleared up, and that depended on him. I dangled some vague threats over his head — pressure from MPs, and the possibility of a resolution in Parliament — but I doubt if this made much impression. The last thing he said was that if I wanted him to go in to the Court every day he was quite willing. Our discussion was friendly, but useless. I came away with the feeling that the impasse was as complete as ever.

JAN. 29. A talk with Gibson about a letter he had written to the Scottish Home Department to the effect that our Department would take no action about launching the law reform Bills we had discussed at the meeting until we received drafting instruction from them. This would leave complete control of the situation to St Andrews House, and is contradictory of the arrangement I made with Ross. I could see no justification for Gibson's writing such a letter without consulting me, and told him so. His excuse was that he wanted to get St Andrews House bogged down on these proposals, so that he could demonstrate that we could do the work better — oblivious of the important factor of having this job properly done. I suggested that we required some proper liaison in our own office before we started worrying about liaison with St Andrews House.

FEB. 2. O'Brien came to see me about a fraud case he has been conducting, involving a company formed to run piggeries in which investors would have their own pigs allocated to them. The case has ended with a derisory verdict against one of the three accused, on a minor charge. Cameron fined him £50, and has been critical throughout of the Crown's case and aspects of its presentation. O'Brien recounted to me the points Cameron had made, but I did not think any of them of much importance: the rather footling difficulties Cameron is inclined to make when in an awkward mood.

FEB. 4. A draft of a long answer Gibson had prepared on reasons why it was useful to us to have a copy of official Whips — in response to an enquiry for reasons, from someone in the Whips' office. I put all this aside, and wrote a brief note to Short asking him to deal with the matter soon, as it was inconvenient to me to be without this information. There seems to be some personal feud between Miss Howat and the Whips' office, which has led to a hold-up of this extremely simple request.

FEB. 5. Inverness solicitors Faculty dinner. After the final toast of the Chairman, a man from Kingussie got up and asked leave to speak. He was slightly the worse of drink, but rather funny. He asked a riddle: "What goes up the road, and down the road, and never touches the road?" The answer is: "The roadman". There were cries for a speech from a solicitor from Nairn, who was obviously drunk but had the presence of mind to start singing "God Save the Queen". This brought the dinner to an end.

FEB. 12. I had phoned Kissen last night and arranged that he would come up and see me when he finished his divorce proof. I waited till 3, then made some enquiry and found that he was in one of the side rooms drafting a judgment. I accordingly went in search of him, feeling rather annoyed, and was still more annoyed by his attitude towards the suggestion that he should become chairman of the Law Reform Commission. I was prepared for his preferring to stay as he is, but what irked me were his reasons: the poor salary compared to England, and the possibility that he might do better by going into industry some time during the next three years. He said he would think it over. As chairman of the existing Law Reform Committee, he is the obvious first choice, but I should be much happier to have Kilbrandon.

FEB. 13. Kissen confirmed that he did not want to take the chairmanship; he had talked it over with his wife, and she was against it.

FEB. 14. To Lady Stair's Close to see Kilbrandon. He seemed interested in the Commission, and we had a useful talk.

FEB. 15. Rents Bill committee. Controversies are gradually being resolved, and matters had reached a stage at which Crossman was able to put before us workable proposals. Surprising how a solution to problems gradually emerges from these discussions and periods of reconsideration. Dickson Mabon as usual intervened on every point, even purely English ones, displaying not only great enthusiasm but a lot of knowledge and ingenuity. His self-confidence among senior colleagues is astonishing, but what he says is always worth saying. Went in to the debate on Sunday observance. An earnest young Conservative, Mr Alison, supported Sunday cinemas and dancing but did not want ballet, theatre or concerts, because they were

156

centralised and would lead to an increase of traffic and more noise in what he called "metropoli" — an odd word to be used by a Member with an Eton and Oxford education. A very empty House: perhaps an indication that the time is ripe for ignoring the sabbatarians and going ahead with something more appropriate to the present day.

FEB. 16. Legislation Committee. Ross was there to support his Highland Development Bill, which gives inquisitorial powers to the Board which he is setting up. He succeeded in bulldozing his proposals through the committee, against the doubts of the lawyers, by talking generally about Tory landlords, and concern for deer as against concern for people, while saying nothing about the point that had been raised. I had an appointment with him to explain the position about the chairmanship of the Law Reform Commission. He had no objection to amending the Bill, if necessary, in order to frustrate a threat by Clyde that if any of his judges went off to the Commission they would find themselves when they came back at the foot of the Outer House so far as seniority was concerned.

FEB. 17. I had been invited to a Cabinet committee dealing with overseas affairs, in connection with an item relating to the Vienna Convention on consular privileges. I knew nothing about this and had never heard of the Convention. The Foreign Secretary having outlined what he proposed, and the Lord Chancellor having made a negative comment, Wilson turned to me. I said I had nothing to add, and left the meeting, as mystified as ever about why I had been there. Lawson came to see me about a man named Todd who has been giving wide circulation to unsavoury allegations against Lawson, Judith Hart and Tam Dalyell. All three had at one time or another written in about Todd's grievances against the Legal Aid Committee, and Dalyell had been assiduous in pursuing Todd's case after being assured time and again that there was nothing in it. In view of this, I had no great sympathy with Dalyell's complaint of persecution, thinking he had largely brought it on himself by encouraging Todd, who obviously had no merit in any of his complaints. Nor was I much concerned with Lawson, who is a pompous ass. There was not much I could do for them anyhow, there being no such thing in Scotland as criminal libel; but I undertook to communicate with the English authorities and see whether they would do anything about letters posted by Todd to MPs in London.

FEB. 19. A copy of next week's House of Commons Whip arrived, thus ending a long controversy. In response to my letter to Short, Miss Howat had had an impertinent letter from someone named Freddie Warren to say that he had not put my letter to the Chief Whip as he was waiting for her to send on reasons why I required the Whip. In view of this, I wrote a personal letter to Short,

157

saying that he might if he pleased inform his Mr Warren that I did not put myself to the trouble of writing just for the fun of the thing. The reply today was a rather ridiculous attempt to save Mr Warren's face: that in view of the confidentiality of the Whip it could not be sent to my secretary in London but he was prepared to send it to me personally in Edinburgh. I wrote thanking him, saying that I was content to have it sent to me personally and adding " Please address it to me at 3 Deans Yard, SW1 " — as it was not convenient to have it addressed to Edinburgh. Short's letter had apologised for the delay, which he said had been caused by my secretary's unwillingness to let his office know what I wanted; and in reply to this I said I was sorry I had not made it clear what I wanted, but if this was so it was entirely my own fault and not due to any unwillingness on the part of my secretary. A precognition in a Glasgow case: the witness, after recounting how he saw a man set upon by the four accused, who stabbed him, knocked him to the ground, and kicked him on the body and face, added: "I immediately ran towards the group and shouted 'That's a liberty' ".

FEB. 25. Johnson and Law came to see me about the Law Commission, and the proposal I had in mind for safeguarding any judge who may be chairman against the threat which Clyde is rumoured to have made that any judge going to the Commission will lose his seniority and miss any vacancy that may arise in the Inner House. I had thought this might have to be dealt with by an amendment to the Bill, but on being referred to the 1825 Act came to the conclusion that promotion to the Inner House was statutory and not subject to the Lord President's control. My visitors were perturbed by a violent article in last week's Scots Law Times, inspired as I thought by Clyde and suggesting that the whole proposal was a betrayal of the Scottish legal profession, particularly in allowing the Secretary of State any part in the appointment of the Commission. The writer thought that the Commission should be appointed by the Lord President, but failing that that the Lord Advocate should have undivided control. Johnson and Law wondered if anything could be said to allay the profession's fears. I pointed out that in bringing in the Secretary of State we had fully appreciated the effect on the legal profession, and that we had just to accept it. I felt at the time that Ross's insistence on his participation had probably made things more difficult, and there might be a risk of not getting a judge to take on the chairmanship — Kilbrandon indicated to me on the phone on Monday that he had serious doubts. I had written him this morning, urging it on him as a public duty, and told the St Andrews House people about this, but made it plain that on account of the feeling against St Andrews House extending its empire as proposed in the

Bill it was doubtful whether we should get Kilbrandon to accept. This seemed to shake them, and I was amused by their obvious worry at what seemed to be the consequence of the policy they had insisted on. Clyde was occupied in the Justiciary Court, where he made himself unpleasant to James Leechman, appearing for the Crown. Even Gordon remarked on it, saying that Clyde cheapened the court by that kind of conduct. James is not all that tactful in handling him: apparently when he had given some answer to Clyde's badgering, and Clyde said, "You might have told us that five minutes ago", James retorted, "I haven't been speaking for five minutes". At 4.15 I went across to Blackie House, where Kilbrandon asked a number of questions and then, much to my relief, said that, as his motto had always been never to volunteer but never to refuse to take on a responsibility, he would accept the chairmanship. He obviously was not keen, and I appreciated his attitude, particularly after I had made it clear that he could expect no cooperation from the Lord President. He made what I thought a sensible suggestion: that it might be a good idea if he were to be in the Lords. I had been keeping my approach to Kilbrandon dark, so that Clyde will have no chance to interfere, and had to go to considerable pains in avoiding Gordon's efforts to find out what was happening, no doubt so that he could pass it on to Clyde, whom he sees almost daily in the Crown Office or downstairs. Mentioned the problem to Wheatley, who pointed out that, despite his friendship with Clyde, Gordon had always been very loyal to all his Lord Advocates, defending them and supporting them both in office and after they moved elsewhere. This is perfectly true.

FEB. 26. A lengthy interview with Clyde. He made it clear that so far as he was concerned no Law Commission chairman was going to have a seat reserved for him in the Division, and was indignant at the idea of amending the Bill, saying that he was not going to be dictated to. I observed that the position might be governed by statute already, but he obviously had no idea what I was talking about. I reported to Law, who not unnaturally seemed surprised and annoyed at the President's attitude. I told him in confidence that Kilbrandon had agreed to accept. Oddly enough, Kilbrandon had made no objection to the inclusion of the Secretary of State in the Bill, and had remarked that it seemed a good idea to keep the political people in on this and make the appointment a joint one. I did not repeat this to Law.

MAR. 8. A visit from the four lay members of the Land Court, to ask that something be done about the chairman. No doubt as a result of my visit to him, Gibson attended a sitting at Inverness, but according to the other members was unable to give any guidance on the questions that arose. He sleeps on the bench during the hearings; and during the Court's stay of two days in Inverness was unshaven and disorderly in his dress. He was found fully dressed in the vestibule of the hotel at 5 am by one of the hotel servants, who had to conduct him to his room — he goes to bed fully clothed because of inability to dress himself. He retired to bed in the afternoon while the members of the Court were away inspecting a holding, and on getting up at 7 pm came down and ordered grapefruit, porridge, bacon and egg. I undertook to write Gibson. To the University library to look up Hansard debates on the Tribunals and Enquiries Bill of 1958, which is the precedent for giving the Lord President of the Court of Session a hand in the appointment of chairmen of independent tribunals. The civil servants want to do this in regard to chairmen of the panels to be set up under the Rent Bill, but as the choice of chairmen has to be carefully made if rent fixing is to proceed without serious political repercussions I had suggested cutting the President out and having the appointments made by the Secretary of State. This was accepted by Ross, and the immediate result was a wail of anguish from Deans Yard: Mitchell on the phone, followed by Miss Howat, then a Minute from Gibson, all proclaiming that this was a terrible departure from what had been accepted by everyone in 1958. I found as I had hoped that there had not been the amount of general agreement in 1958 that Gibson wanted me to suppose. Indeed Soskice in the debate on Second Reading had queried the introduction of the Lord President, who was not answerable to Parliament. Farquharson came up in the afternoon to consult me about common grazings on rocket ranges in the Western Isles.

MAR. 9. Amused to read a speech in Hansard by Forbes Hendry, the Conservative member for West Aberdeenshire, made about midnight on the Backing of Warrants (Republic of Ireland) Bill, when in connection with some point that had come up affecting Scottish practice he asked, "Where is the learned Lord Advocate? Probably in his bed in Edinburgh".

MAR. 11. A letter from Robert Gibson, saying he had been thinking about retiring for some time and had come to the conclusion that he should ask me to accept his resignation. Also a note from Douglas Johnston, whom Gibson had apparently consulted, suggesting I might write him a letter of appreciation and offer to remove the other letter from the files, since it no longer required an answer. I wrote on Tuesday narrating briefly all the grounds of complaint, asking what he proposed to do, and requesting him to treat it as a matter of urgency; but I had hardly expected an immediate reply — indeed I had been turning over in my mind what the terms of the next letter would need to be. I had a short talk with Douglas, and got his approval for a letter I had written accepting the resignation and expressing my personal regret and appreciation of what Gibson had done in the Land Court and Parliament. To Harald Leslie's, to sound him out as to the possibility of his becoming chairman of the Land Court. He seemed favourably disposed, saying he would prefer it to being a judge of the Court of Session. I did not tell him Gibson was resigning, but indicated that I was pressing him to do so.

MAR. 13. A letter from Douglas Johnston, to say that Robert Gibson had shown him my second letter, which had given Gibson and Muriel "the greatest pleasure".

MAR. 16. Legislation Committee: the Rents Bill, a long, complicated piece of legislation which Bowden got through with startling rapidity, taking it clause by clause. I expect it was felt by most of us to be beyond us. I attempted to raise the point wrongly decided in *Pender v. Reid*, when the Court introduced a ridiculous distinction between "house let together with land" and "land let together with a house", but the draftsman explained that if they were to attempt to rephrase the existing Rent Acts it would mean a Committee stage of inordinate length, and I got no support for my attempt to make legislation intelligible — though the Committee seemed interested and sympathetic. To the House for the debate on the Bill to set up a Highland Development Commission. Malcolm Macmillan twitted Noble entertainingly, saying that like Moses he had always been going up into some mountain to bring down tablets of stone, and all he brought were sleeping tablets.

MAR. 17. An appointment with the Secretary of State at Dover House at 10. Johnson was with Ross when I went in, and warmly approved my idea of Leslie as chairman of the Land Court. Johnson at first seemed dubious about my news regarding Gibson, and was much surprised to hear that I had his resignation in writing. On the Underground to Richmond I was reading a book about Wavell, and a railwayman looking over my shoulder proceeded with the usual London friendliness to strangers to tell me he had served with Wavell in France before Dunkirk. I felt his remarks were based on false premises, since so far as I know Wavell did not have a command in France before Dunkirk.

MAR. 19. Among the letters that had come in was rather a pathetic one from Lord Gibson, in his own handwriting, asking if I would allow a portrait to be completed which is being painted of him in his robe of office. This of course I assured him I should arrange for.

MAR. 24. In the absence of the Foreign Secretary in America I was having the use of his car. The driver had come over with Stewart from the Ministry of Education, and had a high opinion of him: "a very brainy chap, never gets flustered". To the House for question time. Houghton's skill in dealing with his questioners was a revelation: he was witty, astute, and in complete command of the situation. The main heckling was directed to the Ministry of Agriculture. Following an unpopular farm prices review, the Minister has been subjected to great pressure by farmers and their organisations, and described as the most hated man in England. It was obvious however, as soon as Peart came in, that he was popular on both sides of the House, and the Tory attack had a synthetic air. He stood up to his hecklers well, more by a frank, friendly manner than by any artistry in dealing with the questions. John Mackie gave him some bluff, commonsense support. Hoy, the other Under-Secretary, intervened occasionally in a painstaking, pedestrian manner which in its way was almost equally deadening to the critics. My impression that Labour ministers are on top of their opposite numbers was clearly confirmed.

MAR. 25. A meeting of Ministers to consider whether there should be some investigation into the working of the Tribunals of Enquiry Act. Houghton made a long, rambling speech which seemed to come to no conclusion, and when the Chancellor asked whether he favoured an investigation or not said that he could not make up his mind. It was agreed to have a small Royal Commission.

MAR. 26. Saw Clyde and told him about the Land Court. He seemed pleased at Leslie's appointment — no doubt relieved at being free from any risk of having him in the Court of Session. He and Leslie have always been at daggers drawn. Gordon told me that Leslie had been up at the office while I was away, obviously delighted and saying that he would not have considered being "downstairs" — in the Court of Session — "with these people". Nice that everyone is satisfied. Interviewed three Procurators-Fiscal who were the most senior of the applicants for Glasgow. We had already decided to appoint Herron, but as he is junior to the other two it was thought advisable to interview them. There was no doubt that on the interview Herron made the best showing. Law Society dinner in the North British Hotel. I sat on the left of the chairman, Sir Hugh Watson, and had as my other neighbour Sir Robert Maclean, a Glasgow manufacturer. I found him interesting and fair-minded, and rather neglected the chairman — who has a reputation for conviviality but whom I always find heavy going. Maclean spoke highly of George Brown, who he said seemed greatly to have increased in stature since becoming a Minister, and whom industrialists thought highly of. He was an admirer also of Lord Eccles. Noble he obviously held in complete contempt. He thought

Wilson was probably able to get through his immense amount of work without undue wear and tear because he himself realised that he was intellectually fit for it. He doubted if the same would apply to Sir Alec Douglas-Home.

AP. 6. Leslie's appointment in the *Scotsman*, with a report in the agricultural column, above the fat-stock prices, of an interview in which Harald recounted how he had been transplanting wallflowers in his garden when he found the Lord Advocate standing beside him with news that "came like a bomb". A visit from Halliday, Professor of Conveyancing in Glasgow University. He seemed the very man to have on the Commission, but as I had expected he was extremely unwilling. He is a partner in a leading Glasgow firm of solicitors, and his work there, along with his university work and the chairmanship of a Government committee on conveyancing reform, is more than enough for any man. At first he turned it down flat, but eventually agreed to consult his partners. Whereas Smith, so long as he thought £6000 might be on the cards, was certain that he could not look at £5000, Halliday's worry was that with a salary of £2000 he would not feel that he was not able to spare the time for £2000 worth of work.

AP. 7. A visit from Donald Macleod, who thinks his status and salary should be raised from C to B because he has to do two days a week at Edinburgh in addition to his work, such as it is, at Selkirk.

AP. 8. St Andrews House had had cold feet as a result of a letter from Clyde saying he could not possibly agree to an amendment providing that the chairman of the Law Commission should retain his seniority for the purpose of going into a Division. He was sure that Lord Kilbrandon would not be a party to any proposal to interfere with succession rights of Outer House judges. I had been content to pass on a copy of this to Kilbrandon, and to reply saying that no one was proposing to interfere with judges' succession rights; but Johnson took it much more seriously, and suggested that in view of what the Lord President had said we could not proceed with the amendment. I told him we had known all along that the President was opposed to the idea, and nothing had happened to relieve me of the necessity of trying to carry out my obligation to Kilbrandon. If they could get Kilbrandon's assent to going on without the amendment I agreed that it need not be put down. Kilbrandon is thought to be in Argyllshire, and as this is the last day for putting down any amendment they may have some difficulty; but having put the onus on Johnson I thought I had done sufficient, and left the office to its own devices for the next ten days. We left shortly after 1 for Stranraer, en route for Ireland.

AP. 9. Sligo: Imperial Hotel. As we arrived, the corridor outside our room began to be filled with smoke. After some toing and froing, a woman remarked to us that it was all right — they had thought the place was on fire, but it wasn't.

From Mr Sinclair Shaw:

Aberdour 10th April 1965
Dear Gordon
I understand you are holidaying in Ireland so you may not have seen the enclosed cuttings from "The Scotsman" and the "Daily Herald". I have no doubt that the "pre-October" Gordon would have found them as nauseating as I do.
If I am right in thinking you had a part in having Ross McLean made a knight (which your Tory predecessor notably failed to do) what a very strange action to take. What has he ever done to deserve a knighthood? And, much more important, what in any event is a Socialist Lord Advocate doing en-titling people?
I regard, as you once did, Leslie, as the Complete Humbug. . . The Labour Party owes him precisely nothing, but you choose to make him Chairman of the Land Court!
Some of us e.g. myself, James Forsyth, Harry Wilson and others, have worked long and faithfully for the Party which we love. Five minutes on the phone would have enabled you to find out whether any of us would have liked to be considered for the post. . . I am genuinely shocked by your behaviour.
We have a right to expect from a Labour Government higher standards of conduct than those upon which a Tory Government usually acts, and I think your two "appointments" are a reflection upon the Labour Government, and upon you, both as a Socialist and as a man. I hope your holiday has been a success — and that you have returned with a determination to do a great deal better in the future!!

AP. 11. A concert of local talent groups — advertised to start at 8.15, but I had noticed in the local paper that they assumed the starting time to be 8.30. This was optimistic. About 8.30 there was some hammering, and someone started working on the curtains and testing microphones, but it was 9.15 before the concert started. The audience waited with complete patience until the show began — without any mention of the delay.

AP. 14. I have grown quite thirled to this little town, but was unable to be of any help when a man stopped me and asked where he could get a few ham sandwiches.

AP. 17. Learned with surprise that Robert Gibson had died while I was in Ireland. The same thing happened with regard to Hendry, who died just as Gibson did almost immediately after we had succeeded in getting him removed from office. Law had commented that contact with the Lord Advocate was apparently equivalent to the kiss of death. The difficulty about Kilbrandon's seniority had been settled — an arrangement had been come to, agreeable to him and also to Clyde. I did not ask what the arrangement was. Professor Halliday had indicated that he would like to come on the Commission. Leechman told me that Shaw had been to lunch with him, and treated him to a diatribe on the lines of his letter to me. He had got Shaw to admit that he probably would not have wanted to be chairman of the Land Court, but he thought he should have been offered it.

AP. 28. Elizabeth for some reason wanted to see the Conservative television broadcast. It turned out to be a talk by Sir Alec, made up entirely of generalities and so far as I could see completely harmless, not to say useless. Though his manner was pleasant, a patronising attitude of mind keeps breaking through, though he himself obviously has no consciousness of it.

AP. 30. Tried on several pairs of old trousers from our wardrobe, and was able to discard four pairs as too tight, and put them aside for Nancy to take to the Scouts' jumble sale tonight.

MAY. 4. Law Commissions Bill in the Lords: everyone in a good humour, shouting "Order, order" goodnaturedly at the Chancellor when he proceeded to address them from in front of the Woolsack instead of taking a step to the Opposition side, as apparently he is supposed to do when making a speech. The only cantankerous note came from Lord Silkin, but he had no real point except dislike of any agreement with Dilhorne. Lord Selkirk raised the Scottish position, upholding the Lord Advocate's status and suggesting that if I did not want to be a member of the other House I might be made a member in the Lords.

MAY. 5. Committee stage of the Bill to abolish capital punishment. Soskice is often a curiously naive speaker, and puts his points oddly. Speaking of his intention to consult the trial judge before deciding on release of a prisoner serving a life sentence, he remarked that it might "not be possible to have access to the learned trial judge", because he might be dead.

MAY 9. To Ampherlaw for tea. Barney told us about one of his surgeons at Law Hospital, an Indian from the south, very dark in colour. He had been interviewed for a Government post in one of the new African states; and Barney asked him if he had got the job. "No", he replied, adding with a twinkle in his eye, "I don't think they liked the colour of my skin".

MAY 13. St Andrews House draft press release prepared in readiness for the announcement of the names of the Law Commission. I had to point out that, though Mr Fairbairn's middle name was certainly Douglas, Douglas Fairbanks was a different person.

MAY 17. Mrs Spence told me they had bought a house near Farnham, and the Richmond house was being put up for sale; so I shall have to look for new lodgings.

MAY 18. Legislation Committee: Steel Bill. I intervened to support an objection by Elwyn Jones to the form in which the Bill has been drafted, reviving certain provisions of the 1949 Act, with amendments in a schedule. I pointed out that it would allow amendments to be put down to include any other provisions of the 1949 Act and to amend these provisions, so that they could be faced not only with amendments to the present Bill but with a vast number of amendments to the 1949 Act as well. This argument was effectively countered by Diamond, who said it might be all right in theory but experience had shows that if Members had lenghty provisions set out in black and white in front of them they were much more likely to table amendments than if the provisions were less obvious. Nobody at these meetings ever makes any reference to the political difficulty that the Government has no majority for the Steel Bill. Discussions invariable proceed on the footing that everything will go on as planned. Car at 2 to take me to the airport. The Lord High Commissioner's dinner at Holyrood tonight — about 100 guests, at one long table. I had omitted to look at the card showing me where we were to go, and had to abandon Lady Milligan's arm in order to show the card to the purse-bearer, Major Blair, and get his directions. A band played from time to time, and when Harald proposed the loyal toast it played the National Anthem. When he went on to propose the health of the Moderator, the band played the Old Hundredth. The only other toast was " Her Grace ". The band did not play anything for her. Conversation was brought to a standstill when two pipers marched round the table once or twice, making a terrible row. After the ladies had withdrawn, I was landed with Sir Maxwell Inglis of Glencorse, who told me how dishonest the Africans had become since they had gained their so-called independence, as compared with the old days when he was a District Commissioner in Nigeria and regarded by the natives as their father and mother. Blair was of course bearing the " purse " — a big pouch with tapestry on it — and Nancy asked him if there was anything in it. He assured her there were various things, including a list of the guests and a Rhodesian penny which he brought out and showed her. Mrs Paton was keeping house, and we arrived home to find a strong smell of burning, with an empty, clean frying-pan on the gas stove and the gas full on under it. Mrs Paton is getting rather peculiar.

MAY 21. The Sheriff-Substitute at Elgin has resigned, and we had agreed to offer the post to young Kermack. Gordon explained to me that it would not do for me to phone Kermack; the proper procedure was that Kermack should phone me. He accordingly rang Kermack yesterday and arranged that he should phone me this morning, which he did — and accepted without further ado. I had to tell Clyde about his new judge, to take Kilbrandon's place. I have nominated James Leechman. Clyde made no comment, but he was up shortly after, having a discussion with Gordon.

MAY 22. Elizabeth's school essays show a remarkable command of language, and descriptive and narrative power. There is a weird poem, "Cruel Courage":

> "Bold spirits that do wax so strong above
> Come thither, take away my earthly love.
> Tonight I must depart — not here! not here!
> And ride across this land, no fear
> Must on me rest if it be done.
> So pledge yourselves to me in homage all.
> First on the spirit of forgetfulness I call.
> That I forget he gave his love to me
> And set to do the awful deed may be.
> Next venom fill my soul with hate
> With malice strong, before it is too late
> To kill, with gory dagger through his breast.
> 'Tis done; but still I have no rest.
> For stealthy swiftness summoned to my aid
> Will let me flee, with night to be her maid,
> To blanket me in darkness. No moon shall shine.
> Ho! dancers hence, for now you are all mine".

MAY 24. The annual meeting of Dr Guthrie's Schools Trust, in the girls' school. I spoke to several of the girls, and formed a more favourable impression of the place than on my previous visit. No doubt the regime is monotonous and unimaginative, but the girls all seemed friendly and reasonably happy. For a girl of moderate intelligence, it may be about the best that can be done.

MAY 25. Deans Yard: Moran brought a young lady in to see me: Miss Gray, whom the Law Society of Scotland have just appointed to be their Public Relations Officer. She was good-looking and charming, and seemed an excellent choice for such a post. Bus to Chelsea, where I made for the home of Mrs Patricia Watts-Jones — one of those who had replied to my "Times" advertisement last December — but got no answer to my ring. Bus on to Kensington, where I had an address at Abingdon Gardens: a more luxurious affair — a block of Edwardian flats in a pleasant cul-de-sac. Again no one was at home.

MAY 26. The House sitting in Committee on the Murder Bill.

Interesting to hear David Steel, the new Liberal member for Roxburgh, discussing with Bessell, who had spoken for the Liberals, how he should vote. Bessell had spoken in favour of the new clause, but the discussion which I overheard ended with Bessell waving Steel into the Labour lobby while he himself turned to join the Tories. Appointment with Ross to discuss who was to be Solicitor-General. Despite the rocket I expect to get from Kirkcaldy, I do not think there is any alternative to Ian Robertson. Ross was worried that he might not be a member of the Labour Party. He is expecting a General Election in the autumn, saying he did not see how the Government could go on beyond that after the trouble over the White Paper on steel.

MAY 28. Downstairs to see Clyde about a draft Bill to raise judges' salaries. This appeared unexpectedly from the Lord Chancellor's department in the course of the week, and gave power to the Chancellor to appoint nine additional judges — a provision that no one had heard anything about. I had had Johnson on the phone, worried because Clyde had not been consulted about a possible need for an increase in the number of Scottish judges. He thought it important that Clyde should be told about the English provision right away, and as I was not to be back in Scotland till the evening I suggested he might tell Clyde himself. This he had done; and my purpose in seeing Clyde was simply to apologise for not having been here to tell him myself. Clyde objected to the "unfairness" of the English provision when nothing was being done for Scotland — oblivious of the fact that we already have power to appoint two more judges and that, as he agreed, there was no need to appoint any, except a judge to take the place of Kilbrandon.

MAY 31. John Wheatley phoned, to report a complaint that Clyde had been making to other judges, that none of them had been consulted about the Judges Salaries Bill. Despite my talk with him on Friday, I had a letter from him on Saturday to the effect that it was unfair to Scotland that the Lord Chancellor should be given power to appoint nine more English judges while nothing was done for Scotland. I replied that I thought his letter must have been written before our conversation — obviously it had been written after it — and that in writing about unfairness to Scotland he might have overlooked the power that the Secretary of State already has to appoint two additional judges — a greater number in proportion to the total of judges of first instance than is envisaged in the power given to the Lord Chancellor.

JUN. 1. Legislation Committee. Gardiner mentioned to me — what he said was none of his business, but he thought he should say it as one lawyer to another — that he understood that the Scottish judges were critical of the proposal to put the Solicitor-General on the bench. It looks as if Clyde, although making no comment to me, has been doing some lobbying behind the scenes. I was surprised but in no way perturbed, and assured Gardiner that the appointment was a good one, in no way merely political. He seemed to understand my reference to certain quarters from which opposition was to be expected. The Committee discussed the attitude to be adopted to a motion by Sir Cyril Osborne for leave to introduce a Bill to provide compulsory health tests for Commonwealth immigrants. It was thought that a responsible private member on the Government side should be briefed to oppose this, but that if a division followed on the two speeches the Government side should be advised to abstain. A sensible intervention by Marsh, the Parliamentary Secretary to the Ministry of Labour, who pointed out that if there was a speech against Osborne's Bill, and feelings were whipped up, and then advice to abstain, the result would be complete confusion, with some voting against the Bill and some not voting, and the Bill being carried amid some chaos on the Government side. Gardiner took a vote round the table; and when equality resulted Elwyn Jones said he was impressed by the fact that the two Ministers most concerned thought abstention the proper course, and so he would change his vote to support them. The Committee went on to consider what to do about a private member's Bill to modify the law of abortion. We were warned by Lord Pakenham that any suggestion that we supported abortion would arouse grave disquiet among a large section of the community, the Catholics — of whom of course he is one. Ross remarked that we had no problem in Scotland; I added that that was because we dealt with the problem administratively along lines that would probably appeal to the Member sponsoring the Bill. "You mean you don't prosecute?" said Elwyn Jones. "We don't prosecute," I said. To Buckingham Palace to attend the Privy Council: the summons to attend an elegantly printed document:

"LET the Messenger acquaint the Lords and others of Her Majesty's Most Honourable Privy Council, That a Council is appointed to meet at the Court at Buckingham Palace, on Tuesday the 1st Day of June at 11.40 of the Clock, A.M. Ordinary Clothes".

We stood in line while the clerk read out the titles of Orders, to each of which the Queen said "Approved". She had returned on Sunday from a state visit to Germany, and Griffiths asked how she had enjoyed her trip. She said it had been very interesting — great enthusiasm everywhere — but she did not think too much should be taken from it. It was a strange experience to visit the Berlin wall. Hamburg she had liked: a more outward-looking place, as seaports were apt to be. Her conversation was lively and uninhibited; she talks, seemingly, just as she thinks, and with an air of enjoyment and interest which is most attractive. I was much impressed with her. Back to Deans Yard, where a phone call had come from my correspondent in Abingdon Gardens. I had addressed my letter to "Mrs Carlisle" — seemingly a mistake, my correspondent, signing "Esme Carlisle", being in fact the Countess of Carlisle. George Mitchell said that his wife had met Lady Carlisle, and she seemed very nice. The flat is close to Kensington High Street station, and George remarked that if I went there I would be on the Inner Circle in every sense of the term. We arranged that I should come and see her between 4.30 and 5. The daughter let me in: a nice-looking girl of about 17. Lady Carlisle said she had done nothing more about letting the room since she answered my advertisement in December, and appeared to be willing that I should have it. She seemed friendly, and nicely got up, probably in her late forties. She showed me the room, but I got so interested in talking to her daughter that I did not really look at it, and did not notice anything about the bed, or heating or lighting. My proposed terms of £4 a week were apparently acceptable, and Lady Carlisle said she could give me breakfast. Nothing was settled, but I left with what appeared to be the general impression that I would come there in September.

JUN. 2. Home Affairs Committee. Judith Hart was there to present a Scottish Office paper asking authority to announce acceptance of the Kilbrandon Committee's recommendations on juvenile delinquents, and to set up a working party to decide how the proposals could best be implemented. The Home Office are objecting, and asking that the announcement be delayed until they are in a position to put forward their proposals to deal with the same problem in England. Nobody knows when that time will come, and when it does it seems obvious that the English proposals will be on different lines. But, after Alice Bacon had put forward the Home Office objections, Douglas Houghton, who was presiding, weighed in with an appeal to Judith to postpone the announcement for a month. He was discussing similar problems with English local authorities, and it would be embarrassing for him to have the Scottish announcement at this stage. Judith continued to put up a good fight, but with Houghton against her it was plainly impossible to defeat the Home Office objection at the moment. Houghton suggested that the proposal be held over till next meeting, and accepted some vague murmurs of assent as indication of agreement. I had promised Judith to support her, but in view of Houghton's attitude thought it useless to say anything today. A lengthy interlude during which Barbara Castle harangued us about some proposal of Crossman's dealing with compensation for people who had purchased houses scheduled for demolition. As Minister for Overseas Development she is not concerned with home affairs, but had invited herself along to urge the point, which she did at considerable length. Crossman made a reasonable reply, and Houghton announced approval of his proposal with the Minister for Overseas Development dissenting. She continued to dissent, volubly and bad-temperedly, as she made her way out. There was a long agenda, and I left with Judith when Soskice was about to embark on one of his longwinded explanations — of a Home Office proposal to provide additional prisons. Judith was indignant at what happened about the Kilbrandon Report: the Home Office will be no further on with their proposals in a fortnight's time, and the delay may make all the difference in getting consultations going before the holiday period. This was the opening day of the Suffolk Farmers Show at Ipswich; and my taxi driver, resourceful and enterprising, reached Liverpool Street in time for me to catch the 12.30 train. A bus for the Show proceeded into the town, through streets with such intriguing names as Silent Street and Dogs Head Street, to the bus station. Another bus took us to the showground. I spent the afternoon there, getting back to Liverpool Street before 7. The House was embarking on another all-night sitting, and I thought it a good opportunity to have a word with Ross. Found him with Judith, who was telling him about our troubles of the morning. He agreed to see Houghton and try to square him before the next meeting. He seemed to be persuaded that the Solicitor-Generalship should be offered to Robertson. I had mentioned the matter to Robertson last week, when he said it would need to be carefully considered; I am not sure that he would accept, in the precarious position in which the Government stands. A useful, pleasant talk with Ross and Judith. Ross remarked on the good impression that the Scottish law officers had made on his colleagues at committee meetings.

JUN 3. Coming through Westminster Abbey, I stopped to look at a monument commemorating " Ann daughter of George Fielding . . . the truly loving (& as truly beloved) wife of Samuel Morland Kt & Bart died February 20th 1679 Aetatis XIX ". The early death of this young wife seemed pathetic, but I noticed that the monument next to this one commemorated " Carola daughter of Roger Harsnett, Esq. Ye truly loving (& as truly beloved) wife of Samuel Morland Kt & Bart, died October 10th 1674 Aetatis XXIII " — only five years before the death of his next wife.

JUN. 4. James Leechman told me he had had a quarrel with

Clyde a year or two ago on some Justiciary Office matter, and they had not since been on speaking terms.

JUN. 11. The police college at Tulliallan Castle — addressing students leaving at the end of their course. In one of the lobbies I was shown a picture, *The Death of Raphael*, which had been left by the castle's former owner and which I had been warned was giving rise to some controversy — the Commandant wanted to remove it and replace it with a display of police batons. It did not strike me as an attractive picture, and as it is enormous one cannot just ignore it. I had been provided with a draft speech from St Andrews House, but Johnson remarked that the most interesting part of ministerial speeches was always the part that was not in the brief.

JUN. 13. The *Observer* has an article, obviously inspired by Clyde, about "disquiet among the Scottish judiciary" at the practice of elevating law officers to the Bench. "In the eyes of the profession there are others more deserving of judicial preferment". The article goes on to propound a "simple solution" proposed by "those who express concern at the present state of affairs": that the Scottish law officers should again be allowed to engage in private practice, in which event there would be less reason for quarrelling with their appointment to the Bench. No explanation is given of this odd statement.

JUN. 14. To Kissen's, to see him about the future of the existing Law Reform Committee. We spoke about the *Observer* article, and a similar one in today's *Scotsman*, where the reporter — no doubt with better knowledge of local conditions — had toned down some of yesterday's extravagances. While expressing "widespread concern" about the practice of elevating law officers to the Bench "automatically", the article in forecasting James' appointment says: "Although it is the prerogative of the Lord Advocate, Mr Gordon Stott, Q.C., to take the appointment, there may be too much important legislation requiring his attention to permit his elevation at present". Despite Clyde's claim to be expressing the view of "the judges", Kissen said Clyde never consulted the judges as a whole, and had not held any meeting of judges since the date of Kissen's appointment.

JUN. 15. Legislation Committee: the Bill to increase judges' salaries. Gardiner had slipped in his proposal to appoint nine more judges, and by drawing attention to three other matters he diverted everyone from dealing with this new point, which was not mentioned. He is astute in the way he handles his colleagues so as to be sure of getting his own way. Underground to Hampstead: "Sundays and Cybele" at the Everyman cinema. Whoever directed this picture has a profound understanding of the mind of a child, and he is brilliantly supported by his child actress: wise, matter-of-fact, unsentimental, utterly real and completely captivating. It is a harrowing picture, for one knows from the start that the happiness with which it is so full is bound to end in disaster; and it is played with such faithfulness to life that the tension is almost unbearable. The final tragedy, through no conscious fault of anyone, is heartbreaking.

JUN. 16. A reception by the High Commissioner for Uganda, in the Colonial Institute. Ugandans are a particularly attractive shade of dusky black; and it was nice to see a lot of pretty black girls in tasteful, varied dresses.

JUN. 18. Melrose: the annual dinner of the Scottish Law Agents Society. I proposed the toast of the Society, and took the opportunity to make some fun of Clyde's press campaign — without mentioning his name.

JUN. 23. Clyde's campaign against Leechman had gone the length of a long centre-page article by a "special correspondent" in the *Times*. This talked about the "indignation which has inflamed Scottish lawyers of all categories". "Private representations to the Government have been brushed aside. . . 'I have never seen them so angry at the Bar as they are about this appointment', said an eminent judge". The appointment of the present Solicitor-General to the bench was "the last straw which may break the system". There was a sneering reference to James as having held the part-time post of Clerk of Justiciary, "an official who sits in Court for important criminal cases", and the writer remarked that if Mr Leechman were not Solicitor-General it was extremely improbable that he would be considered. I was sorry about this for James' sake, but from Clyde's point of view I thought he had perhaps gone rather far in allowing himself to be quoted so obviously. Gordon came in brandishing his *Times* and genuinely indignant about what he thought was a shocking article.

JUN. 25. A *Sunday Times* reporter came to see me, and discussed judicial appointments for nearly an hour. He had found it difficult to understand the *Times* article, which suggested to him that the information on which it was based had come from someone with a personal grudge against the Solicitor-General.

JUN. 28. A visit from Dalgetty and two St Andrews House colleagues to discuss the propriety of promoting a Regulation under the Food and Drugs Act defining what is meant by "whisky". The Scotch Whisky Association are perturbed by the sale in Japan of imitation whisky passed off as the genuine article. A pleasant surprise when I went down to look at the papers — finding in the *Glasgow Herald* a centre-page article, evidently by Watt, demolishing the case Clyde has put up in the other papers. He says it is surprising to hear it said to be among the judiciary that disquiet has arisen, when the majority of the present judges got on the Bench either because they had been in the Crown Office or because of political services. The substantial ground for disquiet was that "either Law Officer may be elevated direct to the chair of the Lord President or of the Lord Justice-Clerk . . . in effect placing himself in a position senior to Judges who have served on the Bench for many years, while he may have no judicial experience at all". Reporting that even before Lord Kilbrandon's appointment to the Law Commission it had been widely known in legal circles that James was the most probable candidate for the vacancy, the writer goes on to say that it is rather hard on Mr Leechman that the age-old issue should be canvassed again now as if it were a source of grievance arising for the first time. "The fact is that as regards both his academic attainments and his equipment to judge with impartiality, fairness, and complete integrity, Mr Leechman is ideally suited to the post. What is more, there is precedent, politics apart, for selecting a man who for years served as Clerk of Justiciary. Lord Walker, Mr Leechman's predecessor in that office, is recognised as one of our most eminent judges".

From the Editor of the Times:

Printing House Square, London, E.C.4 June 28, 1965
My dear Lord Advocate,
I am most obliged to you for your letter. The news report did not attempt to set out *The Times*'s own views on this matter. Were we to do this, it would be in the form of a leading article. If we have inadvertently been unfair to anyone, then we would naturally regret it. Our inquiries did show, however, that there was disquiet about the matter, and we thought it should be reported in the public interest.
Yours sincerely,
W. J. Haley

JUN. 30. Going out on the Terrace for a breath of fresh air, I encountered Norman Wylie. He said he was finding parliamentary life not too disappointing, though he thought there was very little publicity for the work that was done: surprising, since Norman always seems to get himself quite a lot of publicity. Report stage of the Rents Bill. Elwyn Jones was pleasant and affable, but I observed from the copy of the official brief that I had with me that all he was doing was reading out the words of the brief. Mabon was representing the Scottish Office — perky and enthusiastic as ever.
JUL. 1. Packed all the things I had at Richmond into my bag, and

left with mutual expressions of regret and appreciation of how well we had all got on together. The 10.20 flight had no first class; this meant that seats were not allotted. I settled for the one next to the best-looking girl travelling on the aircraft. Though an American, she was not forthcoming, but she was certainly pleasant to look at. To Holyrood for the royal garden party. Talking to Ian Dickson about Craigie Aitchison, I happened to remark that Craigie was the outstanding example of the stupidity of current criticisms of "political" appointments. Dickson at once launched into a violent condemnation of the *Times* article; he thought it shocking, and could not understand how the *Times* had printed it. He had been horrified to learn the source from which the article had come — a matter on which everyone seemed agreed — and said that feeling in the west of Scotland was very strong in regard to the malicious attack on the Solicitor-General. Dickson did not know him, but said everyone who did had been most indignant. This from a Tory like Dickson confirmed my view that Clyde had overreached himself.

JUL. 7. Abingdon Gardens: Lady Carlisle appeared at 8 with a breakfast trolley — wearing a dressing-gown, but as elegant as usual.

JUL. 8. A meeting of the Scottish ministers in Ross's room. Ross raised the question of the adverse publicity arising out of the appointment of the new judge. I said this was my fault, since I had foolishly accepted advice from my people that I ought to tell the Lord President, in confidence. I assured them that I should not do it again. Nobody seemed to be worrying. To 10 Downing Street for a tea party. George Brown joined us, and with his notorious tactlessness at once asked James when introduced to him whether he was the man that "the scurrilous articles" were about. I introduced Nancy to Alice Bacon, and remarked that I was glad to hear that she and Judith Hart had made it up after the Kilbrandon Report controversy — Judith told me this yesterday. Alice Bacon is in difficulties of her own over a Home Office paper on treatment of young offenders. She said she found that when her officials did not like what she was doing they went and told officials of some other Minister, who put him up to oppose it. I am sure this is right, and I have no doubt it happens in my own office. We went downstairs to the garden — secluded and not very large. Wilson came out soon after, and we had quite a long talk with him. He said that most of his good ideas — if ever he had anything he could call a good idea — he got at Chequers, in his bath, or more often when he was just getting into his bath, and then he thought about it in his bath and as soon as he got out rang for his secretary and had a note made. This was the origin of his idea for a Commonwealth mission on Vietnam. Nancy raised the subject of his cat, which he takes to Chequers for the weekend. He said he was once having a very secret meeting when the door of the Cabinet room slowly opened; but when they looked round only the cat came in.

JUL. 10. Watt says that the *Times* Scottish representative was on holiday at the relevant time, and the *Times* must have accepted distorted information as reliable because of the apparent eminence of its source. A Minute from the Home and Health Department on a proposal to improve the keeping quality of milk by allowing them to inject steam into it at high pressure and then extract the water — extracting of course also much of the flavour and nutritive value. I had protested strongly about this, and wrote a Minute to which the officials have replied. On this reply James has minuted: "L.A. no choice but to get own cow".

JUL. 13. Ewan Stewart came to tell me what Clyde was doing in regard to James Leechman's installation on Thursday. Clyde had decided that, in accordance with "tradition" that he had just invented, any Court taking a proof or trial would sit at 10 despite the installation, with the result that there would be a semi-boycott of the ceremony by judges and counsel. Ewan was in a criminal trial on Thursday before Cameron, who has intimated that his court will sit at 10, as also has Hunter. I did not think there was anything we could do about it; and in any event if there was a small attendance for James' installation Clyde's silly instruction would afford a good excuse for it. But I was surprised that Clyde had the support of Cameron and Hunter. McVicar, who is in Thursday's case, was very annoyed, and wanted the Dean to take the matter up. Ewan told me also that Bennett, who according to himself never attends installation ceremonies, had said he would certainly go to this one. James had gone down to see Clyde last week, on Lionel Gordon's advice, and told me that as usual Clyde was quite pleasant, to his face — no reference made to what had been going on behind the scenes.

JUL. 14. Sorry to find that a silly, completely erroneous answer that I gave to a question from Griffiths at Friday's meeting was down in the Minutes; I suppose a correction will have to be issued. Peter McNeill came to see me about a complaint he had been dealing with as Advocate-Depute, from a woman charged with indecent behaviour in a Glasgow close. Two policemen had seen her go into the close in what the senior of the policemen thought was a suspicious manner, and followed her in. She asked why they were looking at her, and some argument ensued. They advised her to go home, but she followed them out of the close and into a shop. As she refused to go away, they charged her with indecent behaviour. The younger one now admits that he saw nothing improper but merely said he did, to back up his colleague. It seems clear that the policeman simply became exasperated and made a charge which he then proceeded to embellish. McNeill had given an elaborate instruction about proceedings under the police discipline code; but having confirmed from Bowen that we had nothing to do with that I altered the instruction to "No Pro". At an earlier stage the complaint had gone to James Leechman, and I was surprised to find that he had given rather an odd instruction: that the P.F. should find out from the Chief Constable what the Chief Constable would do if a disciplinary charge was preferred. I should have thought the only answer he could get would be that the Chief Constable would have to see what the evidence was. It did not seem that anything had been done to follow out the instruction. We were grieved to hear that Adlai Stevenson had died this morning in Grosvenor Square while on a visit to London.

JUL. 15. James Leechman's installation: an excellent attendance of counsel and members of the public. Cameron and Hunter did not turn up, but apart from Grant, who is ill, all the other judges were on the bench, and shook hands with James — most of them with apparent cordiality. Just after 4 John Wheatley appeared, to say how distressed he had been at Clyde's foolery and presumption in claiming to speak for the other judges. I was not impressed by this: it had been open to him or any other judge to disclaim the views attributed to them, or at least to speak to Clyde about it. He did not seem to realise that in complaining to me about what a feeble lot the judges were he was including himself in the condemnation. I accepted his assurance in the spirit in which it appeared to be given, and motored him home.

JUL. 22. Ross was shocked by a reference to James Leechman by Noble, speaking from the back benches on the Judges Remuneration Bill in the early hours of the morning. Luckily the speech does not seem to have been reported except in Hansard, so that I do not suppose James will see it. When Nancy was speaking to him yesterday and remarked that it appeared from the attendance at his installation that he had a lot of lady friends, he replied that at any rate he seemed to have a lot of gentleman enemies.

JUL. 23. Home Affairs Committee: Fugitive Offenders Bill, which will make it possible to refuse to return Commonwealth nationals for trial in their own country if their offence has been political or if they are to be subject to the death penalty. I pointed out that the second condition led to the anomalous result that a man who had committed murder and escaped to this country would get off scot free, whereas if he had merely committed an assault he would be sent back to be tried. Soskice accepted at once that this was the result, but said we must accept anomalies if we were prepared to take our stand on moral principle. As usual, he went on and on, repeating points already set out fully in the papers. He has no sense of the passage of time.

JUL. 24. The family had gone to Patrick Ritchie's wedding, and on to the theatre, and arrived home about 11. "It's been a super day", Richard said; "the path up to the front door's all flooded". Richard and Elizabeth had been great social successes at the reception, and told how Charley Alexander had told Nancy he had seen her parking her car in Charlotte Square, and when she denied this had said he had been sure it was she, for there could not be two such beautiful women in Edinburgh.

JUL. 26. To Granton to join *Pharos*.

JUL. 27. Peterhead: cars there to take us to Rattray Head. The lighthouse stands on a concrete stump rising from some low rocks about ¼-mile out from the shore, and we had to wait until the tide went down and a tractor arrived from the shore station to take us through the shallow water — a bumpy journey. The tractor could not get right up to the concrete because of a ridge of rocks with water flowing over them; and each of us in turn was carried on the old tractor-driver's back and set down on the rock under the lighthouse. The door reached by a vertical climb of 20 horizontal iron bars set in the lighthouse wall.

JUL. 29. Kirkwall. Noticed in several shop windows a notice inviting the citizens to attend some woman's funeral, and in one window some bottles of whisky with a label on which the seller was described as "Wine merchant and ironmonger", Alastair Robertson was recalling an occasion in the war when he was stationed in Orkney and had flown in to one of the islands. There was an elaborate regulation whereby aircraft came in in two clockwise spirals, so as not to be mistaken for enemy aircraft, but Robertson had forgotten this and came straight in. On landing he was hurried off to the shelter, as an air-raid warning had just sounded; and then realised that it was his aeroplane that had given rise to the warning. At dinner we had Stanley Cursiter, the Queen's Limner, who painted the fine portrait of Craigie Aitchison that hangs in Parliament Hall. He said that as a boy he had come across Geikie's book on geology and had been fascinated by it and its subject; and from studying the structure of the land he had come to paint it. He thought a landscape painter should have a knowledge of geology just as a portrait painter studied anatomy — geology being the anatomy of landscape.

JUL. 30. Hellier Holm: a most attractive station on a grassy cliff above a rocky cove. When I was jumping down into the boat there was a splash and Emslie shouted "Your camera!" On looking over the side I saw the camera floating in the water between the boat and the pier. I was able to catch it and haul it aboard, where water

178

continued to drip out of it during the sail back to the ship. I hastily snapped two photos to complete the film, and having taken the film out handed the camera over for John to take to the Chief Engineer to be dried out. As Alastair remarked, it was fortunate that it was not an expensive camera, but simply an empty box with sufficient air space to keep it afloat.

JUL. 31. As I had expected, there was a great stack of stuff in the office, and with Mr Gordon back from holiday it was not easy to get on with it. He comes into the room and asking — absurdly — "Are you busy, Lord Advocate?" proceeds with a long dissertation on some trivial matter. I went through the files, dealing with those that could be disposed of without much consideration; and leaving the others till Monday left at midday for the Border Union Show at Kelso.

AUG. 3. A meeting in the Secretary of State's room to discuss the question of releasing prisoners serving a life sentence. Following the lead of the Home Office, the Scottish Office agreed earlier this year that before releasing any such prisoner we should consult the judge who presided at the trial. If he were not available, the Lord Justice-General would deal with it. The Justiciary Office were informed about three prisoners whom it was proposed to release within the next year. The judge in each case was Sorn, who has retired, and Clyde has taken this to mean that it falls to himself to give the adice. Taking the safe, easy course, without regard to the individual concerned, he has advised that none of them should be released — on the ground, as it seems, that it is never safe to release a murderer. This general advice, we were all agreed, the Secretary of State must disregard. I suggested that when next the matter arose it could be pointed out that the advice we wanted was that of the trial judge, even if he had retired. Ross agreed to the officials' proposal to the effect of releasing two of the men, but jibbed at the third, although the man has been in prison for 11 years and there is some doubt whether he was guilty. Knowing Ross, I realised it was useless to try to change his mind once it was made up, so I suggested that this case might be reconsidered at the end of the year. This was agreed. I proceeded to back him up against Hogarth, the Scottish Office representative present, on fluoridation. The officials want him to issue an extremely one-sided circular urging local authorities to fluoridate all their water supplies because experts think it would be better for people's teeth. Hogarth had to agree to withdraw the circular and produce a more judicious version.

AUG. 4. Home Affairs Committee: quite a violent argument between Soskice on the one hand and Mabon and me on the other. Soskice had this week produced a paper on long-sentence prisoners without any consultation with the Scottish Office and wanted it approved today — although we had had no chance to consult our officials about the many changes in procedure which he proposed. He urged that Scots and English law differed, and it would be absurd to hold up the English reform because the Scottish Office might disagree: a strange argument from the Home Office, which has so often wanted Scots proposals held up because they might "embarrass" the Home Secretary. When Houghton sided with us and asked him to take it away and have a talk with the Scottish Office he became distinctly annoyed. There was a meeting tomorrow, he said, and it must be set down for consideration then. He would explain to the Secretary for Scotland what he proposed, and it was essential that he get approval. Houghton was quite blunt with Soskice, telling him that was not the way to have business done; and whatever happens tomorrow I am hopeful that our set-to may have a useful effect for the future. An appointment with the Prime Minister: the subject of discussion the Solicitor-Generalship. As between Robertson and Wilson, I have a fairly open mind. Ross had seemed to favour Wilson, but when the Prime Minister asked which should be approached first I replied "Robertson", and Ross did not demur. The difficulty may be that neither Robertson nor Wilson will be prepared to take on such a precarious appointment — least of all Wilson, who would have to give up his position as Sheriff-Substitute.

AUG. 5. As I was not to be back in London for some time, I asked Lady Carlisle to send my pyjamas to the laundry. She said she had thought of washing them herself, but wondered if I would regard it as rather presumptuous. "Mummy's very good at washing", said Susan. Home in time for lunch. Surprised to find that apart from the exposures I completed in a hurry to finish the spool the film that was in the camera when it fell in the sea was quite all right, except that the colour was somewhat exaggerated. Phoned Harry Wilson, and told him the position about the vacancy. To my surprise, he was most enthusiastic, and without any hesitation said he would certainly take it if it were offered. In view of this, I had to do my best to discourage Ian Robertson; but he, though by no means so enthusiastic, said he would certainly like to consider it and have a talk with Ross.

AUG. 6. I had been telling Nancy about my visit to Downing Street, and mentioned that when waiting in the hall I had met the tall girl we had seen with Wilson at the party — Marcia Williams. Ross introduced me to her, and she said that though she had not met me she remembered me well as the man who came up to the Prime Minister and said, "I really must shake hands with you because I'm a member of your Government".

AUG. 7. Ellon Show. Nice to hear Aberdeenshire voices again: "Bein' on her ain, she's naebody to news to".

AUG. 8. Looking through the *Sunday Express* I observed with some dismay that Lord Carmont had died suddenly while on holiday in Kirkcudbrightshire. A godsend for the First Division, where at the age of 85 and in a state of senility Carmont has been wholly under the influence of Clyde, sleeping much of the time and rousing himself only to giggle with Clyde at some puerility and to say "I agree" when Clyde has given his opinion; but it means all the bother of filling another vacancy on the bench.

AUG. 9. Inverness. I was able to find Mr McBean and borrow a Parliament House Book. I wanted the book so as to go down the list of counsel and see if there was anyone I had overlooked as a likely Senator of the College of Justice; but I did not tell Mr McBean.

AUG. 31. The Nethy Bridge policeman was on holiday this week: a notice on his door, "In case of crime, contact policeman at Boat of Garten".

SEPT. 7. The report of Board of Trade investigators into the collapse of the Cadco group of companies, which brought near disaster to the New Town of Glenrothes and a loss of £500,000 to the Royal Bank of Scotland: a fantastic story of gullibility on the part of supposedly experienced financiers and business men. The moving spirit was Dennis Loraine, a scriptwriter living in Hove whose wife ran up a bill of over £100 with a local butcher, Mr Thomas. With the help of an obliging solicitor, Loraine persuaded Thomas to accept an unusual method of paying off this debt: by taking Loraine as a partner on terms that Thomas should devote 80 per cent of his time to the business, and Loraine such time as he thought fit. Loraine a few weeks later succeeded in getting another agreement out of Thomas whereby the partnership was dissolved, the business and its assets were transferred to Loraine, and Thomas was to be an employee but to be responsible for all pre-partnership debts. Loraine embarked on a publicity campaign, based on an alleged recipe for sausages said to have won the approval of King Edward VII when staying with the Sassoon family. A letter in which King Edward expressed the intention never to eat any other make of sausage has never been seen — Loraine later told Benita Hume, the film actress, that he had lost it out of an aeroplane. However, the Royal Victoria Sausage Co. was formed on the strength of this recipe, and Loraine succeeded in interesting a number of people in it, including Roe, an international finance lawyer in Lausanne. Through investment companies which he controlled, he provided capital for the company, and a factory was started at Partridge Green in Sussex. This succeeded in producing a quantity of sausages, though at considerable loss — no one concerned having any knowledge of the trade or business acumen. Among the people who became interested in it was George Sanders the film star, Benita Hume's husband, who with Loraine was instrumental in deciding to expand the Company's activities by taking over a big site at Glenrothes where there were to be factories, the biggest piggery in Britain, a supermarket and other activities. Cadco Building Co. was formed to convert two factories erected by Glenrothes Development Corporation and construct other buildings. The Sausage Co. had already lost all the money Roe had put into it, and he was unable to find any more; but they made an agreement for a loan from the Development Corporation and for fortnightly payments on the building work as it progressed; and to cover the gap till the first payments were due got a loan of £40,000 from the Royal Bank. With the help of the name of the Marquess of Linlithgow, who was enlisted as a director, and of a statement from Swiss banks that they were satisfied that neither Roe nor Sanders would embark on any project beyond their means, they got the bank to increase the loan to £100,000, and then by stages to four times that amount. The project had been launched at a press conference in Edinburgh, at which Lord Hughes presided and great play was made of this new industry which was to be brought to Fife. Application was made to the Board of Trade for a grant, but the civil servants proved more wary than industrialists and bankers, and despite great pressure the application was rejected on the ground that the project had no financial basis for success — not surprising, since Loraine besides being penurious had two convictions for fraud, one of them in respect of an incident in which a friend of his had posed as a clairvoyant and prophesied to an old lady that a handsome young man was soon to come into her life. The handsome young man was Loraine, who came into the lady's life and took some money off her. Owing to delay in furnishing the Board of Trade with information, the project was well under way by the time their decision was announced, and the bank had already advanced large sums. A lot of this, instead of being used by the Buildings Company, had been squandered on the sausage company and Loraine's personal expenses; and Loraine arranged for a lot of it to get by devious ways to Italy, where he was supposed to be negotiating with Italian government agencies for support in setting up a large-scale business of growing vegetables and was dabbling in the production of a film. Disaster was fended off through the help of Mrs Elliott, a successful business woman and director of a company called Air-Fix, who until she met Loraine was a person of considerable wealth and was persuaded to lend £240,000; but as bills mounted up, and no one was able to pay, a crash was inevitable. The building company was put into liquidation, and the project came to an end with premises half-built, debts of over £1,000,000, and no pig having been reared or sausage produced. As Roe is still in Switzerland and Loraine in America it may not be easy to deal with them.

SEPT. 9. I had asked Gordon to look out the papers in the case of the life prisoner convicted of murder in 1955 whom Ross has declined to release. The reason for commuting the death penalty having been a doubt as to guilt, I thought I had better read the evidence.

SEPT. 11. McLeod, the Edinburgh Procurator-Fiscal, came to see me about the Canadian bank robbers who were extradited from Scotland some weeks ago. An action has been raised against McLeod in the Sheriff Court by one of the men for recovery of £15,000 which the police got from a safe deposit in his name in a Scottish bank. The position is difficult, since this money is certainly not part of the proceeds of the robbery. The robbers got away with over a million dollars in banknotes of the Bank of Canada, but they were obsolete notes, each marked with two punch-holes. They set to work to repair the notes, but this proved laborious, and ultimately they got themselves flown to Great Britain and there arranged through a firm of solicitors that they would disclose to the Bank's insurance company where the money was hidden, in return for a reward of 60,000 dollars. The reward was paid to the solicitors, and the two men then disclosed the whereabouts of the stolen money, most of which was thus recovered. There is no doubt that the money held by McLeod consists of proceeds of the reward. The transaction was probably illegal under Canadian law, and the Bank and the insurance company have asked McLeod to retain the money. I have advised him to do so on condition that the Bank put in a claim for it and indemnify McLeod against all expenses of the action. If they will not do this, the money will have to be returned to the Scottish bank who had it on safe deposit, and the responsibility of deciding what to do with it will fall on them. No doubt they would have to return it to their criminal clients.

SEPT. 12. Migdale and James Leechman have been on circuit together in Glasgow. He said James had done very well — which conforms with a report I had from the Procurator-Fiscal.

SEPT. 14. Ian Robertson to see me — obviously worried by the worsening of the political situation as a consequence of the death of the Speaker, which if Dr King is appointed to succeed him will result in the Government's majority being reduced to 1. I had no difficulty in getting him to agree that it would not be fair to ask him to come in as Solicitor-General when the Government's position was so precarious. He had wondered if Carmont's death might affect the situation so far as he was concerned — he had seen his own name mentioned in the *Glasgow Herald* as a possible candidate for elevation to the bench. I told him that that was unlikely on this occasion, though it would be useful to have him available on the sidelines.

SEPT. 15. Phoned Harry Wilson, who confirmed that he was agreeable to being appointed Solicitor-General. A meeting with representatives of the Board of Trade and the Director of Public Prosecutions to discuss what was to be done about Cadco. Roe has been arrested in Switzerland on a charge of uttering counterfeit dollar notes and Loraine in America on the basis of a long statement by Roe implicating him in this affair. I do not see how we can have them extradited if they get prison sentences in other countries; and meanwhile there will no doubt be much public clamour for publication of the investigators' report — which in view of its forthright condemnation of Roe, Loraine and Sanders is hardly possible if any of them are to be prosecuted.

SEPT. 16. St James' Park. There was a hut selling refreshments, and I decided to have an open-air lunch: soup, salmon sandwich, and some cake. I fed some of the pigeons which clustered over me, perching on my arm and shoulder in the free-and-easy manner of the London pigeon, and while I was feeding a corner of cake to two of them on my hand I found to my dismay that others had landed on my table and gone off with the whole slice of cake. When I crossed Whitehall, the only traffic at hand was a little cart carrying fruit and vegetables, drawn by a grey horse trotting cheerily towards Westminster.

SEPT. 20. To Trinity to call on Ronnie King Murray and tell him about the Solicitor-Generalship. As he has probably the best claim from a political point of view, and his name has been mentioned in the papers, I thought he was entitled to hear about it from me instead of reading it in the papers. He took the news with his usual complete absence of rancour or complaint, saying he thought Harry Wilson was an excellent choice and he would be happy to work with him.

SEPT. 22. Home Affairs Committee: the Home Secretary's proposals for parole of long-term prisoners. He has come to terms with the Scottish Office, and proceedings today were very amicable. I asked him before the meeting if he had been able to get away at all during the holiday period, and he said he had " in a sense " — he had been going round visiting prisons.

SEPT. 24. Miss Howat phoned to ask whether I was free tomorrow, or at worst had an engagement that could be broken without publicity, as I was required to go to Balmoral for a " hush-

184

hush" meeting of the Privy Council. I had undertaken to open Northesk Church sale of work tomorrow, and thought the breaking of this engagement would not entail much publicity. Douglas Johnson accepted the task without hesitation. Miss Black thought I should have one of the Government cars to take me, but I decided I should prefer to go in my own car and take my own time. To the Roxburgh Hotel to lunch with two visiting Russians: the pro-rector of Moscow University, and the secretary of the British-Soviet Society. The pro-rector was a lanky man with a lock of dark hair and a twinkle in his eye. He asked about the noose used in Britain for hanging murderers, which he had been told was not at all tight, and wondered whether that was better or worse for the murderer. A shoulder of a buck arrived from Richmond Park: a formidable-looking piece of meat. It has to be hung up for a week before being used.

SEPT. 25. Deeside was looking unusually lovely: heather still out, and the woods and bracken turning to brown and gold, with the river surging down in spate. At the Castle I drove to the front door. A man in the dark green uniform of the Balmoral servants was waiting to show me in, and in the hall I encountered a fat, healthy-looking little boy in a kilt who said, " Where are you going? " I replied that I did not really know, but no doubt someone would tell me. At the end of the corridor I was met by an equerry, who took me to a kind of common room where all the newspapers were laid out. Gardiner and Lord Chalfont, the Minister of State for Foreign Affairs, had flown from London and were motoring across from Dyce. Sir Michael Adeane appeared, apologising for not having been there to receive me: they had always a lot of boxes on Saturday morning — the London people seemed to like to get things finished up on Friday. Monday, he said, was their best day at Balmoral — hardly anything came in. The party from Dyce arrived shortly after 12.30, and we assembled in the drawing-room, a pleasant, bright room with Landseer paintings all round the walls, including a terrible one of Queen Victoria in deep black sitting on a horse with John Brown holding the reins, and a big bay window looking out on the garden. The Council was held in a room next door. The business turned out to be an order suspending the constitution of Aden and thus allowing the Governor to arrest the local Prime Minister. The Queen, who seemed to know a lot about it, asked Chalfont about the reasons for the order, and Chalfont trotted out the hoary old excuses that have always been given for putting local patriots in prison on their way to national leadership. We all went through to the drawing-room for drinks. The Queen told us they had been seeing the Beatles' new film, "Help!" She thought it was not as good as "A Hard Day's Night",

185

but spoke highly of the Beatles, whom she regarded as the present-day equivalent of the Marx Brothers. Lunch was announced, and we trooped through with the Queen and without any ceremony sat down at a little table. It was an excellent lunch, simple and in reasonably small quantities — much better than most of those official meals after which one feels that one does not want anything to eat for a long time. The Queen chatted away in her usual friendly, vivacious manner, seriously or frivolously, on any topic that came up — always knowledgeable and sensible, and giving the impression that she was thoroughly enjoying the conversation. I mentioned my Russian visitors and their query about the noose for hanging; she enquired what was the method used to execute people in Russia. None of us knew — shooting was suggested as the likeliest method. There was some conversation about what happened when their air-craft had to land at some out-of-the-way place at 6 o'clock in the morning. Was she to stay in and ignore those who had come to see, or go out and run the risk of saying something bad-tempered that would antagonise them? She said she had tried to arrange before-hand that they would not come out, but it never worked — "all those people come and expect to see us". It was all right going to America, for nobody came to an airport like Gander — "and in any case they've all seen us before". When coffee was being served, Prince Andrew appeared, along with the baby, Prince Edward, who sat on the Queen's lap and was fed with her coffee out of a tea-spoon. Someone asked whether it was the sugar he liked or the coffee. "I hope it's the sugar, at his age", she said; but it looked as if it was the coffee. She asked Andrew to shake hands with the visitors. He shook hands with Gardiner and Chalfont before saying to me, "I've seen you before". I agreed that we had already met, and told him I was now in a position to answer his question. He seemed lively and uninhibited, and proceeded to climb on the table at the window and then to play round the legs of the sideboard with Edward, who fell once or twice but made no complaint. "Oh, well", said the Queen, "he hasn't very far to fall, you know — only if he falls on his nose or his face, he doesn't like that". She said Anne complained that she would never have been allowed to do what the boys did. "I know what you would have said to me", Anne had remarked, "if I'd done something like that". In fact Andrew seemed quite well behaved, though when we went through to the drawing-room after lunch he proceeded to take a big plastic ball which he had in a polythene bag and holding the bag swung it hard into the Lord Chancellor's stomach. "When he does that", the equerry remarked, "the answer is to kick him back — hard". Andrew offered us all a sweet, and then produced some tiddleywinks and settled down on the floor with

Chalfont for a game. There was a lovely log fire burning in the grate, and the Queen occupied herself with flinging logs on it from a hamper on the hearth. She said they had central heating in the Castle, and the only places they had a fire were that room and the nursery. She liked a fire in the nursery so that she could stand with her back to it. I remarked that we were threatened in Edinburgh with the end of our wood fires, when a smokeless zone was introduced; and she said that they had had the same difficulty at Buckingham Palace, where they had given up fires rather than burn smokeless fuel. It made things difficult for their garden rubbish. "We have such a lot of it there, and now we can't have bonfires". She said they saved it all up for 5th November, and had a really big bonfire. The conversation turned to ghosts, and she recalled one night at Holyrood when she had put the dog to bed in the bathroom — she never liked dogs in her room at night — and she had just gone to bed when she heard the dog scratch-scratching at the door; and when she opened it the dog's hackles were all standing on end. She was terrified. She illustrated this story with lively gestures which brought it all very much to life. She said there were some rooms at Holyrood where she never went in the dark; in the daylight it was different. She thought ghosts only came to places where there had been some kind of violence, and of course Holyrood was full of places like that. There were no ghosts at Balmoral — it was quite a different kind of house. Someone suggested there had been a ghost at Windsor, but she had not heard of that. I commented on Queen Victoria's dislike of Windsor, compared with Balmoral; but she said she liked Windsor. It was a great warren of a place rather than a house, but she and Margaret had been brought up there as children, and she always liked going there. Her father had disliked it. We had some discussion with Andrew about where we all came from. He would not believe that Chalfont came from London — he was sure he came from somewhere quite different. "Is that because of his clothes?" someone asked. "No", said Andrew — adding, when pressed, "It's because of his face". Chalfont is very dark complexioned, and I remarked that he had certainly not got his sun-tan in Wales, where he professed to come from. "He might have got it in Wales", said Andrew, thoughtfully. I asked him to guess where I came from, saying he had probably been there; but the Queen said he had never been in Edinburgh. Even Charles — who has gone back to school at Gordonstoun — had never been in Edinburgh till last year; he had always been at school at the time of the royal visits to Edinburgh. The London party had to leave about 2.30, and I left with them. Andrew came out to my car, waving goodbye as I drove off, after what I thought a most entertaining visit.

187

OCT. 1. The Leechmans came in the evening to share our venison, which Nancy had roasted and which turned out very nicely.

OCT. 4. A visit from Clyde about the vacancy on the bench. The usual practice is for the Lord President to notify the Lord Advocate that he needs another judge, but Clyde was obviously in a dilemma. He has always campaigned for more judges on the view that the Court of Session is undermanned in comparison with England, but on the other hand he would not want another judge to be chosen by me. So he did nothing; and Lionel Gordon, no doubt after consultation with Clyde, assured me that as the first move should lie with the Lord President it was not necessary for me to do anything either. However, knowing that if the Court got into difficulties I should be blamed by Clyde for not having had a judge appointed, I wrote him and asked his views. He sent a stalling reply, to the effect that he did not have the figures available. Realising however that it would be hopeless to try to put off the evil day, he came up today to say that they would need another judge. He undertook to write me to that effect. He canvassed the claims of the Dean of Faculty, saying he hoped I should give them a good judge this time. I replied that I had given him a good judge last time, and had never understood what all the fuss was about. His reply was that he had heard that the new judge had done very well on Circuit. I did not tell him what I thought of him and his campaign of denigration, as perhaps I should; and our conversation was amicable. Law came to see me about a proposal to introduce spot checks on motorists to see whether they had been drinking — the police stopping a motorist on the road and making him breathe into a tube in which there is something that will change colour if there is alcoholic content in the breath.

OCT. 5. Air services much disorganised through fog at London; but luckily the car meeting me was the Secretary of State's car with his driver Daphne, a persevering, indomitable young lady who had made three trips to London airport for the purpose of collecting me, and got me speedily to Deans Yard. A meeting with Ministry of Labour people — Ernest Thornton, the Parliamentary Secretary, with one of his Permanent Under-Secretaries, Mr Singleton, a representative of the Ministry's legal department, and a private secretary — to discuss my proposal to restore the old law of employers' liability for failure to provide safe plant, which the Ministry's legal department have been doing their utmost to shoot down and about which I had a dusty answer from the Minister, prompted no doubt by their advice. Thornton however turned out to be a very nice little man — an old trade unionist and textile worker — who was distinctly sympathetic to my proposal; and Singleton also seemed friendly. So despite efforts by the legal department's man to reintroduce some controversy we found ourselves in general agreement. The meeting ended with the only point in issue whether the Ministry or the Lord Chancellor should initiate the consultations with workers' and employers' organisations. I was pleased with this meeting, which I had at Dick Marsh's suggestion and which has demonstrated the value of personal contacts as against correspondence with Ministers. Charing Cross station full of youths and girls saying farewell to one another: every nook and corner had its young couple locked in a melancholy embrace.

OCT. 7. On my way to the Commons cafeteria I went through Westminster Abbey and stopped to look at a monument to Sir Richard Bingham, who "suppressed dangers rebellions and that with smale charges to Her Ma_{tie}". The inscription has an odd postscript: "This is done by S_r John Bingley Knight sometimes his servant".

OCT. 8. Dalgetty came to see me about a small problem arising out of a booklet on law for journalists by Watt of the *Glasgow Herald*. Watt had expressed the view that in the light of a ruling by Clyde about newspaper comments on pending criminal cases it would be dangerous for a newspaper to report that a particular prisoner had escaped, since escaping from prison was a crime and to report that someone had escaped might be held to prejudge his case if he came to be tried for that offence. This perturbed the Scottish Information Office, who are in the habit when a prisoner escapes of giving a hand-out to the press stating the name of the prisoner and details of his conviction and sentence. We took the view that Watt had probably overstressed the danger, but that in future hand-outs it might be prudent to confine the information to the name of the prisoner and his home address. I took the opportunity to enlist Dalgetty's help about an objection raised by the Ministry of National Insurance to an item in the draft programme of the Scottish Law Commission, who were proposing to examine, on a comparative basis and for fact-finding purposes only, the possibility of replacing the existing law of liability for negligence by compulsory insurance. I think the Ministry's real objection was to a more comprehensive proposal in the draft programme of the English commission, and we agreed that so far as our Commission was concerned the objection would probably be met by persuading Kilbrandon to leave out the reference to compulsory insurance, while still examining the whole question of liability for negligence. Gardiner has caved in and instructed his Commission to shelve the whole matter, but I should be sorry if we had to follow suit, on a subject in which law reform would probably be more in the public interest than any other.

OCT. 9. Coming along the new motorway at Whitburn I was

surprised to see what looked like a young couple walking along the motorway, with the man giving an indication that he wanted a lift. It was a young man and a girl, and he asked if I would take the girl to Edinburgh. They had been driving to Edinburgh to introduce the girl to his sister, and the car had broken down. He took a snapshot of himself from his pocket, wrote the sister's address on it, and bundled the girl in beside me. She seemed a nice girl, and must have been a brave one to set off on a long drive in pitch darkness with a complete stranger whom she could not even see, to visit someone she had never met. She said she had been a bit frightened at first. Her name was Margaret Doyle, and she was 18. Though she had lived all her life in Glasgow, she had never been to Edinburgh, and was delighted with the floodlit Castle. "It's just like what you read about in the history books". I thought I had better take her to her destination, so we made for East Thomas Street and climbed the stair at No 9, where on the first floor we found a door marked "Gunn" and knocked. The door remained closed while someone inside enquired who it was; but when we replied the door was opened, and a woman and some young people poured out. We explained who we were and Margaret displayed the snapshot. "And he wants my man to go out and pick him up — well, he can't. But you'd better come in". So Margaret went in, and I, having explained where the breakdown was to be found, came away.

OCT. 11. Home Affairs Committee. The Scottish Office were proposing a Bill to bring the law of burial grounds up to date. When this came up, Willis asked me to present the case for it. It looked as if Willis' journey to attend today's Committee was not really necessary: he came south for that purpose, and is going back to Edinburgh tonight. Soskice presented his paper on amendments in English law relating to criminal appeals. I was dubious about one of Soskice's proposals: that a convicted prisoner should be given the right to apply to the Court at any time for a re-hearing on the ground that fresh evidence had been discovered. I think it is asking too much of human nature to put such a right in the hands of a convicted criminal and not expect him to use it; and the more experienced the criminal the readier they will be to find "fresh" evidence — they always do, generally evidence supposed to reflect in some way on the credibility of some Crown witness who may have played a minor part at the trial. I do not know how the courts will be expected to set about re-assessing credibility on the basis of "fresh" evidence — it certainly looks as if they will be kept busy. In Westminster Abbey I made a brief halt to continue my examination of the monuments: the sad story of "William Wragge Esqr of South Carolina" who when the American colonies revolted "maintain'd his loyalty to the person and government of his sovereign and was therefore compell'd to leave his district family and ample fortune. On his passage to England by the way of Amsterdam he was unfortunately shipwreck'd and drowned on the coast of Holland". A visit from Colonel Hogan, who is in charge of the legal services of American forces in this country, to discuss a case that has arisen at Dunoon, where a US officer driving a car came over the brow of a hill at a fast speed and was confronted by a lorry coming up on its own side and a woman pushing a pram on the other. He was going too fast to stop or control the car, crashed into the pram and threw it into a field, killing a baby in the pram and taking one of the mother's legs off. I proposed that he be tried in Dunoon Sheriff Court on a charge of causing death by reckless driving. The Americans claim that the offence arose in the course of his duty as member of a visiting force, and by the Visiting Forces Act such an offence cannot be tried by a United Kingdom court. At the time of the accident the driver was proceeding home to Dunoon from his work at the American depot at Holy Loch, and the Americans say that according to their rules a man going to or from service by direct route from his home is regarded as being on duty. This they say has been accepted by all the NATO countries, including England. The first letter they wrote was a snooty one, merely saying that the man was on duty and I was not to interfere; but on my replying that I proposed to have the case tried in the Sheriff Court, and the accused could enter a plea of " No jurisdiction" if he liked, they became much more amenable and wrote a reasonable letter arguing that servicemen had to be given accommodation away from base but had to be ready for duty at any time and hence were regarded as being on duty from the time they left home until their return. I explained today the importance of having justice seen to be done, in the interests of good relations with the local population, and asked for an assurance that the man would be dealt with by the American authorities. Americans as individuals always seem pleasant, and my visitors today were no exception. We had an interesting discussion, and I agreed to hold my hand until they let me know what they would do about the case if I conceded jurisdiction. One of them was doubtful, saying they had always in these cases had the jurisdiction point decided first; but when I pointed out that the alternative would be to have it decided in Dunoon Sheriff Court he came round to his colleagues' point of view.

OCT. 12. Legislation Committee. On a Bill dealing with pensions, I was foolish enough to interrupt MacDermot in correction of something he was saying in explanation of the Bill. I ought to have known better than to suppose MacDermot would make a mistake in such a matter. He was right and I was wrong, and he shot me down without any compunction.

OCT. 15. Spoke to the Dean of Faculty, who had no hesitation in accepting the offer of the vacant seat on the bench. A television report of the Conservative conference, with Sir Alec in great form. Now that he is out of office, he seems happy and relaxed, remarking on what a nonsense this business of an "image" was. "I can put on my spectacles now without somebody telling me I'll lose the next election".

OCT. 16. Lionel Gordon showed me a proposal from the English Law Commission for repeal of some ancient criminal statutes: an Act against eavesdropping or being a common barrator or a common scold or a common night walker. It might not be a bad idea to revive the Act rather than repeal it.

OCT. 19. Glasgow University Union: a students' meeting in support of the candidature of Lord Caradon in the Rectorial election. A raving mob filled the hall, showers of paper darts were pouring in on the platform, and when we sat down we discovered that a pool of water had been left on the chair of each member of the platform party. I felt the dampness at once, and was able to move forward to the edge of the chair without giving any indication that I had got wet. The noise was continuous. I succeeded in getting it across that if they gave me a hearing I would try to answer questions; and eventually said I should be better than my word, and try to answer questions even though they had not given me a hearing. But most of the questions were inaudible in the uproar. Arthur Woodburn had remarked to me on Sunday that in dealing with questions I was obviously a disciple of Willie Graham, who had always adopted an attitude of sweet reasonableness towards hostile questioners, saying he quite sympathised with the questioner, explaining what it was that the questioner really wanted, and then going into the pros and cons. No opportunity today for practising such a line; I thought it all rather silly, but not having anything special to say did not feel bad tempered about it.

OCT. 21. Cabinet meeting — the topic for which I was in attendance drink and driving. Nobody spoke at much length, and most of what was said was reasonable and to the point. Frank Cousins was the only one whose remarks seemed doubtfully relevant. He was opposed to police checks, but the effective opposition was led by Crossman. I was impressed by Wilson's handling of his colleagues. He let everyone have his say, but never allowed the discussion to get out of hand, and accomplished the remarkable feat of cutting off Soskice in mid-flight by telling him that he had explained it all very lucidly and everyone now understood. It was obvious that Wilson did not like the proposals much, and he tried to steer the decision in the direction suggested by Short, starting off with more modest powers of enforcement with spot checks to follow in a year or two. But as soon as it was obvious that this was not going to work he switched to a different tack and got general agreement for random checks, with the right of jury trial in England for those charged with the new offence. At the end he suggested that the Legislation Committee might consider leaving it to a free vote of the House — which would make the proposals more acceptable. Next to Wilson, I was impressed by George Brown, who made a thoughtful, fairminded little intervention. A meeting with the Lord Chancellor to discuss arrangements for coordinating information about pending reforms of the law. Thinking this would be a good chance of introducing our Solicitor-General to him I had told Miss Howat to let the Chancellor's department know that I was bringing him. Harry made a useful contribution at the end, when Gardiner raised the question of whether it was desirable to do away with the dock in criminal courts. From his experiences as a sheriff, Harry was able to explain the dangers from the police point of view. He was obviously enjoying himself in London, and remarked as we were going back across Parliament Square on how interesting it was to have one's work centred all round about there.

NOV. 3. In consequence of a disaster last week to one of the Edinburgh-London Viscounts, which crashed in flames at London airport on a foggy night, with the loss of its complete complement of passengers and crew, Nancy had urged me to come home by train. This was illogical: the Viscounts have a good safety record, and presumably all the more care will be taken as the result of such an accident. We had an excellent flight today.

NOV. 8. Earls Court: my unsuccessful efforts to get a milk machine to work aroused the attention of a gang of youths, who watched me putting a succession of sixpences into the machine and getting them all returned. I should have concluded that the machine must be empty, but they were not so easily deceived, and by shaking and banging the machine succeeded eventually in extracting a carton of milk.

NOV. 9. An appointment with William Hannan, MP for one of the Glasgow divisions, about a case at the last Glasgow Circuit in which four men were charged with the murder of one of his constituents. There was no evidence as to which of the four had a knife, and as the evidence came out it did not establish anything against any of the four in particular except pushing and jostling. The four QCs who were appearing on Legal Aid for the defence succeeded in browbeating Peter McNeill into accepting a plea to this modified form of assault, and Strachan sentenced each of them to 3 months imprisonment: received by the accused with laughter and derision. I cannot see why Strachan did not give them at least 12 months: they had criminal records, and had been concerned in an affray in somebody else's house which had resulted in a man's death. The relatives of the dead man, egged on by the *Daily Express*, were scandalised by the result, particularly as some of them had given evidence at considerable risk to their own safety from the accused men and their friends. I had written a conciliatory letter to Hannan, in which I explained the position about the Advocate-Depute's discretion and said that on the evidence he had exercised it properly. Hannan accepted this, but wanted to know how far he could make the explanation public. I saw no objection, and we had a friendly chat. He seems a sensible man.

NOV. 10. A meeting on the question of enforcement of an incomes policy. There is a voluntary arrangement with employers and trade unions whereby wage claims or settlements are notified to the Government, and if the Government refers any of them to the Prices and Incomes Board there is a standstill for a few weeks to allow the Board to pronounce on it. Brown wants this procedure to be made compulsory, and penalties imposed on employers who breach the standstill. The effect in law would be to make it a civil wrong for trade unions or their members to seek to induce employers to breach the standstill, and they would also — in England at least — be liable to a criminal charge of conspiracy. The consequences would be extremely serious for unions, their funds and their members; and Elwyn Jones had proposed that, instead of the unlimited liability of the common law, employees who tried to induce a breach should be liable to a fine or imprisonment for 6 months on conviction for a new offence. I felt that Elwyn's proposal was politically impossible, for what the unions would see was a Labour Government legislating to the effect of making it a crime, punishable by 3 months imprisonment, for men to go on strike. I thought too that there would be difficulties in defining the crime and in enforcement. Not wanting to be merely negative, I tried to think of some alternative, and wrote a brief note suggesting as a possibility that on receipt of information that there had been a payment in breach of a standstill the Minister should be entitled to go to the Court and get an immediate interim order setting aside the award or agreement on which the payment had proceeded. Only then would it be illegal to continue to make the increased payment, and except in that case unions and men would be free to agitate for increases without running any risk under the conspiracy laws. The officials, according to their custom, were concerned mainly in finding flaws.

They had not much difficulty in finding flaws in my plan, but though my idea was shot down in the end nobody produced any workable alternative. I found it all very interesting, and was gratified to find I had as good a grasp of it, to all appearances, as the specialists with whom I was arguing.

NOV. 11. Haddow to see me about a proposal to include Cameron's name in the New Year Honours list. The proposal had been that he get a KBE, but someone had suggested it would be better to make him a Privy Councillor. Haddow wondered whether I thought it might lead to trouble with other judges. This was not a matter on which I could express any opinion, though I said I saw no reason myself why they should not make him a Privy Councillor if they wanted. McNeill had been successful in getting a conviction in a murder case in which I had instructed proceedings, though the evidence was so thin that Gordon and Bowen had agreed with the Advocate-Depute that there ought to be no proceedings: particularly satisfactory since the accused was one of the four who got away with the assault plea in McNeill's other case. The murder of which he has been convicted followed a visit by the murdered man to a night club on the south side of Glasgow which has become notorious for such happenings. Nicholas Fairbairn, who had been defending, had remarked that there were two kinds of members: life members and death members.

NOV. 16. Ross McLean died suddenly during the week-end. I lunched with him on Thursday, when he spoke cheerfully of having been at a dinner in Dublin on Tuesday and at the Faculty dinner to the Queen Mother on Wednesday, while on Thursday he was to attend the dinner of the Merchant Company. I had been feeling thankful that I had declined invitations to both the latter events, but he was delighted to be participating in all these festivities. Never standing on his dignity, he was at home in any company. He particularly liked the company of pretty girls, but he could be equally charming to anyone. Despite his reputation as something of an enfant terrible, he was fundamentally a responsible person, with a serious view of life along with his capacity to enjoy it to the full. I shall miss him quite a lot.

NOV. 18. St Giles': memorial service to Ross McLean. The address was given by Kilbrandon, in a chatty, matter-of-fact, almost jovial manner, a pleasant change from the sanctimonious stuff one usually gets. The complete absence of humbug was most appropriate to a service in memory of Ross McLean. Phoned Sinclair Shaw to offer him the vacant Sheriffdom, a full-time pensionable office. He accepted with alacrity.

NOV. 23. A debate on Commonwealth immigration. The best

speech came from Mrs Shirley Williams, who put the problem in perspective by reference to what happened in other European countries. Another excellent speech from Roy Hattersley, one of the new Labour members for Birmingham. Dr Shirley Summerskill, giving a kind of lecture on health checks for immigrants, suddenly and in an equally deadpan manner introduced a comment on Powell's advocacy of repatriation of unassimilable immigrants, remarking that some considered that Powell himself was unassimilable.

Nov. 27. Gordon told a story about Lord Strathclyde, who when a member of the Government was observed having a drink at the bar at 11 am. Someone expressed surprised at seeing him drinking at such an early hour, to which he replied that he had just been having an hour with permanent officials.

Dec. 2. Law Reform (Miscellaneous Provisions) Bill in the House of Lords. Guest attacked a Clause allowing a trust to be set up wherein income will be accumulated for 20 years from the date of the settlement, as imposing restrictions on accumulation. This seemed to me rather odd. Guest however said he had information that "the judges of the Court of Session" did not approve of the alteration, so presumably Clyde has got on to him. He asked for the Clause to be dropped until somebody like the Law Commission had had a chance to consider it. The debate was listened to by a surprisingly large number of peers: a far better attendance than there would have been for a similar debate in the Commons. I had a look at some authorities, finding to my surprise that there was something in what Guest had said. Moran, who had been responsible for this Clause, explained that he had taken the Law Society with him. Their representative had seen the Clause, and had not suggested any objection.

Dec. 3. Home Affairs Committee; a proposal by Soskice to have an enquiry by a departmental committee into censorship of stage plays. Ross had put in a puritanical paper arguing that this was a bad time to set up such a committee, since it would mean that we should have to consider also censorship of the BBC, some of whose recent productions had aroused a lot of public indignation in Scotland. Judith Hart and I spoke in favour of the paper's conclusion, but from the opposite standpoint: that a committee might well recommend a much stricter censorship. I cited the well-known precept for cross-examiners — never to ask a question unless you had a good idea of what the answer was going to be. I suggested that the same might apply to appointing a committee of enquiry. Douglas Houghton took up this point right away, with great gusto, asking Soskice what was his motive in wanting a committee, and what recommendation he expected to get. He did not answer this, but rambled away in his usual longwinded manner. Wedgwood Benn came nearest to answering the question, saying that what he thought we should aim at was something like the present film censorship, with A and U certificates for plays. The Committee decided that a debate should be arranged in the Lords in January, and nothing else done meantime. Next came a paper by Griffiths, who wanted the Welsh language to have equal validity with English in things like Post Office forms issued in Wales. Though not quite as longwinded as Soskice, Griffiths is even woollier and more irrelevant. Bowden wanted to know whether it meant that anybody could go into a post office in Wales and demand a postal order printed in Welsh. Griffiths, though denying it, was vague as to what it did mean. Despite a plea for precision from MacDermot, the Committee gave its approval in principle. The Lord Chancellor then spoke to a paper recommending a short course of training for Justices of the Peace. In England, as I saw with surprise in Gardiner's paper, over 90 per cent of criminal charges came before Justices. When everyone interested had spoken, I intervened to say that as we from Scotland sometimes caused a bit of trouble in matters of this kind it was right that I should say that we welcomed this attempt by England to bring their standard of justice a little nearer what prevailed in Scotland. This little joke was well received.

DEC. 4. Left a note in Ian Fraser's court asking him to come and see me. He had read some report of Guest's speech about accumulations, and was dismayed when I told him I was thinking of dropping the Clause in view of Guest's statement that the judges were against it. He had heard nothing of any opposition, and it was obvious to him as to me that this was just nonsense that Guest had got from Clyde. He undertook to phone Guest and urge him to drop his opposition.

DEC. 13. The technicalities of drafting parliamentary bills are generally beyond me, so that today I was pleased with myself for spotting a weak point in a highly technical Bill dealing with housing subsidies. A paragraph in one of the clauses did not seem to me to make sense; and Mitchell, after undertaking to look into the meaning of the paragraph, came back to say that it had been agreed to delete it altogether. I had to interview Gibson about a query that had been put to him: whether a female was entitled to be included in the roll of Baronets. I saw no reason why she should not, though it was a matter of indifference to me.

DEC. 14. A meeting with Brewis, MP for Galloway, who has a complaint against Sheriff Peter Thomson that he ought not to be taking an active part in the Scottish Plebiscite Society, a society

197

organised to run a plebiscite in various localities in Scotland on whether we should have Home Rule. Basically it is no doubt Scottish Nationalist, but it makes a show of impartiality, professing to recruit members opposed to Home Rule as well as people in favour of it, and I did not agree that Thomson's activities were political. Anyhow he has been carrying them on for years without objection. Brewis admitted that he was raising the matter at the prompting of Wendy Wood, who is interested in one of the numerous Scots Nationalist bodies antagonistic to Thomson's. There are two societies claiming to be the genuine Plebiscite Society, and from time to time there is acrimonious correspondence in newspapers between Thomson and one Colonel Gayre of Gayre and Nigg who runs the rival society. To the House to hear a debate on Orders removing the Governors of the Reserve Bank of Rhodesia. The Opposition were concerned to find out whether the Government accepted liability for paying interest on Rhodesian stock, which the Smith Government were unable to pay because they had no longer any control over Government assets in the bank. This question the Government spokesman, John Diamond, set himself resolutely not to answer. He did not decline to answer it, in so many words, and gave way repeatedly to Tory interrupters, but none of them succeeded in framing the right question. One, for instance, when Diamond explained that like any other bank the Reserve Bank of Rhodesia could act only as an agent, asked for whom the bank was acting as agent. "For its customers, of course", replied the innocent Mr Diamond, adding that he had not expected that it would fall to him to explain to Members opposite the elementary principles of banking. "But surely", said the questioner, "the position of a Reserve Bank is different". "Yes, of course", said Mr Diamond, "it has different customers". Nobody managed to put the critical question: whether, on the British Government assuming responsibility for the government of Rhodesia, it had put itself in the position of the customer and so was responsible for failing to give instructions for payment.

DEC. 17. Sinclair Shaw told me he had just been dealing with a public-spirited citizen and had thought it right to commend his action not only on his own behalf but on behalf of the Lord Advocate. I was beginning to be perturbed at what he might have committed me to, when he went on to explain that the man had pled guilty to breaking into Conservative party headquarters and stealing £50. I am told that his appointment had caused indignation among the Sheriffs but this had been completely dissipated since he had been there. He was getting on well with everybody, and pleased the Fiscals by listening to evidence without interruption and giving appropriate sentences. He seems to be enjoying himself.

DEC. 20. Ewan Stewart to see me about a 2-page article in last Thursday's *Daily Express*. The general tenor is that instead of being limited to five advocates, not all expert in criminal law, the prosecution should be free to draw, like the defence, from the whole range of counsel and solicitors. The article states that I was asked to comment, but chose to decline. "But there is reason to believe that, far from being complacent, he is deeply concerned at failure to convict to the full extent of the indictment. Nor, we believe, is the Lord Advocate under any illusion about the anxiety that exists in the police force in face of repeated discouragement". Ewan had taken all this as a reflection on his forensic skill, and with the agreement of his solicitors was preparing to get them to write the *Express* demanding an apology. I had not seen the article; but after reading it I was convinced that he was talking nonsense. However unpleasant, I am sure it is not slanderous; nor is it any worse than what public men have to put up with from the press throughout their careers. Harry Wilson told me he had had Sinclair Shaw in to see him. Nancy Wheatley had been at his installation, and had expressed the hope that he would not find the work too heavy — in reply to which he told her that he was installing a computer so that they could feed the evidence into it and get the right answer. To her remark that she hoped the computer would make provision for appeals to the Inner House of the Court of Session, he replied, " Oh, no. It's a scientific instrument, not a gambling machine".

DEC. 23. Some conversation in the office about Heath's failure to keep his party together on the Rhodesia issue. Harry Wilson remarked that he had heard they were grooming Sir Alec for the leadership. A shocking letter from Gardiner suggesting that we do nothing more about my proposal to legislate on the *Davie* case. I had written telling him that I had cleared the Ministry of Labour's points and sent him a draft of a paper to be put up to the Home Affairs Committee. Moran warned me that he had heard Gardiner's officials were again trying to get at him to turn the proposal down; but it is pitiful that at this late stage he should again give way to them so readily.

1966

1966. Seizing the opportunity afforded by a favourable showing in the Public Opinion polls, the Prime Minister went to the country in early Spring; and a General Election confirmed the Labour Government in office with a greatly increased majority. Ministers, including myself, could thus look forward to a reasonably secure tenure for some years ahead. As Lord Advocate, I was not confronted with any serious problems, and spent a pleasant and relatively indolent year. With the heat taken out of party politics, the Government seemed to have a first-class opportunity to look and plan ahead, and work out the principles by which a socialist Government would want to be guided. But this they failed to do; no consistent principle or policy emerged. The position of the pound as an international reserve currency made it vulnerable to foreign financial influence, and our policy was subordinated to the unsatisfactory and fundamentally irrelevant aim of reassuring our foreign creditors. Machinery was hastily devised for freezing wages and prices. Obviously there is a great deal to be said for having such machinery: it would be a remedy for creeping inflation, and social justice would be better served by a national incomes policy than by a system depending on the relative strength of big trade unions and the militancy of their members. But the success of any policy of wage restraint must depend on keeping prices steady also, and the taxation measures introduced by the Chancellor of the Exchequer had the opposite effect. The sudden reversal of Government policy from expansion to restriction did not seem to have greatly affected its standing with the electorate, but it was a bitter disappointment to Labour supporters who had looked for a more imaginative and drastic way of dealing with a highly artificial crisis – which had little to do with the real problems of production, distribution and exchange. On Vietnam, the Government gave the appearance more and more of being committed to support the United States, whose bombing aeroplanes continued for no intelligible purpose to lavish on that unhappy country an increasingly powerful but futile demonstration of the American way of death. I myself did not succeed in finding a seat in Parliament. With some misgivings, I allowed my name to go forward to the Modlothian selection conference – some prominent Labour men in the constituency, including Mr Methven, the county convener, had asked me to stand. Throughout my life I had done things for the most part because I wanted to do them, and had not sought to delude myself or anyone else with the idea that I was actuated by any sense of duty; but I think that in accepting Mr Methven's invitation I did

*so more from duty than from inclination, and in the end I was
thankful that it did not come off.*

JAN. 13. Norman Wylie to see me about a circular issued by the
Scottish Information Office which professes to record "a new
ruling" by me restricting information to be given to the press on
escaped prisoners. They consulted me about this some time ago,
when I advised that they would be safe to tell the press the name and
home town of an escaped prisoner, the date and place of conviction,
and the length of sentence. This was for their own information; I
had no idea that they were going to issue a circular to newspaper
editors, and had never been shown a draft or even a copy. As any
sensible person should have realised, the circular has been denounced
as an infringement of the rights of the press: a ruling that, as the
Scotsman puts it, only "carefully edited facts" on escapers will be
published — whereas of course newspapers are at liberty so far as I
am concerned to publish anything they like. All I was interested in
was the extent to which the Information Office could safely assist
them. Norman thought the decision was wrong, and I offered no
objection to his writing to the newspapers on the subject.

JAN. 14. Wylie had a long letter in this morning's *Scotsman*, and
Dalgetty came to see me about it, with his assistant, Hogarth, and
Ballantyne, the head of the Information department. They were all
very penitent, and promised not to mention me in any more circulars
without my express approval. A *Daily Mail* reporter managed to
evade Gordon's vigilance and got himself shown into my room. I
explained the position, and later he phoned me and read back quite a
fair resumé of what I had said. The *Daily Express* phoned in the
evening, and I told my caller pretty much what I had told the man
from the *Mail*. Early to bed; and at 11 was awakened by a telephone
call from a man who said he was a reporter on the *Daily Record* and
had been told by his editor to find out whether I had said what was
ascribed to me in the early edition of the *Daily Express*. I told him I
was certainly not going to be rung up at my house at that hour of the
night. He rang off hastily, without pursuing his enquiries.

JAN. 16. We all motored to church, where Dr Mowat preached
on James 4,14. Any time I turned my attention from reading
Genesis, he seemed to be booming away melodramatically on some
aspect of the weather. Johnson rang up asking if he could come and
see me at 3.30. The first to arrive turned out to be Dalgetty, followed
by Hogarth, Johnson and Ballantyne, and finally Haddow. I brought
all my visitors into the drawing-room, where there was a nice fire,
with the cat and dog lying on the rug by the fireside. All that this

imposing deputation required was to be advised what they should do in response to Wylie's letter. My advice was that they should do nothing. Some discussion about the Secretary of State's programme for the week: Haddow and the others thought that Ross attempted to do far too much — the amount of work put in by his predecessors bore no relation to what he tried to do.

JAN. 17. To Dundas Street to look out Lord Rosebery's letters to my father: an exhibition relating to Cramond is being organised locally.

From Lord Rosebery to Rev. G. Gordon Stott,

Dalmeny House, Edinburgh. Dec 3, 1911
My Dear Mr Stott,
I am honoured by your invitation. But, though I hope to be present at the opening service, I am afraid I cannot accept it. I have reached the age of 64 without ever having done this and am too old to begin! Moreover I am not worthy. For a layman to take such a position implies a certain superiority which I certainly cannot claim Believe me Sincerely.

Rosebery, Gorebridge, Midlothian. Jan 1 1917
My Dear Mr Stott,
It has suddenly occurred to me that I received a kind letter from you with regard to my acquisition of Craigie Hall, with a simultaneous doubt as to whether I have answered it. Anyhow the doubt enables me to send you and Mrs Stott my best wishes for the year that broods over us. I must explain that since my secretary was taken from me, at a time when it is vain to seek for another, my correspondence has been in a state of chaos. I ought to apologise for such an act of madness as the purchase of land at this time. But there were many reasons, too long to set forth.
I hear you are lecturing at St Andrews during the week, which I suspect you love, and on Hebrew too, a pleasure I can never enjoy. But I came across your name in Dummelow's Commentary, an excellent work I ignorantly think.
Believe me Sincerely

JAN. 18. A meeting of a committee of ministers dealing with amendment of the law on abortion, the subject of a private member's Bill at present before the House of Lords. A tremendous improvement through the absence of Soskice following his demotion to Lord Privy Seal. Instead of his rambling dissertations, we had short, business-like observations from the new Home Secretary, Roy Jenkins. He sat beside Kenneth Robinson, and it was obvious that the two knew exactly what they wanted and were able to expound their views in the fewest possible words. The committee accepted my proposition that we should not make any decision on the principle but consider what would be practicable to carry into effect any decision on principle which the House of Lords might adopt. This shortened the discussion. Gardiner asked if I was coming to a meeting in his room about committal proceedings. I had never heard of the meeting, but he said he thought it would be helpful if I came, and gave me a lift in his car to the House of Lords. Preliminary hearings held in England before people are committed for trial involve immense newspaper publicity in sensational cases, and leave one with the impression that it must be impossible to ensure an unprejudiced hearing for the accused when their cases come to trial. I said to Gardiner I had not been thinking about this at all, and would come simply as an interested observer; but in the event I had to explain in some detail what the Scottish procedure was and how I thought it would be difficult to apply in England where there is no machinery for centralised control or for independent enquiry by Procurators-Fiscal.

JAN. 20. Committee on the Prices and Incomes Bill — George Brown's committee. He arrived five minutes late, contrary to the usual practice at these Cabinet committees, which always start on the dot; but his chairmanship of the meeting was exemplary: business-like, good-humoured and sensible, allowing everyone his say and wasting no time. This committee includes argumentative characters like Jay and Cousins. I did not hesitate to intervene, in preference to Elwyn Jones, who admitted he had not studied the papers. I had some lively interchanges with Brown, and quite enjoyed myself.

JAN. 25. Legislation Committee: Road Safety Bill. I launched an attack on a ludicrous clause setting out in great detail the machinery by which it was proposed to get specimens at a police station from which the alcohol content in the blood stream might be ascertained. I pointed out the impracticability of proving that all the procedure had been carried out, and the many opportunities that all this rigmarole would afford an ingenious defence counsel for having the prosecution laughed out of court. Barbara said the clause was designed to ensure that the most reliable specimen was obtained; presentationally it was most important that this should be in the Bill. I replied that whatever the argument regarding the presentational aspect of the clause — and even in the House it seemed to me they would have to expect some fun and games about it — I was concerned with presentation in court, which in many cases would be made ridiculous. I was glad to observe that my reference to what might be expected to happen in the House gave rise to a general murmur of assent; but at that point Bowden announced that the meeting would have to adjourn, to meet again at 4.45. Walked back down Whitehall with Reid, Mitchell and the Attorney-General's assistant legal secretary, to whom I held forth on the consequences of the clause — much to the amusement of my department members, who are in agreement with me on this. When I got back to Deans Yard, Miss Howat told me I was wanted at the Scottish Office to sit in at a meeting Hughes was having with Lord Drumalbyn, to discuss another amendment Lord Inglewood has put down to the Miscellaneous Provisions Bill, whereby the Sheriff is empowered to refuse a marriage licence to young applicants not domiciled in Scotland if he thinks their primary object in coming there is to evade the marriage laws of their own country. The amendment is open to every conceivable objection. Hardly any of the runaway Gretna marriages with which he is concerned are on licence by the Sheriff: only 8 out of 500 per annum. Then it seems obvious that the primary object for which the young people come to Gretna is to get married, the evasion of their country's laws being incidental. In any event the Sheriff could not know the marriage laws of all the countries these young people come from, nor could he decide a difficult question like domicile off the cuff on every application for a licence. I had already taken a strong line on this amendment, urging that it would be monstrous to upset our own marriage arrangements for the sake of bolstering the antiquated English law of parental consent; and this morning Hughes had no difficulty in getting Drumalbyn to agree that the amendment should be resisted. Drumalbyn, the former Neil Macpherson, is now front-bench spokesman for the Scottish Conservative peers, and Hughes with his usual caution had asked him along so as to make sure beforehand that there would be no trouble with the Opposition on the committee stage of the Bill. In the afternoon to the Home Office for a meeting with Jenkins. Barbara Castle did not attend, but her Parliamentary Secretary, John Morris, was there, and a formidable array of officials. The officials argued strongly in favour of their clause, saying that it embodied the procedure at present followed by the police in England. But Jenkins, who had grasped the point at once, simply said, "Yes, but do you have to prove it?" — to which they had to reply in the negative. Taking advantage of a helpful intervention by Morris, he overruled the objectors and agreed that the offending words should come out of the Bill, and procedure dealt with in instructions to the police. Everything was settled in about 15 minutes; and George Thomas, the Minister of State at the Home Office — who used to back up Soskice loyally — remarked with a sigh of relief on how different meetings at the Home Office now were from what they used to be.

At Legislation Committee, Thomas announced the result of our discussions, and the Bill was approved without further argument. Barbara observed that it was perhaps academic, as everyone, knowing that the blood test was more accurate, would of course prefer to give a specimen of blood. "Provided", I added, "that he hadn't been drinking more than he should". I was pleased with the result of the day's work, which I thought justified upsetting my Edinburgh arrangements in order to be in London today. Harry Wilson a fortnight ago was present at a meeting about testing for alcohol, but had been unable to make any headway; and I had thought it would be worth while to make a last effort at the Legislation Committee to get rid of a clause which seemed likely to make a laughing-stock of the Government. I heard afterwards that MacDermot had remarked that he was glad Scottish commonsense had after all prevailed.

JAN. 26. A meeting with the Attorney-General, on the Prices and Incomes Bill: the usual gathering of officials, including Sir Norman Skelhorn, Director of Public Prosecutions, who seemed level-headed and fully capable of appreciating all the difficult problems that arose. They have solved the problem of limiting unions' liabilities by devising a new crime consisting of any action designed to persuade an employer to implement a wages settlement in breach of an interim pay pause, with the penalty of a fine, and sub-clause designed to prevent any extension of civil or criminal liability. I had been critical of the Scottish application clause, but Gibson had produced a neat and simple alternative. On what was a price increase, the clause referred merely to comparison between prices of goods, without mention of time; it seemed essential that there should be something to indicate that the comparison must be with the price charged at some earlier period. On this the draftsmen took up a defeatist attitude, insisting that it was impossible to give effect to in drafting the Bill. Elwyn Jones gave me a lift to the Home Affairs Committee, and said he wished he had more time to read his papers; in most cases he had to leave everything to the departmental lawyers and hope they had got it right. He is always friendly and likeable.

JAN. 27. A letter from the surtax office, intimating that instead of my being due them £1067, as they told me not long ago, they were due me a repayment of £533.

FEB. 8. Legislation Committee: a Tory private Member's Bill to make it illegal for anyone to take away a boat without the owner's permission. A meeting with Ross to discuss a restriction which has been put into all feu charters granted by the Secretary of State of crofting land, whereby no licensed premises are allowed. In view of difficulties which have arisen in individual cases, officials have recommended that a decision be taken to waive all these restrictions and allow the position to be regulated by the licensing court. I rather agreed, thinking that a feu restriction was not a sound way of enforcing temperance; but Ross was concerned about the effect on local opinion in the Highlands. It was agreed that we wait for the Halliday Committee's report, which is expected to recommend a general relaxation of feu restrictions.

FEB. 9. George Wigg quoted a remark that Chuter Ede had made to him about Gaitskell, when Gaitskell was electioneering against the Tories and involved in controversy with his followers. "He's like the Lancashire cricket team", he said; "he can never win because he's so afraid of losing".

FEB. 12. I had to write to a patient in the mental section of Bangour Hospital, who had written complaining that the doctors there prevented him from getting out. He had written to the Scottish Rights of Way Society, but they replied that it did not come within their province. Oddly enough, he is a voluntary patient and can come away any time, but he probably does not realise it. Mr Gordon had dictated a letter to that effect, but I thought that in his state of health it was tactless to give him that information; I dictated a substitute letter, merely referring sympathetically to his grievances.

FEB. 14. I had had a letter from John Taylor, asking if I could help to arrange a meeting with Judith Hart, who is on the House of Commons committee on the Land Commission Bill. He thinks that mineral development should be exempt from development levy, and having failed to get anywhere with the Ministry officials wanted to put his point to a Scottish Minister. This morning I gor on the phone to Judith in London, and got her to agree that either she or Willis would fix up a meeting with Taylor before the Committee stage on the Bill on Thursday. This apparently caused consternation among the officials when it got known, and it became obvious as the day went on that strong pressure was being put on Judith to back down from this undertaking and leave any meeting to the officials. I would not accept this when it was reported to me, and had a somewhat acrimonious conversation on the phone with a Scottish Development Department official. He could not produce any valid reason why Judith should not see representatives of the Confederation of British Industry, except that she could not be compelled to meet them; but whether she has been got at to the extent of giving in to their advice remains to be seen. I made it clear that Taylor had no desire to meet any officials, and if a Minister was not to see him would have to brief an Opposition MP.

FEB. 15. More phoning in connection with John Taylor's affairs. Judith had stood out against the pressure to the extent of being prepared to give him half an hour, but she has since succumbed to the prevailing epidemic and was reported to be in bed with flu. I phoned Taylor accordingly, and found him quite pleased that the matter had been stirred up — he was of the opinion that it had got lost in somebody's in-tray. First Division: *Kilmarnock Cooperative Society v. Inland Revenue.* The question is whether the Society are entitled to investment allowances on the construction of a coal depot, and this depends on whether it is an "industrial building or structure". I was not hopeful, but got a fairly good hearing, though at one stage I became involved in an acrimonious wrangle with Clyde. I succeeded in shooting him down, to the general amusement; and Guthrie poured oil on the waters by asking an innocuous question to direct me to a safer topic. At 3.30 Clyde brought me to a stop by saying he had a meeting. He likes to stop always at 3.30, and I did not believe he had a meeting; but his intimation was a nuisance as I wanted to consult him on another matter. Meeting him in the lobby, I suggested I should come to see him after his meeting. As I expected, he proposed that I come right away, offering the explanation that the people for his meeting had not turned up. He was as always perfectly pleasant in a face-to-face talk, despite our contretemps in court shortly before. Rather exhausted after a day in the First Division, but pleased to find that after a long absence from any court work I was in no way inhibited from presenting a forceful argument and bringing a hostile court at least to the point of thinking about it.

FEB. 16. I brought my speech to a speedy conclusion, and they gave judgment in favour of the appellants. They all had their judgments already written, and read them out as "extempore" judgments; Migdale seemed to have wearied in the task, and towards the end of his Opinion had no manuscript to rely on, with the result that he rather lost his way. The judgments sounded good, and I think they may well be right.

FEB. 23. Lady Carlisle called me into her room, where Susan was sitting on the foot of her mother's bed in a very abbreviated nightie and joined in to back up Lady Carlisle when she said they had been worried about talk of a General Election. I said it was I who had to worry about that, but both in chorus assured me that it was very much their worry because they didn't want to lose me. Lady Carlisle said Mrs Robin Day had told her that although Mr Thorneycroft said the Conservatives would win he could not suggest any point of policy on which a win would be based.

FEB. 26. Kilbrandon told me that the Law Commission was about to come into head-on collision with the Lord President, having indicated to him that they proposed to abolish the antiquated law of corroboration in accident cases. Clyde has said this would mean that insurance companies would take their business elsewhere — "I don't know what he means by that", Kilbrandon said. I assured him that I would back him up, with great pleasure.

FEB. 27. Phone call from Methven the Convener of Midlothian County Council, who wanted to see me about the Labour candidature for Midlothian, vacant through the decision of the sitting MP, James Hill, not to contest this election. Hill is a miner, and the constituency has always been regarded as a miners' seat. Methven was perturbed at the poor quality of representation which this limitation has entailed, and wanted a strong candidate to put up against the miners' nominee. He had with him Bailie Heaney from Pumpherston, and it was arranged that I should be nominated by Pumpherston Labour Party. If I were to get the nomination, there would be no further difficulty: Midlothian has a big Labour majority. With some misgivings, I agreed to fall in with this plan. Once I get going on it, I shall no doubt feel I should like to win; but there is obviously much to be said for losing.

FEB. 28. The Prime Minister today announced 31st March as the date of the General Election.

MAR. 2. Methven phoned to say that the miners had seen the red light, and decided to put forward Alex Eadie instead of the local man they had intended to support and who everyone agrees is hopeless. Eadie would be an excellent candidate, and the decision ensures that whatever happens Midlothian will have a reasonably acceptable MP — no doubt the main object of Methven's exercise.

MAR. 7. Norman Wylie asked if he might have a word with me, and said that if he should be defeated in the Pentlands division at this election he would like to come and see me about the possibility of his becoming a Sheriff-Substitute. This seemed to me to be taking a very pessimistic view of Conservative prospects.

MAR. 8. A complaint from Kilmarnock about a case heard by Levitt in December 1963 in which no judgment was given until January 1966. I thought this utterly shocking, but it seems to be supposed that it is not out of line with what happens quite often in some Sheriff Courts. McDonald undertook to look into the position at Kilmarnock. To Free Gardeners Hall for the Midlothian selection conference. Six candidates had been nominated; and we were left in the lower hall while the conference of about 160 delegates deliberated overhead. The conference began at 7, and shortly after 7.45 Marshall came down with scraps of paper bearing the numbers 1 to 6 which he placed in his hat. I drew No 1. 10 minutes for each speech and 5 minutes for questions; and I started off by dealing with the position of the Lord Advocate, then, after saying that the point was important but not the most important — for I had been a socialist long before I was a lawyer — went on to general issues and my one joke, a quote of Willie Hamilton's remark in the House of Commons that "nothing quickened the Tory social conscience more than to find their backsides on the Opposition benches". This went down well, and while realising that it would make no difference to the result I was pleased with my speech and its reception. My place was taken by Provost Smith of Dalkeith. Eadie had been drawn third, and after we got back to the lower hall I went off with him and Smith to a cafe in Leith Walk, leaving the other three to their pieces. Eadie confirmed my previous impression of him as thoughtful and sensible: a first-rate candidate. He said some interesting things about his work at the coal face, which he was doing until he became a full-time organiser 9 months ago, at the same time occupying the position of Convener of Fife Education Committee. After walking back to the hall, we had not long to wait until someone summoned us upstairs. Eadie was received with applause which at once indicated that he had won. No figures were disclosed, but I was unofficially told that a second ballot had been required before Eadie got a clear majority. He made an astute little speech, with a touch of sentiment, and a gesture of appreciation to his defeated rivals. Smith followed; and I, saying I had just one sentence to add, said I should tell them what I had said to my wife before I left home tonight: that if they got Alex Eadie as their candidate they could not have a better man. This was true, and was received with general laughter and applause. Several people spoke to me as the meeting came out, congratulating me on my "presentation"; and in contrast to what one would have expected from press reports of what was happening in Midlothian Labour Party everything was friendly and civilised. The *Scotsman* was on the phone as soon as I got home, wanting me to say I was disappointed. All I would say was that I knew Eadie well, and that he was a goof friend of mine and an excellent candidate. In fact, though it is always disappointing to lose, and it would have been fun to fight a winning election and sit in the House, I knew well that it would have been a hard, trying way of life, and that in many respects I was much better off as I am.

MAR. 12. We went to the Assembly Hall to hear the Prime Minister address an election rally. The hall was full, but we got nice seats in the back row. We had a speech from Ross: forceful, witty and effective. He got a great ovation. The Prime Minister gave the impression of being tired, but he livened up when dealing with a few Tory interrupters; he played with them like a cat with a mouse, egging them on to say something before delivering some devastating retort. The bulk of the audience was enthusiastically pro-Wilson, and we lined the stairway to give him a rousing send-off.

MAR. 16. The Second Division today endorsed my views on Glasgow Councillors' telephones, holding that the Corporation was entitled to pay for them out of the Common Good. I was pleased about this, since the Glasgow telephones case was the first important issue on which I had overruled the St Andrews House solicitors.

MAR. 17. A phone call from London about an oil tanker said to be heading for Beira with petrol for Rhodesia and expected to dock there on the evening tide. It was flying the Liberian flag and owned by a Panamanian company, a subsidiary of Neeff Shipping Co. in New York for which Denholm & Co. of Glasgow are agents; and it was suggested that I get into touch with Mr Thomson of Denholms and point out that it would be an offence against the Rhodesia Orders if they facilitated the transit of oil to Rhodesia. The ship, I was told, had been chartered to convey oil from the Persian Gulf to Buenos Aires, but they had word that it was making course for Beira and a frigate had been sent in pursuit. I got Mr Gordon to phone the Procurator-Fiscal in Glasgow, and he contacted Mr Thomson, who denied all knowledge of any tanker bound for Beira. He put the Procurator-Fiscal on to Mr Barclay, of another company, Denholm Agency; but Mr Barclay knew of only two tankers, both at present in the Clyde. I reported to London, and said we could do nothing more. The consent of the Liberian Government had been obtained to the frigate's intercepting the ship if necessary.

MAR. 18. With Nancy to Gullane for golf: conditions ideal — sunshine and larks singing and no wind to speak of.

MAR. 20. North Morningside Church. Dr Lewis Cameron preached on Romans 5,20, with his customary vigour in his pleasant Buchan voice, talking his usual good sense. Some of his quotations were odd — one example of sin wherein the offender cheated at dominoes by covering one of the spots with a piece of chewing gum and so got away with the kitty of £39.

MAR. 24. Dunn to see me about a Revenue case which James Mackay took in the First Division. This was decided against the Crown, and they want to appeal it to the Lords. We agreed that Mackay should continue to be responsible for it. I should quite like to take it myself, but that would hardly be fair either to Mackay or to the case.

MAR. 29. A visit from two matronly Conservative canvassers who after some innocuous conversation about the weather said "I suppose we can put you down for two Conservative votes". "No", said Nancy, "we're supporting the Labour Government". "It's a Communist government you're supporting", said one of the ladies angrily. I was standing at the garage door while this was going on, and heard Nancy assuring them cheerfully that they would be getting

212

themselves run in for slander if they said things like that. They turned hastily and fled.

MAR. 30. With Nancy and Elizabeth to Stenhouse School for Pentlands final rally. The audience was packed into a tiny schoolroom, not a suitable place for oratory, and on the other hand it was a full meeting, with people standing, so that it was unsuitable for a "fireside chat" style of speaking. I spoke on trade unions, making what I thought a moderately good speech, but it got little response. There seemed to be quite a few opponents, and when the candidate was speaking one of the opponents erupted into an excitable and irrelevant string of interruptions. The candidate, Councillor William Wallace, was a solid, kindly, well-meaning man who kept his temper and dealt painstakingly with such points as were within his range of knowledge. I did not enjoy this meeting, and was surprised to find when we were motoring home that Elizabeth had enjoyed it very much. She had been sitting next the violent Tory supporter, and found it most exciting. She had also been much impressed by my speech.

MAR. 31. Called at the Keir Hardie Hall and arranged to bring the cars at 6.30 to help in taking voters to the poll. Nancy had one voter to take in the course of her operations, but agreed that everyone had been extremely nice and it was a good thing we had gone and given them a bit of encouragement, however ineffectual the use they made of our services.

AP. 1. We went to bed with the wireless and hung on till some time after 2. By then it was obvious that Labour would have a substantial majority, and this was confirmed in the morning paper. Pentlands had been held by Norman Wylie by only **44**.

AP. 4. Shaws to tea. He told me about a meeting of Sheriffs at which they considered a suggestion I made that they get monthly returns from the Sheriff Clerk of cases at avizandum, so as to try to get rid of delays in the issue of judgments by Sheriff-Substitutes. Campbell in the course of the meeting had kept saying that they should leave the matter over till after the election when they might have a more sensible Lord Advocate.

AP. 6. Going into the Deputes' room I found Croan, who is on duty this week, obviously depressed by the amount of work facing him. His tray was piled with stuff which he said was from the North, and the Glasgow stuff had still to come in. So I picked up the tray and carried it down to my room, where I got through it in not much more than an hour — quite enjoyable to be reading Sudden Deaths and precognitions again and marking the appropriate instruction as I used to do when I was an Advocate Depute. In fact the tray included the Glasgow cases as well as those from the North.

AP. 9. We moved from the drawing-room to the study to leave the way clear for a party Elizabeth was having — a very odd party, as apart from Penelope, and Nigel Cook, she had invited people she did not know. Everyone accepted: 5 youths and 4 girls. It seemed to be a sedate party — somewhat unsocial, all those present engaged in different pursuits. Richard told us he had been playing chess with one of them. But both he and Elizabeth seemed to agree that it had been an excellent party.

AP. 21. The state opening of Parliament. Miss Howat had arranged for us to see the procession from the balcony of Dover House. We were escorted on to the roof balcony, where, finding duckboards and iron ladders, I climbed up to the flagstaff. Richard came with me, Nancy and Elizabeth preferring to remain on the balcony overlooking Whitehall. We had a colourful vista of the whole line of the procession.

AP. 22. From Deans Yard the children went across to the House, where Miss Howat had arranged for them to take part in the climb up the Clock Tower. They are getting quite accustomed to the place — the policemen are beginning to know them without their having to say they had an appointment with the Lord Advocate.

AP. 26. I was interested to notice, in some papers that came in, a copy of a letter from Clyde in which he mentioned the probability that an additional judge would have to be appointed. I suppose he reckons that I would choose to appoint myself, and that if he is to be saddled with me for four years, I should do less harm as a judge than as Lord Advocate.

AP. 27. Johnson and Fearn to see me to discuss the Sheriffs' request for an increase in their salaries. The difficulty was that if I went down to the floor of Parliament House next week I could invite the busiest and most popular counsel I could find to be a Sheriff and he would accept with alacrity, at the present rates, so that from the public's point of view there was no necessity for an increase. I agreed however that Johnson should put the Sheriffs' case to the Treasury, on the basis that since their emoluments were last considered other people, including Sheriffs-Substitute, had had a 40 per cent rise.

AP. 29. Dalgetty and three other officials to see me on whether the Highlands Development Board have power to form themselves into a limited company. I thought that as their powers had been set out in the Act in detail it was impossible to construe the Act in such a way as to give them further powers by implication.

MAY 2. Commonwealth Law Ministers' dinner at Lancaster House. I had a little table with 5 guests, including Barbara Stonehouse, an attractive blonde who is the wife of the Under-Secretary for the Colonies. She drank nothing but water, but her abstemiousness was amply made up for by Tan Sri Abdul Kadir bin Yusef, Attorney-General of Malaysia. He told us he had had three whiskies before coming, and during the dinner he had sherry, white wine, champagne and port, in considerable quantities, followed by a double drambuie. None of it had any effect on him: he continued to talk brightly and rapidly, so that most of what he said was lost. Fortunately he did not seem to mind whether anyone paid attention to him or not. Hon. Dr K. K. Konoso from Zambia, rather overwhelmed by Kadir, sat glum and silent; but later he livened up, and his broad face broke into a cheerful grim as he entered into the conversation. He too drank only water. Towards the end of the dinner he asked if we thought he could slip out. As our table was next the door, and his seat was nearest the door of all those at the table, Mrs Stonehouse said he was probably the only person who could slip out without being noticed; and with a parting smile he proceeded to do so. We did not see him again.

MAY 3. Conference at Marlborough House. Gardiner was presiding and got through the business with reasonable expedition, despite the Attorney-General of Australia, a boring fellow named Sneddon who felt it incumbent on him to intervene whenever it looked as if the delegates were about to come to a decision. He never had any point of the slightest importance. I was impressed by the leader of the British delegation, a QC named Taverne who has just been appointed Under-Secretary at the Home Office. He had everything under control, and replied to questions competently and persuasively, without any fuss or appearance of superiority — a very nice man. Impressed too by the competence and suavity with which the lawyers from the black countries — Uganda, Jamaica, British Guiana — put their points. To Dover House: a sherry party for Scottish backbench Labour MPs. Assembled thus together, they offered a convincing demonstration of what — apart from a few exceptions — a hopeless bunch they are. A glass of milk had been laid on for me.

MAY 5. No one came in before about 2 a.m., but when Lady Carlisle appeared with my breakfast at 8 she looked as fresh as a daisy. She said she was going to Edinburgh next week, and Susan had offered to look after me.

MAY 6. Kilbrandon to see me about the Commission's tentative proposal to abolish the rule of corroboration in civil actions. This has met with strong opposition from the Lord President and the Faculty, and Kilbrandon wrote me to ask if they could expect Government support if they pressed on with it. I could not guarantee this in advance, but wrote a memorandum expressing my own view and pointing out that the grounds of opposition were nebulous rationalisations of prejudice against change and that as any substantial reform would be likely to encounter organised opposition in the legal profession it might not be a bad thing to start with one that was obviously sensible and easy for the public to understand. Kilbrandon did not seem to be worrying much about the professional opposition, and indicated that the Commission would be going ahead with their proposal.

MAY 9. To Muirfield for the Bar Foursomes; I was drawn to play with Morris Rose. Speaking of left-handed players, Rose remarked that the Kerr clan were traditionally left-handed, so that they built the staircases in their castles to go round in the opposite direction from usual in order to gain the advantage over their visitors when swords required to be drawn.

MY 15. To church: Dr Mowat on James 1,25. I occupied myself in reading the metrical psalms. Psalm 5 includes a rather naive anticipation of reciprocity:

"Lord, thou shalt early hear my voice:
I early will direct
My pray'r to thee; and, looking up,
An answer will expect".

MAY 16. Home Affairs Committee: a Ministry of Transport proposal to continue the experiment of a speed limit of 70 mph till August of next year. There was some grumbling from Jenkins, Crosland and MacDermot, who wanted to be able to cruise at 90 mph when the road was clear; but in the end everyone agreed that the experiment should continue. An appointment with Dean, principal assistant solicitor to the Board of Trade, to whom I communicated my view that practical difficulties in the way of prosecuting Loraine and Rowe were such that the best course would be to publish the Cadco report and give up the idea of prosecution. Loraine has been sentenced by a court in Los Angeles to imprisonment for 6 years on a charge of uttering counterfeit dollars and is now out on bail pending an appeal — which may take years to complete — while Rowe has for some time now been in prison in Lausanne awaiting trial on a similar charge. I think it might be difficult to bring home to Loraine any specific charge of fraudulent misrepresentation. What he did was to generate a pervasive air of euphoria under the influence of which the Glenrothes authorities fell for his scheme, hook, line and sinker, without any specific inducement held out to them. Rowe had to be more specific, particularly in his dealings with the bank, but by that time both Glenrothes and the bank were well along the road to disaster and more concerned with a desperate effort to get their money back than with any figures supplied by Rowe. Dean thought the Board of Trade would be pleased about this decision.

MAY 17. Miss Howat had fixed up a meeting with the Lord Chancellor in his room at the House of Lords; I found him there alone. As usual, when divorced from his officials he was the soul of urbanity and agreeableness. Despite the letter they had got him to write me, he made no difficulties about my Bill to reverse *Davie v. New Merton Board Mills*, and readily agreed to sponsor a paper to the Home Affairs Committee, either along with me or along with the Secretary of State for Scotland. On the path past Westminster Abbey I encountered Guest and his daughter, an attractive girl who might be in her early 20s. He introduced her to me as his wife, and she had to correct him. I seem to have been promoted at the Legislation Committee, my card having been set down at a place near the head of the table while Dingle Foot was at the foot of the table where I used to be. I made a short intervention on the provision of off-street parking places: a bad point, as MacDermot was at once able to point out to me. He always understands exactly what the situation is. Lunched at the Commons cafeteria; and on the Terrace afterwards encountered Mary Mackie, now in London helping her father with constituency correspondence. I was able to tell her the state secret that her father's Ministry had been entrusted with the responsibility for licensing of dogs, other than Scottish dogs, a decision reached rather in a spirit of levity by a committee of senior Ministers none of whom wanted to take on the task — the Treasury wanted to get rid of it. To Kensington to change into flannel trousers. As I was leaving the flat, Susan was just going out, and walked along with me. She wanted me to see her false eyelashes — surprisingly effective.

MAY 20. Harald Leslie to see me, with Mr Wilson, the principal clerk to the Land Court, to discuss the possibility of extending the legal aid scheme to include the Land Court, a project that I have been urging on the Scottish Home Department. My visitors did not think legal aid was required; they thought it would be a disadvantage, interfering with the informality of Land Court procedure and giving rise to questions of expenses which do not at present arise. They did not think anyone was prejudiced by the absence of legal assistance, and felt it would be better not to pursue this unless there was some public demand for it among the crofters — which they assured me did not at present exist.

MAY. 21. Kilbrandon to see me. I told him there was a possibility of a private member's Bill to restore the law to what it had been before the *Davie* decision, and I wanted to know whether this would cut across anything the Commission were doing. Kilbrandon said he would mention it to them, but he was sure they would have no objection to such a sensible proposal.

MAY 26. Home Affairs Committee: a proposed amendment of the Red Deer (Scotland) Act. I explained to the committee what was meant by "marauding" deer.

MAY 30. Harry Wilson had been at the Assembly service at St Giles' and had been sitting next the Pursebearer — who had come without any money, so that Harry had to lend him 2/6 for the collection.

MAY 31. Letter from the Lord Chancellor agreeing my joint paper about the *Davie* case.

JUN. 1. A long-delayed visit from Peter Thomson. I showed him a copy of a letter I had written to Brewis, and he agreed that he had been wrong in saying that I had ganged up with the MP against him. He apologised for misrepresenting me, and undertook that he would not again engage in public controversy. I did not challenge his chairmanship of his Plebiscite Society, about which he made some peculiar remarks, justifying it as a necessary expression of a Christian's freedom of action. I hope the whole thing can now be allowed to fade out.

JUN. 22. To Buckingham Palace for Privy Council: Lord Cromer, the governor of the Bank of England, was sworn as a member of the Council, and Jenny Lee affirmed. She was neatly got up in a white coat and skirt, but my driver criticised her for not wearing a hat on such an occasion.

JUN. 24. Home Affairs Committee: the paper about my Bill to reverse the *Davie* decision fourth on the agenda. There seemed a good chance that I would get my Bill considered, but Houghton was at his wordiest, and we seemed to be plagued by a superfluity of Welshmen, all of whom spoke at length. I had thought that with old Griffiths out of the Government we had got rid of the worst of the Welsh garrulity, but Cledwyn Hughes, the new Secretary for Wales, seemed about as longwinded, though he does not speak as often as Griffiths spoke. Anyhow, discussion of the Lord Chancellor's paper, for reforming the method of appointing JPs, took up an inordinate amount of time; and item 4, Houghton announced, would have to be left over. I did not mind much, for having got to this stage I think I shall probably get my Bill eventually. I remarked going down in the lift that there were too many Welshmen on the committee, and this led to some discussion. Albu remarked that it was funny that today we all seemed to have been thinking in terms of the Committee's ethnic composition. At Deans Yard I was just thinking of going across to the House for lunch, preparatory to flying back to Scotland, when there was a sudden flap on the phone from Bruce

Millan, who wanted to know if any legal point arose on a proposal to requisition ships under the Emergency Regulations, for the purpose of transporting goods and passengers to the Hebrides. The Regulations, made under emergency powers given to deal with the situation brought about by the seamen's strike, include a power to requisition moveable property, including ships. My office had not been consulted on this, and I knew nothing about it; but I undertook to look at a paper that the Scottish Office delivered to my room at the House. As it contained no clue as to what legal difficulties were expected, I did not think I could do more than undertake that Moran would look into the matter.

JUN. 27. Harry Wilson has rented one of the reconditioned cottages in Cramond village from the Corporation. They agreed that there was damp in one of the walls, and that tradesmen should be sent to deal with it. The Wilsons had not yet moved from Drymen, and the Corporation arranged to deliver the keys to him so that he could let the tradesmen in. This they did by having the keys put through the letter-box of the cottage, so neither he nor the tradesmen could get them.

JUN. 28. Dalgetty to see me about requisitioned ships. An Act of 1920 enables orders in council to be made for securing essentials of life of the community, and the question is whether transport of tourists to and from the Western Isles falls within that purpose. I should doubt it very much; but as the regulation gives some discretion to the competent authority it may be that, if Ministers decide in good faith that requisitioning for this purpose came within the Act, the Court would be excluded from looking behind the Ministers' decision. I said I should be prepared to defend the decision on that ground, though with no great confidence.

JUN. 29. Holyrood: the royal garden party. We were seized on by Kenneth Middleton's wife who wanted to discuss vandalism that the East Lothian planning officer was perpetrating next to her house in Haddington. Her complaint seemed to be that when she had gone to the planning enquiry to give her version of the matter counsel for the local authority had cross-examined her. "I might just as well have been a criminal!" she said. We met Norman Wylie; and I expressed sympathy with his attempts to put back into the Miscellaneous Provisions Bill the sub-section about accumulations that Guest had got us to take out. I said that if he could square matters with Guest I should be delighted to accept his amendment. Sidney Lockhart told us that the seamen's strike was settled.

JUL. 1. Home Affairs Committee: our paper on employers' liability. "The Lord Advocate had better introduce this one", Elwyn Jones remarked, but I thought it politic to leave it to

Gardiner, who introduced it neatly and briefly, soft-pedalling on any possible difficulties. Houghton seemed prepared to make some trouble, but he was quickly suppressed — Neil MacDermot joining in to support me in a useful little contribution confirming that until the *Davie* case the law in England had been thought to be the same as in Scotland. Gardiner had mentioned consultation, saying that the Ministry of Labour had suggested consultation with the TUC and CBI. He himself was doubtful about whether a full-scale consultation was necessary on such a minor proposal, but if it was he thought the Ministry of Labour should hold it. Bowden remarked that consultation was obviously necessary; unless we got agreement we had not a hope of getting the Bill through — anyone could object to it. Shirley Williams protested that the Ministry of Labour had not the expertise required for consultations on a purely legal question; but she was overruled, and the committee decided that consultations should be conducted by the Ministry. I imagine that their approval will not be wildly enthusiastic, but the important thing was that the principle of the proposed Bill was unanimously approved.

JUL. 7. To Victoria to call on John Taylor. I left him a memorandum dealing with my Bill, and he promised to take the matter up with those in the Confederation of British Industry who would be concerned in the consultations. He seemed not unnaturally disgruntled about peerages conferred on industrialists hostile to the Government while those like him got nothing but trouble.

JUL. 8. Home Affairs Committee. The committee approved a proposal to abolish from the law of England the crime of eavesdropping — listening at someone else's door or window.

JUL. 9. Reading today's *Scotsman*, I was surprised to find I had hit the headlines of an article on the judicial work of the House of Lords, in which the writer recorded that "certainly one can recall the present Lord Advocate, when in private practice, going off to London with some gusto to 'have the Division put right'".

JUL. 15. A meeting with Bowen and Macleod, the Edinburgh Procurator-Fiscal, to discuss a suggestion by the Scottish Law Commission that Crown precognitions should be available as of right to the accused's solicitors. This would be a breach with long-standing practice, and would present difficulties, but I thought there was something to be said for it if it could be combined with a rule that an accused who got copies of the Crown precognitions should be debarred from seeking to precognosce or make any contact with the Crown witnesses. This, if practicable, might go some way towards getting rid of the intimidation and pressuring of witnesses that certainly goes on in places like Glasgow.

JUL. 17. Harry Wilson and I were featured in "Crossbencher"'s column in the *Sunday Express* today, which, after pointing out that there are two H. Wilsons in the Government, "both, by a further merry coincidence, born in March, 1916", goes on to say that the second Mr Wilson is Solicitor-General for Scotland. "But, of course, you never see him in Westminster. Any more than you see the other Scottish law officer, Lord Advocate Mr. Gordon Stott. For these are the Government's invisible men. They simply cannot find seats. No constituency ever wants them. Wretched Mr. Wilson. He has fought three elections — 1950, 1951, and 1955. And been thrashed each time. Miserable Mr. Stott. He first stood for Parliament 31 years ago. No dice. He tried again in 1945 and in 1959 — and took two more beatings. And last March he could not even get a candidature". The writer goes on to ask about the future, and lists 5 Labour backbenchers over 70, all holding safe seats, who might be willing to make room for us in return for life peerages. "Alas. Cross-Bencher's disheartening view is that before that happens pigs will fly". St Catherines in Grange: Rev. Brinley R. Evans preached on Psalms 23,1. The psalm, he said, contemplated an old sheep looking out of the pen and not at first recognising whether it was friend or foe that was coming, then saying to the others, "It's all right; it's Jehovah". It was wrong, he said, to say the psalmist was at fault — suggesting that a shepherd may lose his sheep by leading them instead of following. There were two sheepdogs, "Goodness" and "Mercy", which the sheep realised would follow them. All utterly useless, but rather quaint. He seemed to have been a missionary in Madagascar. Finished reading *Last Exit to Brooklyn*, by Hubert Selby jnr. The Attorney-General was asked about this book by a Tory MP who wanted to have it banned as obscene; and after a negative reply the publishers advertised the book by quoting what the MP had said about it — much to his indignation. Stodart has now put down a question to me about the same book; and by what I think must be a unique mistake the question appeared on the Order paper of the House addressed to a Minister who was not a member. I arranged for a stalling reply to be given by a Scottish Office Minister: that my attention had not previously been directed to this book, but I should now consider it with a view to deciding whether to institute proceedings. The book is a study in intellectual and moral degradation, devoid of glamour or any other redeeming feature. It contains a large number of words seldom seen in print, and the incidents which it relates are disgusting and shocking. It is fair to say that the author's purpose is obviously to make sure that his readers are shocked and disgusted, not so much at the book as by the kind of life lived by the type of people it portrays. Read by the right people — people in authority or a position of responsibility — it might be regarded as highly moral. I thought myself that the author had overplayed his hand, portraying characers not one of whom had any spark of humanity or humour, and I certainly was glad to reach the end of it. I doubt if it is the kind of writing that would lead anyone to imitate the practices he describes.

JUL. 20. A balance-of-payments "crisis" has suddenly blown up and led the Government to take panic measures involving increased taxation and a cut-back in trade and industry. I have never had any doubt that these balance-of-payments crises are phoney, and that the sooner we get clear of international finance and banking mumbo-jumbo the better. What seems to be required is the imposition of a firm limit on prices of imported goods, so that if foreign exporters are not satisfied with the price they are getting here our imports will be cut down automatically, whereas if they are content to export to us at our prices — as I should suppose they would have to be — we should have a definite, limited liability. The Government are to aim at a price standstill, but how they are to do that while increasing purchase tax is a mystery. Of course no solution is possible so long as we insist on trying to keep London's position as a centre of international banking.

JUL. 22. Lady Carlisle told me she had been glad to hear me come in last night, as she had just been rung up three times by some young man unknown to her who had not given his name but claimed to have seen her in a Family Planning Association advertisement a year ago. He had said nothing objectionable but obviously was mentally unstable. She seems to be alone in the flat; Susan has gone to join her boy friend, James Buchanan-Jardine, on the Riviera. Home Affairs Committee: a scheme which the Home Secretary is proposing, to recover contributions from those who get legal aid in criminal cases. We in Scotland think it will be difficult to recover anything like the sums that Jenkins anticipates. We felt too that it would be impossible to put on the Sheriff Courts the burden of assessing contributions. Bruce Millan explained the Scottish position, justifying our refusal to cooperate on the basis that we had only recently started to operate criminal legal aid. The Treasury was prepared to accept this, so it was not necessary for me to argue the matter. I intervened at the end of a lengthy discussion on a proposal by Dingle Foot that contributions should not be sought from those who had been acquitted — on the ground that it was bad enough to be tried for something one had not done, without being asked to pay for it immediately after. As no one had a good word to say for Foot's suggestion, I remarked that I suspected the Solicitor-General might be right in thinking that it would be difficult after the event to recover a contribution from an accused who had been successfully defended. It would probably be equally difficult to recover anything from someone who had been unsuccessfully defended. The Home Secretary's proposal seemed to me to be very much over-optimistic, but I wished him joy of it, and we should see what happened. Everyone laughed, and Houghton passed on to the next item. A visit from Douglas Fairbairn. I took him in to hear the debate on the Abortion Bill which David Steel is promoting. Mrs Jill Knight, the new Conservative member for Edgbaston, was speaking against the Bill: a youngish woman, with a pretty, babylike face and a self-assured manner. I have never had any great enthusiasm for the Bill, but hers was the kind of speech that would make me want to vote in the Aye lobby. Joan Vickers, a more elderly Conservative noted for her bright mauve hair, made a thoughtful speech, in sharp contrast to the smarmy, "oh-so-sympathetic" attitude of Mrs Knight.

JUL. 23. The Castle: a Government banquet in honour of King Hussein of Jordan. I was lucky enough to be set down next a young lady who was, I think, the best-looking and most vivacious of all present: Mrs Adams, wife of the man who has just been appointed British ambassador to Jordan — a daughter of Lord Oaksey, but much more imaginative and advanced in her views than Oaksey could possibly be. Ross proposed the health of the King in an excellent speech.

JUL. 25. Rizza, a persistent correspondent of ours from Inverness, regularly complains of perversion of justice to his detriment, and in his latest letter does so in picturesque terms:

"The 'Nelson Eye' which has indeed added lustre to Naval tradition, can only tarnish the reputation of justice, who's figure, you must agree, would look most inelegant wearing one eye patch and a monocle".

JUL. 26. Dalgetty to see me about a small trade association — I think he said the Pigskin Hides Association — which was suspected of having broken an undertaking given to the Restrictive Practices Court. It was thought that they could be proceeded against for contempt of court. We agreed that counsel should be asked to draft a petition, and I would then consider it.

JUL. 28. An afternoon meeting with Johnson to discuss Home Office proposals for release of long-term prisoners on parole. I thought release should be decided by the Secretary of State, not by a panel of judges and other legal luminaries, who I thought had no qualifications to determine such a matter. Johnson mentioned a proposal to recommend McLeod and McNicol for inclusion in the

Honours List as representatives of the Fiscal service. A snag had been found in respect that McLeod's seniority and salary were above OBE level and he could be considered only for CBE; and as others had prior claims on this particular honour they felt unable to put his name forward — in other words, all the CBEs had been pinched by St Andrews House. They therefore proposed to put forward only McNicol, who could be considered for OBE. I demurred, pointing out that McLeod was much more deserving and it would be regarded as a snub to McLeod if McNicol got OBE and McLeod nothing. Lionel Gordon supported me, and recommended that if McLeod could not get anything it would be better not to put forward McNicol's name. I made it clear what I thought of this ridiculous red tape: a typically Civil Service problem in which a commonsense solution is virtually out of the question. Between these meetings I was kept fully occupied on a big pile of papers that had come in, including a number of Minutes from Home Office about proposals they are putting before Home Affairs Committee tomorrow. It seemed reasonable that the odium of opposing the Home Office's impracticable schemes should fall on someone else for a change, and I contented myself with writing a series of Minutes to be teleprinted to Mabon for his guidance at the meeting.

AUG. 1. A card from Lady Carlisle, written at London airport on her departure for a 3-week holiday in Virginia. Hoping that I will be all right if I come to London, she says: "There's a faint chance that Susan may be back & though a bad housemaid is a good cook".

SEPT. 6. A meeting with Dalgetty to discuss an amendment put down by Norman Wylie to the Local Government (Scotland) Bill, to exclude night storage heaters from the value of a house for assessment purposes. When the amendment came up in Committee, Dr Mabon was pressed from all sides to accept it, and had to fall back on the argument that it was contrary to recognised principles of valuation law. I did not think there was much in this argument. Valuation law is so anomalous that it did not seem to matter if another minor anomaly crept into it; and if everybody wanted to exclude space heaters I could not see why we should not please them by agreeing. I pointed out however that Wylie's amendment would have precisely the opposite effect. He had devised an ingenious amendment to omit the reference to industrial buildings in the machinery definition, so that in houses as in industrial buildings machinery would not be treated as heritable if it could be removed without injury to the structure. But he had omitted to notice the phrase "Save as herein provided", and that it was provided in the clause that machinery and appliances for heating the building were heritable. So the effect of his amendment would be to exempt space heaters only if they were not used for heating the building. J.P. Mackintosh, in a conversation about the problem of finding seats for law officers, told me that Marshall had done all he could to stop his being selected as candidate for Berwick and East Lothian. He argued that Marshall should have been pressing the claims of the law officers, but I pointed out that his example proved Marshall's intervention was ineffective and might do more harm than good. After supper motored with Nancy and Elizabeth to the Salmons' — a number of people crammed into a small room. We were told by Salmon that there was more space in a room at the back. This turned out to be right: hardly anyone in the room, mostly relatives, including a pretty girl — things much improved. Norman Wylie put in a short appearance, and I told him his amendment was nonsense.

SEPT. 8. Lady Carlisle made a tentative approach to me to see if I would pay a higher rent. She claims to be hard up, though that I should think is a relative term in the case of anyone just back from a fortnight's holiday in Virginia. She has fallen out with Susan following on Susan's wish to go for a motor tour round Italy with James. This was stopped by James' mother, who told the young people that Lady Carlisle had forbidden it. Lady Carlisle is annoyed about this, for though she was opposed to the idea and advised Susan against it she thought nothing could be worse than to forbid it. "What can you expect from a Buchanan-Jardine?" I asked. "Exactly", said Lady Carlisle.

SEPT. 9. To Paddington for the 9.10 train to Birkenhead. Underground train to Liverpool, where I embarked on a steamer leaving for New Brighton. I enjoyed my sail down the Mersey, and was back at Liverpool in time for the 5.45 train to Edinburgh.

SEPT. 10. Signed the nomination of Ian Robertson as an additional judge in the Court of Session. King Murray, having talked things over with his wife, said he had decided not to be a Sheriff-Substitute. He said he thought he could do more useful work elsewhere — which in his case is, I think, a completely genuine attitude.

SEPT. 13. Lillie, to consult me about Fife Valuation Appeal Committee. The Vice-Chairman of the County Council, who is a member of the committee, recently made some criticism of the Assessor at a Council meeting, saying that a lot of the assessments were unintelligible and similar properties had been assessed at widely varying figures. The Assessor is annoyed about this, and has threatened to object to the member's sitting on the committee during the hearing of valuation appeals, on the ground of his prejudice against the Assessor. The committee secretary had written to Lillie asking if he would speak to the member of the committee and suggest that he might stay at home on the day of the meeting. In telling me this, Lillie talked a lot of nonsense about whether the speech had been made on a privileged occasion and without malice — which seemed completely irrelevant — and actually suggested that one way of dealing with the matter would be for me to bring an action of interdict against the Assessor prohibiting him from challenging the Vice-Chairman's right to sit. After looking at the Act, I wrote a note to Lillie telling him it was no business of his, and he should advise the secretary accordingly. I referred him however to an opinion of Lord Salvesen, which seemed to make it clear that the Vice-Chairman could sit and hear appeals if he wanted.

SEPT. 20. Balmoral. A meeting of the Privy Council: Crossman in his new capacity of Lord President, Kenneth Robinson, and Silkin, who replaced Short as Chief Whip on Short's appointment to be Postmaster-General. The Lady in Waiting, addressed as "Lady Rose", remarked that there should be fewer Council meetings nowadays — they always seemed to be concerned with colonial matters and we had shed so many colonies. The company for lunch was larger than last year's, but Andrew did not appear. He was apparently resting; and when we were back in the drawing-room the Queen bowed to Edward and apologised for not believing him when he had told her. "He was quite right", she said "and I never believe what he says". Crossman had expressed a desire to go for a walk in the hills. My arrival in an open car seemed to have caused some admiring comment — considerable competition to come in it. We followed a rough track to Lock Muick, a fine loch about 3½ miles long, with quite steep precipices, rather like the Wastwater ones, rising on the other side. I discarded my jacket, and Crossman followed my example, revealing a pair of bright red braces. Our path soon reached a good height, giving a fine backward view of Loch Muick. Here Silkin gave up, pleading an old cartilege injury, and sat down among the heather to await our return. On the skyline at the top we could see a herd of deer. Crossman said it only remained for them to show us an eagle. Adeane led the way down at a good rate, his small, elderly figure skipping agilely from stone to stone and tuft to tuft. The Queen, I thought, looked a little coldly at us, having been kept waiting for her tea, but she relented sufficiently to show us snapshots of the family in bathing suits, taken at Loch Muick in the hot summer of 1956 or 1957, to prove to us that they really had bathed in the loch. At tea Crossman and the Duke were on either side of the Queen, and argued across her about land conservancy. The Queen, who was pouring out, did not offer us a second cup; and as soon as tea was over we were hustled out to the door, where a car was waiting to take my colleagues to Aberdeen.

SEPT. 24. With Nancy to Musselburgh, to open Northesk Church sale of work. We had been told that a special announcement would be made later in the proceedings: that today was the 60th anniversary of my father's induction to Northesk. But no announcement was made.

OCT. 5. A talk with Mitchell about Gibson's retiral date. Regrettably, he was most cooperative, and made it plain that he was content to have his promotion delayed by Gibson's remaining if Gibson wanted to remain. He said that Gibson strongly denied being a Tory, maintaining that he had been a Liberal all his life.

OCT. 6. An appointment to meet Mr Sich, Registrar of Restrictive Practices, who had suggested that the Pigskin Tanners provided a good opportunity for our making one another's acquaintance. He was quite enthusiastic about this absurd case, which he seemed to approach from a somewhat theoretical standpoint. We had a friendly, courteous interchange of opinion, lasting over an hour, but at the end neither of us was any nearer accepting the other's point of view.

OCT. 8. Abbey to see me — saying that the Crown Agent was hostile to him and so had deliberately spread rumours about him in Parliament House. I assured him that he was wrong: the truth is that Gordon is congenitally incapable of keeping any information to himself, and spreads rumours about everybody without any malice whatever.

OCT. 9. To the Shaws' for supper. I got a seat on the sofa next to Paula Menzies, the Belgian wife of a WS, a pretty girl who looked much younger than her 42 years and was most vivacious and agreeable.

OCT. 11. Dalgetty and Sir Matthew Campbell to see me about the position of Mr Frank Thomson as a member of the Highlands Development Board. He is about to accompany the chairman of the Board and a planning consultant to Los Angeles to meet some American industrialists whom they hope to interest in a petroleum chemical project at Invergordon. Thomson was interested in this before he joined the Board, and spent £15,000 of his Distillery Company's money on a report that he obtained from planning consultants. The Act provides that if a member of the Board has a pecuniary interest in any matter, and is present at a meeting of the Board at which it is the subject of consideration, he is not to take part in discussion or voting on it; but it seemed clear that this did not preclude Thomson from going to America and giving the Board the benefit of his advice and negotiating skill. Harry Wilson thought that though not illegal such action would amount to impropriety, and that the Secretary of State should refuse his consent; but I was not prepared to express an opinion without knowing enough about it to balance any possibility of impropriety against the advantage to the Board of having Thomson take part in the negotiations. We contented ourselves with advising that what Thomson was proposing to do up to the present was within the law. We went on to discuss the disposal of the Dryburgh estate near Dundee, which its owner presented to the Secretary of State about 30 years ago for use as smallholdings on which to settle Dundee unemployed. The donor postulated that if "in the distant future" the purpose of the gift should fail, partially or completely, the Secretary of State could dispose of the estate, partially or wholly, and use the funds for other land settlement schemes. With a change in industrial conditions, there is no longer any demand for land on which to settle the unemployed, though one or two of the original holdings on the estate are still occupied. We had no doubt that there was a partial failure, and agreed that this could be regarded as "distant future" from the point of view of the '30s, so that the Secretary of State would be entitled to dispose of most of the estate to Dundee Corporation, who require it for housing. The question remained as to what was to be done with the money from the sale. The answer depended on whether the Secretary of State held the property on trust, or as a gift subject to a condition. G. R. Thomson when Lord Advocate had given a firm opinion that the land was held on trust, but a contrary opinion was later obtained from a professor of Conveyancing. I had no doubt that Thomson was right. The test of trust is whether what is handed over can go into the donee's general fund, or must be held in a separate fund for the benefit of some particular class of persons; and it seemed obvious that this gift was to be held for the benefit of the unemployed. Harry Wilson in drafting an opinion had sided with the professor, as also had the St Andrews House people; but I had no difficulty in persuading Harry that he was wrong, and today everybody agreed that the funds should be treated as held in trust, and application made to the court for a *cy près* scheme. Even if I were wrong, this would be a convenient way of getting a decision from the court and so having the matter disposed of. Dalgetty remained to discuss the possibility of disjoining the offices of Dean of the Thistle and Dean of the Chapel Royal, which George III by sign-manual conjoined "for all time coming", at the same time appointing one Dr Jardine to be Dean of the Thistle and Chapel Royal for the term of his natural life. The conjoined office is now held by Dr Warr, and Dalgetty is worried about what is to happen when he dies. Dr Whitley will presumably have to be Dean of the Thistle so that Thistle services can continue to be conducted in the Thistle Chapel at St Giles' — it being unlikely that Dr Whitley as minister of St Giles would look kindly on having Thistle services there under any Dean but himself. The Queen however regards the office of Dean of the Chapel Royal as her personal appointment. Dalgetty wants the offices disjoined so that Whitley can be Dean of the Thistle and the Queen have someone else as Dean of the Chapel Royal. He argues that on the death of the holder the offices revert to the Crown, and joint or separate appointments can be made as the Crown pleases. It seems to me however that it is impossible to ignore the words "for all time coming", and that it would need an Act of Parliament to alter a grant in those terms. To the Laigh Hall: a meeting of the Council of Law Reporting, responsible for the production of Session Cases. Fiddes, who became editor on Fisher's death, has got hopelessly into arrears: the first part of the 1965 volume has not yet appeared. Apart from being generally inconvenient, this has brought the Council to the edge of financial disaster, for with no Session Cases to sell they have no revenue to pay the salaries of editor and reporters. Fiddes did not attend, but a letter was read in which he said in effect that he was beginning to understand the job and expected to do better in future. Everyone agreed that it was thoroughly unsatisfactory, but no one had any solution to offer. The day is past when one can hope to find someone like Alison prepared to devote a vast amount of time and erudition to editing law reports.

Oct. 16. A leader in the *Sunday Express* complaining about their inability to find out about an incident in Glasgow Sheriff Court, where Frank Middleton fined three policemen for coming late to court and subsequently recalled the fines — actually, though this was not publicised, in consequence of an intervention from the Crown Office. In the public interest, said the *Express*, they had attempted to find out how this had come about, but as always in anything connected with the law of Scotland a curtain of silence had descended and it had been impossible to find anyone who would admit to knowing anything about it. Chief Constable, Procurator Fiscal, Sheriff Clerk, Crown Office — none of them would admit to knowing anything. I thought this was rather a compliment to our criminal law administration.

Oct. 18. The Attorney-General's car came to take me and Gibson to the law courts for a talk with him — I had thought to be about the speed limit, but it turned out that he wanted my views on Part II of the Prices and Incomes Act, which gives immunity to employers who break any contract which would involve them in payment of remuneration to any employee at a higher rate than was paid before the Act came into force. The question is what happens in numerous cases where employers, in obedience to Government directions for a wages freeze, did not pay increases to which workers were

229

entitled by their contracts before the date when the Act came into force. I had not been asked to consider this point before, but expressed the firm view that "rate of remuneration paid" meant the amount a man had actually received in his pay packet, not what he might have been legally entitled to be paid by an employer disregarding the voluntary freeze. Elwyn Jones said he had taken the same view, but went on to read an Opinion which British Railways had obtained from Sir Andrew Clark, which shook me considerably. Clark's strongly expressed view was that he could not conceive of any court reading the section as referring to anything else than what the worker was entitled in law to be paid at the date when the section came into force, and that employers could not possibly be regarded as having put themselves in a better position vis-a-vis a workman, the other party to the contract, through having illegally and in breach of contract failed up to that date to pay what had been due. On reflection, this seemed to me a pretty sound argument; but we agreed that having taken the opposite line, and advised industrialists accordingly, the Government would have to stick to it, on the view that the Act was not concerned with rights and interests of contracting parties but laid down in black and white, as matter of public policy, that no payment need be made in excess of the actual payment being made when the section came into operation.

OCT. 19. Lady Carlisle has said nothing more about putting up the rent, but it occurred to me that she might be "working to rule", for the dirty shirt I had left as usual in the wardrobe had not been washed — an unprecedented omission. A meeting with Miss Herbison about Douglas Campbell, whom her Ministry had put forward for a CBE, as reward for presiding over National Insurance tribunals. Remembering Sinclair Shaw's indignation at the appearance of Ross McLean's name in a Labour Honours List, I had written a Minute suggesting that this be reconsidered. I made it clear to Miss Herbison that I had no criticism of Campbell's conduct of tribunals, which is well spoken of, but made it equally clear that I thought he was quite an unsuitable person to be honoured by us.

OCT. 21. To St Giles' for memorial service to Sir Hugh Watson: the usual rubbish. The thought passed through my mind to ask Nancy to see that I was not prayed over by Dr Whitley or anyone else. To the University Staff Club for Muir Society's wine party: quite a restful evening, and I was not required to drink anything except two glasses of milk. Amused to hear Douglas Fairbairn telling Norwell of his experiences with me as his counsel when some disaster occurred, such as coming up to court on the morning of a jury trial and finding that our principal witness had not turned up. This type of occurrence, which, he said, would drive Kissen frantic if it happened in a case in which he was appearing, never seemed to cause me any worry.

OCT. 22. Ewan Stewart came in to get some advice about an Income Tax fraud case he is conducting. When the trial was in its third week, and the first accused, an elderly Chartered Accountant., was in the witness box, this accused took ill, and it looks as if he will not be able to go on for a very long time. We decided that Stewart should ask the judge to continue with the case against the other. In the course of his evidence the first accused has already said some things to the disadvantage of his co-accused, and there can now be no cross-examination — so that Robert Reid, for the second accused, will almost certainly object to the case going on against his client. I thought that was for Lord Milligan to decide; and it did not seem to me to matter whether the case went on or not, both accused having incurred a heavy penalty already in loss of professional reputation and in meeting the cost of their defence.

OCT.25. I had undertaken to address the Scottish Council of the Union of Post Office Workers on the economic situation — at Queens Hotel, Perth. I addressed them for 45 minutes. The flood-gates were then unloosed, and I was heckled violently for the next hour, during which everyone condemned the Government and its prices and incomes policy, hook, line and sinker. I replied vigorously but to all appearances quite ineffectively — though the response to the vote of thanks was surprisingly enthusiastic. The meeting voted unanimously to go on for an extra quarter of an hour so that heckling could continue, and despite the general hostility everyone seemed pleased.

OCT. 28. Dalgetty and some of his people to see me about teachers' salaries, increased in April in accordance with provisional regulations made by the Secretary of State. In July the increases were confirmed, and the opportunity taken to make some adjustments which provided for minor increases for about 900 teachers. Mean-while the Government wage standstill had been announced. The Secretary of State on the advice of his officials informed the Depart-ment of Economic Affairs that he was to advise authorities that they had to pay in accordance with the regulations, and this has caused a furore in the Department and at the Exchequer, who insist that it is out of the question to "approve" these minor adjustments when increases are involved. Their attitude fails to take account of the position in law, which involves beyond a shadow of doubt that the authorities must pay what the Regulations lay down; no question of approval arises. I readily agreed to write a short Opinion to that effect. We had a talk about the Pigskin Tanners. Everyone agreed that it would be absurd to run this footling case as a test case on breach of an undertaking given to the Restrictive Practices Court; and it was agreed that the case would be dropped. An effusion of 83 pages had come in from McShane, forwarded to us by the Law Society — the typescript of an appeal he is lodging with a court in Los Angeles. A 2-page list of those whom he is serving with copies includes "Dougie Johnston, Jimmy Clyde, Frankie Carmont, Slim Sorn, Eek Guthrie, JOM Hunter, Mannie Kissen", described as "pirate judges" at Scottish Parliament House. "It is averred, alleged and realleged", he says, "that lawyers are neither the brightest nor most honest people in society . . . and most judges so far met by these appellants are not one whit better".

NOV. 2. On my way through the Abbey, stopped to look at some of the monuments in the corner where Dickens and Kipling are commemorated by slabs on the floor. An impressive monument to Elizabeth Dowager Baroness of Lechmere, daughter of Charles Howard, third Earl of Carlisle, and widow of Nicholas Lord Lechmere. "She afterwards intermarried with Sir Thomas Robinson of Rookly Park", and died in 1739 at the age of 44.

> "By an Order in his last Will dated 1775 this Monument was erected to perpetuate his grateful Sense of the Pleasure he had in the Conversation of an accomplished Woman, a sincere Friend, and an agreeable Companion, with particular directions that his Bust should be placed by hers".

This direction has been carried out; the two busts stand overlooking one another. The memorial goes on to relate that Sir Thomas had been MP for the Borough of Morpeth, and later Governor General of Barbados;

> "and tho' he did several eminent Services to the Island yet upon some Complaints sent home he was recalled; Tho', in Justice to his Memory it must be conceded that the Complaints were afterwards substantially acknowledged to be groundless".

Next to this is a monument to what was evidently a royalist family, including Sir Richard Atkyns, Lord Chief Baron of the Exchequer. He

> "retired upon the Revolution to his seat in Norfolk, where He employed himself in reconciling Differences among his Neighbours, in which he obtained so great a Character that few would refuse the most difficult Cause to his decision, and the most litigious would not appeal from it".

A big Memorial to one Mary Hope, who died at Brookhall in the county of Northampton, at the age of 25, and "whose remains unnotic'd lie in the Neighbouring Church at Norton". Her virtues are recounted in a sonnet, beginning:

"Tho low in earth her beautious Form decay'd
My faithful wife, my lov'd Marias laid".

Nov. 3. Miss Howat and I to Ministry of Works premises behind Deans Yard, to select pictures for my room. Up to now my wall has been adorned with photos of former Lord Advocates; these were taken down for the painting, and I refused to allow them to be put back. Miss Howat had heard that someone from Mr Justice Scarman's English Law Commission was to be choosing a picture, and when we got into the room where the pictures were displayed there were two gentlemen in formal dress, one of them remarking jocularly to the lady in charge that Mr Justice Scarman took precedence over all their Ambassadors and suchlike hangers-on. I remarked that that might raise an interesting question as to whether he took precedence over the Lord Advocate. A Ministry of Works official came in, and it at once became apparent that the man I had been talking to was Scarman himself. "You are Mr Justice Scarman", I said, and when he agreed added "I am the Lord Advocate". He seemed agreeable and interesting. He had selected a coloured print of a racehorse, a picture for which I certainly did not want to compete. We selected a Dutch landscape, and a more modern painting of the South Bank.

Nov. 4. On television tonight an interesting survey of the campaign for election of a Governor of California. Brown, the Governor, is being challenged by a right-wing Republican film actor named Ronald Reagan, a handsome, rugged-looking man with an attractive style of speaking and a cosy air of being all things to all men. I should think that women voters would fall for him like ninepins.

Nov. 8. A meeting with Ross, Willis and Department of Agriculture officials to discuss the Hunter Report on salmon and trout fishing. Jack Hunter's committee have proposed a comprehensive scheme of regulation which will prevent anyone from fishing in Scotland without a licence. This, it is thought, will encourage landowners with trout fishings to conserve and improve their stock of fish. Willis and the officials were enthusiastic, but I agreed with Ross in thinking that it would probably mean a lot of regimentation with no benefit to anyone except fishing proprietors. Ross bullied the officials mercilessly and unpleasantly. It was obvious that they were not going to get anywhere with their proposals.

Nov. 9. A chat in the kitchen with Susan, who thought her mother was working much too hard: she is out of the house soon after 8 every morning, and does not get home till 7 at night. Susan said the man she works for, Ronnie Grierson, is an enthusiast for work, and is at his office at 8 o'clock. Susan was afraid that she did not do anything much to help; and we agreed that she could bring my breakfast — though I do not know what Lady Carlisle will say to that.

Nov. 10. Went down to see Clyde about a proposal from England about the tribunals which deal with claims under the Redundancy Payments Act. Many of the claims are obviously irrelevant or incompetent, and the English people propose that these should be thrown out by the President of the Tribunal, with an intimation to the claimant that he can write in, saying why he thinks this should not be done. The Act provides that claims have to be referred to a Tribunal, and it is proposed to get round this by a provision in the new Regulation that the President of the Tribunal should constitute the tribunal for this purpose. Clyde at first approved of this, but later, on prodding by Robert Reid, the chairman of the Scottish tribunal, objected to it as inconsistent with principles of natural justice. I thought there was something to be said for this view, and anyhow saw a more fundamental objection: that tribunals to which redundancy payments have to be referred are tribunals set up under the Industrial Training Act, which gives power to set up tribunals for the purpose of hearing appeals under that Act. It is true that once such a tribunal has been set up any question arising under the Redundancy Payments Act can be referred to it; but the one-man tribunal which they are proposing is not to be set up for the purpose of appeals under the 1964 Act but for a different purpose, and I cannot find any power to set up such a tribunal. I mentioned this to Clyde, who agreed that I was probably right.

Nov. 11. Parliament House. I encountered Robert Reid, who said there had been a new development, and telling me about a discovery he had made about the validity of the new Regulations proceeded to expound to me the point I had made to the Lord President yesterday. He eventually admitted he had been talking to the Lord President; and it seemed obvious that Clyde must have rung him up last night and claimed the point as his own discovery — otherwise Reid would hardly have tried to explain it to me on the view that I had never heard it.

Nov. 16. A Full Bench of 5 judges in the High Court: *H.M. Advocate v. Burns* — a charge of having 17 forged Royal Bank of

Scotland notes, knowing them to be forged, contrary to section 6 of the Bank Notes (Forgery) Act, 1805. Objection was taken that the section covered only Bank of England notes. The section is one of a series taken from an earlier English Act, with an additional section extending the Act to Scotland; and the argument against me was that the whole thing was for the protection of the Bank of England and the extension to Scotland meant only that it was a crime to be knowingly in possession of Bank of England notes there. A court of 6 judges in 1814 held that Scottish banknotes came under the section; but Alison's Criminal Law, published in 1832, included a statement that "this judgment, which was passed by the narrowest majority, is now considered to be bad law; and though the point has not been expressly brought under their notice it is understood that the Court is now unanimously of opinion that the Act applies only to Bank of England notes". This text-writer's view, oddly enough, seems to have had the effect of overruling the earlier Full Bench decision, for in 1882 a normal court of 3 judges held by 2 to 1 that the Act did not apply to Scottish notes. I had found the point interesting, and gone into all the statutes and authorities, most of which I referred to in opening the case; and Nicholas Fairbairn put up a good argument in reply. Clyde however had his "extempore" judgment drafted before the hearing began, and when the debate finished concussed his four colleagues into accepting it as the judgment of the Court. Clyde's judgment was a jejune affair, right enough, I think, in its conclusion that Scottish banknotes were covered, but doing no justice to the argument that had been submitted. As Fairbairn remarked to me earlier, the only matter in doubt was whether the Lord President's dislike of the Lord Advocate was less than his dislike of criminals. We both got a good hearing, and the debate itself was interesting and enjoyable.

NOV. 18. Susan brought my breakfast as arranged. Home Affairs Committee: a report which the Lord Chancellor had obtained from his Law Commission on reform of divorce law — a business-like report which narrows the field to a new ground based on breakdown of marriage. Gardiner on receipt of this proceeded to publish it without consulting any of his colleagues. This caused perturbation in the Scottish Office, who were not even told that the Chancellor was consulting the Law Commission on the subject; and I was annoyed myself to find that the Scottish Law Commission had heard nothing of it. It makes things awkward for us: we may be asked by Scottish MPs why we have allowed the English to go ahead with this without ourselves doing anything. Mabon was supposed to protest at today's meeting on behalf of Scotland, but had slept in. So it fell to me to protest, which I did vigorously, saying this had happened before and the Lord Chancellor's department was the worst I had encountered as regards cooperation. But it was not a good occasion for making this case. The meeting consisted of liberal-minded people who were pleased with the result and not interested in how it had been achieved. Gardiner made some footling excuse, but when I attempted to challenge this Roy Jenkins cut in to ask if we could get to the merits of the case; and it was impossible to pursue the Scottish point. Though Houghton made sympathetic noises, and Gardiner promised to do better in future, I doubt if my intervention did any good either to me or to the case for cooperation.

NOV. 19. I had promised to meet the Deputes this morning and try to appease their wrath against Glasgow Assistant Chief Constables, who have been making foolish remarks reported in the *Glasgow Herald*. It was started off by Kelso, who referred to the "ridiculous" High Court system where senior QCs defended a criminal and the prosecution was left to some "wet-eared junior". I wrote the Chief Constable and extracted from him a somewhat grudging withdrawal. He professed to justify Kelso's remarks by reference to a case in which an Advocate Depute had been opposed by Bennett, A. A. Bell, Carmichael and Macvicar, whom he described somewhat oddly as "the cream of the legal profession". I was not altogether content with this, and wrote asking for clarification. There was no reply; and in yesterday's *Herald* Mr Kelso's colleague, Ratcliffe, was reported to have returned to the attack, stating that the Advocates Depute were all rather young and inexperienced when you saw the people they were up against, and this was a situation in which the battle against crime was being fought in the courts and lost. As I pointed out to the Chief Constable in my letter, this is untrue: the present team of Advocates Depute has an extremely good record of convictions. Ratcliffe's speech has got a lot of publicity, and all the Deputes have been much incensed, with threats of resignations and letters to the newspapers and what not. I thought the best course was to ask the Chief Constable to come and see me. I told the Deputes this when they came to my room, read the letters I had written to the Chief Constable, and had no difficulty in cooling them down. They do not realise the extent to which all these attacks are political, and the necessity for not taking them too seriously. With Nancy to the Castle for dinner in the Banqueting Hall for President Ayub Khan. I sat between Mrs Willis and Major-General Rafi Khan, the military secretary to the President. Though prepared to converse on any topic, he did not himself introduce any, and I was content to leave him to his neighbour on the other side, Lady Hughes, who seemed to be an expert conversationalist, while Mrs Willis and I indulged in more homely topics such as her fear of eating onions and her distrust of J. P. Mackintosh. She told me that as soon as the Labour Prime Minister had been summoned to the Palace Sinclair Shaw had been on the phone to Willis reminding him that Gordon Stott was available for the post of Lord Advocate. Ross made an excellent speech, to which the President replied with some amiable, chatty remarks. The official programme envisaged that after dinner the visitors would go round the historic apartments, and I was surprised to see them get into their cars and drive straight off to Holyrood — a sensible move. Mrs Ross told us about the enormous high bed she was occupying at Holyrood. She recalled a story about James Brown's wife when they were at Holyrood after his appointment as Lord High Commissioner and she was told about the ghost of Mary Queen of Scots which is supposed to be seen there and was asked if she would not be frightened at seeing her. "Not half as frightened", she said, "as she would be when she saw me".

NOV. 25. Lionel Gordon showed me the *Glasgow Herald*, with an excellent letter from Nicholas Fairbairn in which, on the basis of his High Court experience, he defends the Advocates Depute and demolishes Kelso and Ratcliffe: a brilliant piece of invective, fully supported by facts. To North Berwick to address a meeting under the auspices of the local Labour Party, on prices and incomes: a complete flop. Throughout my talk a tiresome, self-opinionated man kept up a running commentary on what I was saying. It was obvious from the questions asked that nobody had had any idea of what I was driving at.

NOV. 29. A meeting in Ross's room about Cadco. Among the civil servants present was Hume, the head of the Scottish Development Department, a quiet, logically-minded man who rather impressed me.

NOV. 30. A meeting with David Steel about his Abortion Bill. This Bill will enable doctors to terminate pregnancies when they find it necessary in the interests of the mother. It is hedged about with stringent precautions, and as it provides that all abortions, other than those carried out in the manner prescribed by the Bill, are to be illegal I had to point out that so far as Scotland is concerned the effect would be restrictive rather than otherwise. He accepted this, but said that even in Scotland the doctors wanted more certainty about their position in law. I think this is probably right.

DEC. 4. To John Wheatley's for a talk about release of life prisoners. He has been annoyed with St Andrews House because in advising about the release of a murderer named Stephens, who was given a life sentence by John about 8 years ago, they had consulted the prison governor and psychiatrists before consulting him, so that when they came to him he concluded, wrongly, that release was a foregone conclusion. He had written a bad-tempered minute, saying that if the verdict had been culpable homicide he would have given Stephens 15 years. Stephens, who had no criminal record, strangled his wife as the result of some momentary aberration; and as his release would obviously not endanger anyone I thought Wheatley's observations were mostly irrelevant. I did not suppose that my talking to him would do much good, but as I had not consulted him about anything for a long time I accepted Harry Wilson's suggestion that I should go and see him. I consulted him about one or two other current problems.

DEC. 5. Chief Constable Robertson came at 11. Though weak in dealing with his subordinates, he is recognised to be an able and efficient officer, and no one could be more reasonable or agreeable to deal with. He made no bones about his regret for the way in which Kelso and Ratcliffe had put their points, and assured me that they had no complaint about the competence of the present team of Advocates Depute. He felt that they were too much inclined to keep the police at arm's length, but otherwise had nothing to say against them, and agreed that they had an excellent record: the percentage of convictions in the High Court in the past 2 years is 81, which I should think is unsurpassed in any court in Great Britain. He seemed willing to allow me to say something to the effect that Glasgow was satisfied with the Depute's performance, but asked for time to consider it, since Ratcliffe had had a lawyer's letter written on behalf of one of the Deputes. This was news to me; and when Robertson left I went straight upstairs and interrogated Ewan Stewart. I had thought that Stewart would be the culprit, but he told me that it was Cox. Cox was sent for, and confessed that he had got a " friend " — which at my prodding he amended to a " solicitor " — to write Kelso and Ratcliffe asking for a withdrawal. I told him in no uncertain terms that he had been wrong to do this without telling me, and explained to him how his silly action had upset my arrangement with the Chief Constable. Ratcliffe's reply was quite good, stressing that no reflection on Cox had been intended, and if Cox could demonstrate that a lot of people junior to him had been appearing against him at the Circuit he would publish a withdrawal of his allegation that the Deputes were young and inexperienced in comparison with those appearing for the defence. Despite this complication, I wrote Robertson with a note of what I wanted him to agree: a single sentence to the effect that the Glasgow police had no complaint against the present Deputes, who were recognised to be exceptionally competent and successful prosecutors.

DEC. 6. Interviewed by a *Daily Mail* reporter on the dispute with the Glasgow police. I declined to enter into any controversy, but said

I had had a friendly meeting with the Chief Constable, when we had discussed ways of closer cooperation between the police and the Crown Office. I said that anyone who had criticised Crown Counsel had made it clear that they intended no reflection on the present team — nor could they, in view of the present Deputes' record. A meeting to discuss the question of release of prisoners serving life sentences. Hunter and Grant have been given a lot of publicity for criticising what they professed to regard as a civil service practice which had "recently grown up" whereby murderers were released after serving $8\frac{1}{2}$ years. There is a political element in this too: both of them must know that these decisions are taken by the Secretary of State personally and that a general practice of releasing lifers after about 8 years has prevailed throughout our lifetimes. Ross has released only one lifer, and that after a longer period than normal — my experience has been that he is unreasonably harsh in such matters, refusing to release people whose release would be very unlikely to involve any danger to the public. Willis however had got cold feet, and thought we should remember that the public regarded murder as a serious crime and would not approve if they knew that murderers were expected to serve "only eight years". He seemed incapable of imagining what was involved in a sentence of 8 years in prison. They agreed not to enter into argument with Hunter. As regards Grant, Haddow and I thought that Ross should arrange a private talk with him. One is always at a disadvantage in public controversy with judges, while it is unlikely that a judge — except, of course, Clyde — would persist in slanging someone with whom he had just had a personal talk. We had a short talk on the Halliday Report on conveyancing reforms. Their proposals are set out in exceptionally lucid form, so that even I can understand them. On arriving at the flat I found Lady Carlisle out and Susan in her little study with James Buchanan-Jardine. I thought James attractive and agreeable. They looked very cosy, with Susan on the floor beside the electric fire and James beside her.

DEC. 7. Lunched at the Commons cafeteria, where I was joined by two men who seemed to know me. One recalled a former advocate who regularly wore the kilt, even on visits to London, until on one visit there he had an unfortunate experience: he had his sporran picked. Bought a *Scottish Daily Mail*, with some misgivings about what they might have thought fit to publish — relieved to find that it was very good. The point about effectiveness of High Court prosecutors is well made, and they have included some complimentary reference I made to the Glasgow police.

DEC. 8. Everyone at the Crown Office seemed pleased about the *Mail* interview.

DEC. 9. Ross had given way to clamour and refused to release Stephens in accordance with the usual programme. He has written a petulant Minute complaining about the judges' observations and adding "I have not been influenced by this" — a fairly obvious indication that he has. It will be a big disappointment for the man, who will know he is due for release and now for no reason will have to wait in vain for the expected intimation. Ross has minuted that the case will be reconsidered in a year's time.

DEC. 13. Hunter to see me about his controversy with St Andrews House, bringing Stevenson. The trouble arose out of a murder case which Hunter tried at Ayr. The Advocate Depute accepted a plea of culpable homicide, and Hunter imposed a sentence of 15 years. He delivered a long, carefully prepared diatribe; that he was informed that the average duration of detention under a life sentence was $8\frac{1}{2}$ to 9 years, and that it was now the practice to release life prisoners within that time, with unjust and dangerous results, when the Court regarded 15 years as appropriate in serious cases of culpable homicide. The injustice of a position whereby a murderer served a shorter sentence than a man pleading guilty to culpable homicide might be the result of a failure of those responsible for administrative action to take account of the length of sentence imposed by the Court for crimes other than murder, and emphasised the need for reconsideration of the administrative procedures. Ross, approached about this by an *Express* reporter, apparently said " I don't think he is aware of the ruling announced at the passing of the Abolition of Capital Punishment Act, when it was stated that before anyone was released the advice of the judge who tried the case or the Lord Justice-General would be sought ". Hunter then got Stevenson to write Ross's private secretary asking him to inform the Secretary of State that he was well aware of the ruling "and of the practice which has followed thereon". It took St Andrews House three weeks to acknowledge this letter, and meanwhile an appeal by the man whom Hunter had sentenced came before the Second Division, where Grant, before dismissing the appeal, remarked in the course of the argument that it was not for the Court to look into the inscrutable working of the minds of civil servants at St Andrews House. He observed that recommendations by judges had not been accepted by the Secretary of State — there were two recent cases. A paragraph at the end of the *Scotsman* report of the appeal read: "Asked to comment on the court's criticism, a spokesman for St Andrews House said he could not go beyond a statement made at the time of the High Court case in Ayr by the Secretary of State for Scotland. Mr Ross had said that he did not think Lord Hunter was aware of the ruling announced at the passing of the Abolition of Capital Punishment Act last year. It was stated at that time that before anyone was released, the advice of the judge who tried the case, or the Lord Justice-General, would be sought ". This comment aroused Hunter's wrath, and he had got Stevenson to write demanding that an opportunity be taken to correct the false impression given by repetition of the statement attributed to Ross. The reply to Stevenson, following my advice, had been that the Secretary of State had noted Lord Hunter's views. This of course did nothing to soothe Hunter. It appeared that he was assuming that the " spokesman " had actually repeated Ross's remark, whereas I took it that the spokesman had merely said he could not add to Ross's statement, and the *Scotsman* had repeated the statement for clarification. We had an amicable discussion, in which I said I was not surprised that Ross on reading Hunter's remarks had drawn the inference he had, and got in one or two criticisms of Hunter's argument — though he said he had not come to discuss that. He did not press any complaint against Ross himself, realising perhaps as the discussion proceeded that he and Grant might be on delicate ground through having made use of confidential information about Ross's consultations with Clyde — which they could have got only from Clyde himself. He agreed that, if all the spokesman had said was that he could not add to what Ross had said before, he would not press the matter. I undertook to find out about this, and we parted on friendly terms. Stevenson throughout sat and said nothing, merely nodding his head now and again to show he understood what we were saying.

DEC. 15. Home Affairs Committee: a Bill promoted by the Minister of Agriculture to increase the compensation payable to agricultural tenants whose land had been compulsorily purchased for development purposes. It was said that this was urgent, as inadequate compensation terms were causing a lot of trouble in the development of New Towns. The Scottish Office were not prepared to accept the proposal unless the improved terms were applied also to tenants whose farms were taken over for afforestation. There is no logical answer to this — it is all the same to the tenant whether the land is taken over for one purpose or the other — but the Ministry of Agriculture have dug their heels in, and insisted that the Bill should be confined to the immediate problem they were concerned with. They claim to have negotiated with the landowners' association on that basis, but this was not a strong argument since the landowners had not actually agreed to anything. Ross was at today's meeting, and put up a powerful argument. He got some halfhearted support from the Welsh Office, but nobody else seemed much interested. Peart was supported by Crossman, who argued that land taken over for forestry was always poor quality: a ridiculous argument which Ross demolished by pointing out that the value of the land was reflected in the rental, which in every case was the basis on which compensation was assessed. Willey seemed to be supporting Peart. Unfortunately for him, however, it turned out that some people thought that nothing should be done at all. This view was expressed by Gardiner, and supported by Diamond on behalf of the Treasury. This led Houghton to think that Peart would have to make some concession. I weighed in, suggesting that there would be some trouble if for no explainable reason well-to-do farmers around the New Towns were to get compensation on the basis of 5 years rental while poorer farmers in Scotland whose land was taken for forestry got much less. " I think there's something in what the Lord Advocate says", said Houghton, and proposed that as we were unlikely to reach agreement Peart had better take the proposal back and have further discussion. Peart and Crossman accepted this with an ill grace, saying that it had all been discussed over and over again, and it was deplorable that there should be more delay in dealing with this very urgent problem. It seemed to me that they had only themselves to blame — if they had come to terms on the forestry point they could have ignored their other opponents, but the combination of the Scottish opponents with those who wanted nothing done resulted in a degree of disagreement which Houghton could hardly have ignored even if he had wanted. Returned to Deans Yard and had a word with Mitchell about the Water (Scotland) Bill. He and Margaret Christie have been doing some concentrated work on this in order to get it ready for Legislation Committee next week, and I found them round a table with two Scottish Office people, in an atmosphere thick with tobacco smoke. I put half a dozen drafting points, in all of which I was pleased to find they found some substance. Susan was to be out late tonight, and Lady Carlisle undertook to attend to my breakfast tomorrow. It was practically the first time I had seen her since she started work, and I asked her whether she was really enjoying it. It was obvious from her answer that she was not enjoying it at all. She thought industrialists compared unfavourably with civil service people: they seemed to take a pride in discourtesy and lack of consideration and thought they should get credit for absurdities like working till 8 o'clock on Christmas Eve, which she regarded simply as evidence of bad organisation. She thought she ought to carry on for 6 months.

DEC. 16. Lady Carlisle brought my breakfast shortly before 8. I had on my black jacket and striped trousers, to attend the Statute Law Committee, and she said I looked just like her husband when he used to go off in the morning to the city. A car took me to the airport. Some of these girls drive through heavy traffic at a most alarming speed, so that it is quite a relief to get into the comparative safety of the aeroplane; but I had to give today's driver credit for getting me to the airport by checking-in time in face of considerable difficulties. Having, as I now always have, a tourist ticket, I chose a seat beside two girls. One was very pleasant, but slept most of the way, having been out until 5 this morning at Sandhurst cadets' passing-out ball. Her telling me about this reminded me of what Miss Reilly had told me when we were passing a site at Knightsbridge. The new building is to be multi-storey, and the idea was to have the mess room on the top floor, with a view over the Park; but they had to abandon this idea because of the tradition that on one occasion each year a horse is ridden into the messroom and this would not be possible when it was so high up. Miss Reilly thought a possible alternative would be to make a lift big enough to take horse and rider.

DEC. 17. A note from R. E. C. Johnson explaining that the spokesman who had replied to the query about Hunter's case had merely referred to the Secretary of State's comment, without repeating it.

DEC. 19. 10.30 flight to London. Several MPs in the first class; but travelling Tourist class I had the more interesting company of a young Indian from Mombasa, a second-year student at St Andrews. He thought the future of inter-racial cooperation might depend on whether the present regime in Kenya, which has been extraordinarily successful in enabling everyone to work together, could last out the next five years in face of Opposition pressures for a more strongly nationalist approach. He expressed great admiration for President Kenyatta, who he said had by the reading he had done while in prison and the philosophy he had formed there had his character transformed; he thought Kenyatta was one of the great men of the age. He told me that while Germany, Switzerland and Sweden organised charter flights to Kenya, the British had not yet realised its attractiveness: fine climate, and miles of practically deserted beaches. He told me that in his own home he had spoken an Urdu language. Teaching in schools was in English and Swahili, so that he had had the advantage of being trilingual without ever really having to learn any of the three languages as such. To the House, where I met Pike in the Central Lobby at 6; he wanted to hear the debate on the Sexual Offences Bill, having been negotiating with its sponsor, Leo Abse, on whether seamen should be excluded. Abse moved the Second Reading in an effective speech. A reasoned amendment for rejection on the ground that the Merchant Navy was not excluded was moved by Simon Mahon, a Merseyside Labour Catholic, who told the House that he spoke with great authority and gave a long disquisition on what might happen at sea, where there were no back doors. Despite an intervention by Abse, assuring him that his point would be met in Committee, he seemed to be saying that he would be bound to vote against the Bill unless he got a categorical undertaking from the Board of Trade. The best speech in the debate came from Dr Owen, a psychiatrist who represents a Plymouth division. He dealt with several points that had been raised, and concluded with a moving, eloquent appeal. A young Merseyside MP, Ogden, while apparently opposing Mahon's amendment, which he correctly described as a wrecking amendment, seemed at the same time to be complaining that as a Merseyside MP, and one of only two ex-Merchant Navy men in the House, he had not been asked to support it. The last speaker we heard was Simon Mahon's brother Peter, who in his own pedestrian style repeated most of what Simon had said in a pontifical manner from the bench in front of him, even saying again that there were no back doors in the Navy. Simon's union, he said, would not accept responsibility for the outcome of the Bill; and it sounded as if he were saying that it would be " salutary " if strikes were caused not by bad industrial conditions but because of moral turpitude of individual seagoers.

DEC. 20. Legislation Committee: Water (Scotland) Bill — Mabon there to explain the Bill. Back with him to Dover House for a talk about Cadco: Haddow, Hume and two other officials. I was amused by the oblique references they made to Ross's prejudices and preconceptions, referring to him simply as " he " — " That's not what he'll think "; " I know what he'll say about that ". Ross, it seemed, was disposed to attack the Conservative ministers who had been in office when the Cadco trouble began, but Haddow remarked that the obvious retort would be an attack on a member of the present Government who had been primarily responsible for Glenrothes at the time: the chairman of the New Town corporation, Lord Hughes. I think it was Hume who observed that " he " might not be displeased by that line of attack, to which Mabon replied that he was aware that not everyone among the Scottish junior ministers was persona grata. Haddow said he realised that. I was again impressed by Mabon, who put relevant points against the officials forcibly and fairly, without the bullying and bad temper that Ross displays in deaLing with officials — conceding that while he thought they might have gone wrong he himself would have done the same in their position.

DEC. 21. A visit from Cox, to consult me about what reply he was to make to Ratcliffe and Kelso. He did not take kindly to my suggestion that he make no reply, objecting that that would mean leaving them with the last word. I could not see anything objectionable in that.

DEC. 23. Amused to find a letter from Clyde, prompted by a remark I made to him when I found him yesterday gossiping with Gordon in the latter's room. Remarking that he had got me into trouble — which, I added, was nothing out of the ordinary — I told him he had persuaded me to get the Secretary of State to give him an extra judge because of the time that Wheatley had to be away, attending to his Royal Commission on Local Government, and now Wheatley had told the Secretary of State that the new judge had been unnecessary, as he would have been able to do all the work required. Clyde explains in his letter that Wheatley is completely wrong, and that without the extra judge we should be in a desperate situation. No doubt he will now complain to Wheatley, and Wheatley will complain to Ross about his repeating Wheatley's remark, and Ross will presumably complain to me about my repeating it to Clyde; but I think it will do no harm that Wheatley should realise he has been making trouble.

DEC. 27. Parliament House. Nothing had come in except letters from two well-established, semi-lunatic complainers, pursuing their complaints. "It is little wonder", one of them observed, "our Democracy is fastly taking the place of a scarecrow".

Index

247

248

250